The Personal Vote

The Personal Vote

Constituency Service
and Electoral Independence

Bruce Cain

John Ferejohn

Morris Fiorina

Harvard University Press
Cambridge, Massachusetts
and London, England

Copyright © 1987 by the
President and Fellows of Harvard College
All rights reserved
Printed in the United States of America
10 9 8 7 6 5 4 3 2

Library of Congress Cataloging in Publication Data
Cain, Bruce E.
    The personal vote.

    Bibliography: p.
    Includes index.
    1. United States.   Congress.   2. Legislators—
United States.   3. Representative government and
representation—United States.   4. Great Britain.
Parliament.   5. Legislators—Great Britain.
6. Representative government and representation—
Great Britain.   I. Ferejohn, John A.   II. Fiorina,
Morris P.   III. Title.
JK1071.C28   1987   328'.331'0973   86-22839
ISBN 0-674-66317-9 (alk. paper) (cloth)
ISBN 0-674-66318-7 (paper)

To Anne

To Christopher, Sara, and Marissa

To Mary

Preface

This project began in 1978 and at times it seemed that it would never end. Two-person collaborations are difficult; three-person collaborations test the bounds of collegiality, friendship, and, on occasion, even civility. The authors are pleased to report that they continue to hold a large degree of respect for one another.

We are indebted to more people than we will remember to acknowledge. First and foremost we thank the National Science Foundation, which provided four years of research support for the project. There is simply no way to carry out a research effort like this one without released time and adequate funding. The foundation also funded the 1978 and 1980 National Election Studies, which were major components of our project. These studies were carried out by the University of Michigan Center for Political Studies under the supervision of the Board of Overseers of the National Election Studies. We gratefully acknowledge their contribution to our work.

Other institutions also gave major support to our efforts. The California Institute of Technology was home base for twelve of the eighteen man-years invested in the project. That enlightened institution provided the kind of research infrastructure rarely enjoyed by political science professors. Caltech secretaries Georgeia Hutchinson and Irene Baldon were especially helpful. The project was finished after two of us had moved on to other institutions. Susan Page and her assistants at Harvard University attended to numerous details in the preparation of the manuscript. Timothy Prinz deserves special mention for his yeoman service in tracking down notes, checking tables, and providing second opinions on the copyediting.

This project undoubtedly would have taken even longer but for the efforts of John Schmitz, a student in the Law and Social Science Program at Caltech. Schmitz helped design the questionnaires, did the bulk of the American interviewing, and contributed much to our thinking. Until he left to clerk for Antonin Scalia, at that time Appeals Court Judge, Schmitz was almost a fourth collaborator.

Kenneth McCue, then a graduate student at Caltech, was of inestimable help in readying the data sets for analysis. Unfortunately, we gave him so much practice in developing special skills that he decided to open a consulting firm rather than follow in the footsteps of his professors. Jill Appel gave helpful instruction on how to function in a new computer environment at Harvard.

The *Legislative Studies Quarterly, Comparative Political Studies, Political Studies,* and *the American Political Science Review* published early reports on various aspects of the research. We thank them for permitting us to incorporate those analyses into this book.

Many friends and colleagues have commented on earlier articles or on the manuscript or portions thereof. For their observations, criticisms, and suggestions we thank James Alt, Brian Barry, David Butler, Heinz Eulau, Richard Fenno, Peter Hall, Gary Jacobson, John Johannes, Keith Krehbiel, Thomas Mann, Roger Noll, John Padgett, Glenn Parker, Gillian Peele, Douglas Rivers, and Philip Williams.

Finally, we thank our wives and children, who listened sympathetically to complaints about how our collaborators were holding up the project. All the complaints were well-founded.

Contents

The Personal Vote

The Marquis had been Secretary of State under the Restoration, and was now making an attempt to re-enter political life. He was preparing for the parliamentary elections by devious methods, with a great many distributions of firewood in the winter and passionate demands at the General Assembly for more and more roads in his constituency.

—Flaubert, *Madame Bovary*

Introduction

Article 1 of the United States Constitution contains ten sections setting out in detail the structure, powers, and duties of the Congress, along with certain prohibitions on the exercise of the legislative power. Aside from specifying a few formal qualifications for membership, however, the Constitution contains nothing on the powers and duties of the individual members of Congress. To be sure, the Founders were operating in the context of an indigenous tradition of representative government, much of which they could reasonably presume would transfer to the new national government. Still, it is noteworthy how little the framing document constrains the individual members of Congress in the performance of their collective duties.

While the Constitution is unspecific about the behavior of individual representatives, political science is not. An extensive literature describes the way in which individual members of Congress carry out their representational responsibilities. For example, studies of the relationship between legislative roll call voting and district interests, as measured by demographic and economic characteristics, have typically found little or no relationship, possibly suggesting that modern American representatives are not very conscientious. More recent studies, relying on survey measures of constituent opinion, have found stronger relationships between constituency preferences and roll call voting on at least some issues. But many constituents have little information about the issues and their representatives' positions, so doubts about the strength of the representative linkage continue to exist.[1]

Another large literature examines how representatives view their "roles," in particular their representational roles. Are representatives trustees, who use their own best judgment to decide what is in their constituents' interest, or are they delegates, who bend to their constituents' expressed will? Moreover, do representatives see their constituencies as the districts which elect them or as the larger whole of which their districts are parts? How do their role perceptions affect their behavior, and how do they resolve the conflicts that surely occur?[2]

The most recent research raises the question of whether prevailing conceptions of representation are sufficiently rich to encompass the observed activities of representatives. Representation is generally viewed as policy responsiveness, as the representative responding to and articulating the policy positions or ideologies of constituents in the legislature. But in the contemporary administrative state representatives increasingly engage in and are rewarded for ombudsman-like activities which are only indirectly mentioned in the Constitution and rarely treated in the professional literature. Indeed, much of the behavior of American representatives has little programmatic or ideological content. The contemporary representative serves constituents individually and collectively, keeps in close touch with them, and generally tries to cultivate a personal relationship with them, based on accessibility and trust.[3]

This newer research suggests that theories of representation must expand their focus. Modern political science has equated representation with policy responsiveness and symbolic responsiveness: how faithfully does the representative respond to the wishes of the district in words and deeds? Representation also includes allocation responsiveness: does the representative work to ensure that his or her district gets a fair share of government projects, programs, and expenditures? This component of representation is generally viewed in a pejorative light, as "pork barrel." Finally, representation includes service responsiveness: how assiduously does the representative respond to individual and group requests for assistance in dealing with the government bureaucracy? Since representation involves all of these components and perhaps others, to investigate policy responsiveness alone would yield an incomplete picture.[4]

The obvious solution is to study what representatives do, regardless of the fit between behavior and prevailing theories. If representatives wish to remain representatives, their behavior will be calculated to please constituents. Thus, what representatives do reveals something about what constituents want them to do, and both in turn provide information about the contemporary representative-constituency relationship. If aspects of the relationship other than policy responsiveness loom large, then either some traditional notions of representation are too narrow, or much of what representatives do and constituents want is not representation.

This book is about the underemphasized aspects of contemporary representation, specifically service and allocation responsiveness—constituency service for short. It describes the behavior of representatives and the perceptions of constituents in two developed democracies with single-member district systems, the United States and Great Britain. Service and allocation responsiveness have come to be increasingly important components of the representational relationship, with consequences far more extensive than simply a change in the nature of representation. Constituency service constitutes an important means by which representatives earn personalized electoral support—votes based not on party membership or association with a particular government but on the individual identities and activities of the candidates. From this simple proposition a great deal follows. Important features of democratic political processes vary with the ways by which members of the national legislature gain and retain their seats. To the extent that members develop personalized electoral support, they are able, should they so desire, to withstand efforts by national leaders to control and coordinate their behavior. This ability has obvious consequences for the style of policy making and the types of policies characteristic of the political system. Moreover, the manner in which members of representative assemblies gain office has broader consequences for the development of governmental institutions. Representatives who believe themselves responsible for their own electoral fate are less likely to accept government practices and institutions which deny them the means to exercise individual influence than are representatives whose fate lies in the hands of the national party or other authority. Again, the consequences for the style and substance of policy making are obvious. In general, a polity's electoral processes, policy processes, and institutional structure are bound together: if one element of the constellation changes, the others will adjust toward a new equilibrium. Before we proceed to a full development of this argument, it will be helpful to review some recent electoral trends in Great Britain and the United States.

Recent Electoral Trends

In 1967 Donald Stokes argued that national forces in elections to the United States House of Representatives were becoming increasingly prominent.[5] A partition of the variance among House districts into national, state, and local components appeared to show that the proportion of variance attributable to national forces had increased over time and the proportion attributable to state and especially to district forces had decreased. Such trends seemed reasonable in that the development of mass communications should naturally work to erode local and regional differences. Stokes then contrasted the interelection swings in party shares of the vote in House elections with those observed in British parliamentary elections. The British swings showed much greater uniformity, consistent with the national character of modern British elections.

Whatever the soundness of Stokes's methodology, his conclusions came under challenge almost immediately. Robert Erikson noted that the electoral advantage accruing to incumbency increased markedly in the mid-1960s, and David Mayhew drove home the point with a classic series of histograms.[6] These diagrams show how a condition of reasonably balanced two-party competition gave way to a condition in which incumbents of both parties won by comfortable margins (Figure I.1). Over the course of a generation the marginal districts largely vanished. Since individual incumbency is by definition a district level force, the Erikson-Mayhew findings demonstrated that the ascendant nationalization process described by Stokes had halted and reversed.

Consistent with the increasing advantage of incumbency, the swing ratio—the relationship between seats won and votes gained—declined during the postwar period from approximately 3:1 (roughly in accord with the venerable if atheoretical cube law) to approximately 2:1.[7] As the number of marginal districts declined, fewer

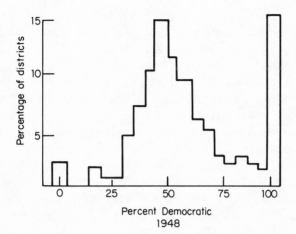

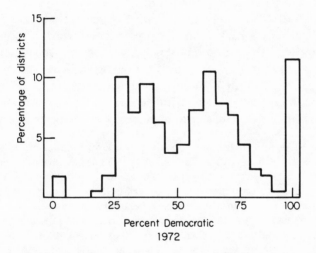

FIGURE I.1. House vote in districts with incumbents running, 1948 and 1972. *Source*: Morris P. Fiorina, "The Decline of Collective Responsibility in American Politics," reprinted by permission of *Daedalus* 109 (Summer 1980).

seats were at risk to vote swings of any given size. Consequently the swing ratio dropped.

Other studies described the deterioration of traditional ties between national conditions and House voting, namely the tendency for midterm elections to serve as referenda on the performance of the incumbent administration and the decline of presidential coattails. Only seven years after Stokes's study, Walter Dean Burnham was describing the increasing separation of the presidential and congressional electoral arenas. Shortly thereafter, scholars using newly available data were asserting that "congressional elections were local not national events," that incumbency was "the most important single factor" in House elections, and that national responsibility in American politics focused on the president alone. Whatever the validity of the earlier findings, their projection failed to forecast the voting trends in American legislative elections.[8]

Meanwhile, the nationally structured British system began to show signs of erosion in the 1970s. The ability of the two major parties to structure the electoral system declined, and the ebb and flow of party competition in mid-1970s British elections made that decline evident to all. The Liberals made a major resurgence, aided in considerable part by a grass roots, locally oriented strategy.[9] Regionally based nationalist parties also emerged with renewed strength. By the early 1980s the new Social Democratic–Liberal alliance took almost as much of the popular vote as Labour. Amid such electoral upheavals the once uniform swing became less so. Concepts familiar to American scholars began to appear in British discussions:

> The 1974–1979 swing was not uniform: it varied more from seat to seat than in any other election since 1950. Because of the greater attention he can command in the media and the constituency services he can render, an incumbent MP [Member of Parliament] is more likely than a prospective parliamentary candidate to be able to establish a personal vote, consisting of those who support him as an individual rather than as a party representative . . . the more important and unexpected change is the reduction in the number of marginal constituencies . . . on average, about 12 seats would change hands for each 1% swing. However, the equivalent tables produced after the 1964 and 1966 elections showed that about 18 seats would change hands for each 1% swing. This dramatic reduction in the number of seats liable to change hands has undermined the "cube law," which if it holds, does result in practice in about 18 seats changing hands for each 1% swing.

> In the 1970s both major parties won more seats by large two-party majorities: the distribution of the two-party vote widened and flattened. Before 1974 it was unimodal with a peak near its centre; the distribution is now bimodal with peaks where both parties win safe seats by moderately safe majorities.[10]

Nonuniform national swings? Incumbency effects? Vanishing marginals? Declining swing ratios? Students of American elections may experience a rush of *déja vu*, although the magnitude of the changes in Britain is small compared to that in the United States. Given the past stability of the British electoral system, however, even such small changes drew notice.

Although the electoral changes within each of the two countries are complex and multifaceted, and undoubtedly derive from somewhat distinct sources, they are nevertheless intimately connected, and the connection lies in the efforts of professional politicians operating within single-member district electoral systems. Consider the modern U.S. House of Representatives. Most of its members view politics as a career and care a great deal about retaining their office, even if most are generally on the lookout for an open Senate seat. As compared to their nineteenth century amateur predecessors, modern representatives serve longer, win re-election more dependably, and work harder at their responsibilities, as shown by the lengthening of congressional sessions, the increase in the number of committee and subcommittee meetings, and the expansion of district activities. Typically representatives struggle to establish a solid personal base of support during their first few terms and work thereafter to maintain that personal base against various sources of erosion, often making strenuous efforts and great personal sacrifices in order to do so.[11] Their efforts are understandable. As politics has become a profession, and service in the House a realistic and attractive career, job security has become as important for the professional representative as for any other professional—but more problematic.

In contrast to the House, the British Parliament has long been a bastion of amateur politics. In recent years, however, the frequency of part-time parliamentarians has declined, age at entry has decreased, and tenure has increased. The voluntary retirement rate now stands at about 10 percent, actually lower than in House elections of the 1970s. Moreover, there has been a steady increase in the number of elections lost before the first electoral success of new members of Parliament (MPs), suggesting that modern MPs are willing to endure more for the prospect of eventual success. As a result of such trends, career politicians increasingly make up the Cabinet and House of Commons.[12]

Career representatives have compelling personal motives to concern themselves with the good opinion and, by implication, the well-being of their constituents. Solicitude for constituents should vary closely with the importance of their votes for the representative's life goals. But if the desire to be re-elected explains why representatives pay attention to those important for their re-election, the fundamental electoral law has much to do with defining the particular individuals who are important. Candidates who run at large or on national party lists in proportional representation systems are not formally responsible for representing a specific geographical area; they have no particular district to represent. By comparison, in single-member district systems representatives have geographical areas to call their own. These systems present an opportunity and create a motivation for relationships between represented and representatives that are more personal, particularistic, and idiosyncratic than in other kinds of systems.[13] Such relationships are often based on relatively nonpartisan, nonideological, and nonprogrammatic constituency service—the various activities carried out by representatives on behalf of individuals, groups, and organizations in the district. Expanding on the traditional legislative role, the representative engaged in constituency service acts as an ombudsman or broker concerned with the particular impact on the district of the policies of the national government.

Building a personal following is not the only source of safety for representatives in democratic societies; it may not even be a major source outside the United States. In most systems there is some security in the fact that electorates manifest a high degree of inertia in their behavior. Party loyalties are sufficiently widespread and stable, and the level of public information is sufficiently low, that violent shifts in partisan support seldom occur, though recent trends in both Britain and the United States lessen somewhat the degree of stability expected from these sources. Electoral fluctuations do occur, however, and such fluctuations need not be massive for incumbents, particularly those who hold marginal seats, to regard defeat as a genuine possibility.[14]

This study explores the connection between constituency effort and the personal following that representatives develop. To reiterate, numerous aspects of democratic politics reflect the process by which members of the national legislature gain and retain their seats. To the extent that members manage to build and maintain bases of personal support in their different constituencies, they are better able to resist attempts by national leaders to control and coordinate their behavior, should members desire to do so. National leaders in turn must take this independence into account when attempting to formulate and secure the passage of legislation. Moreover, the processes by which members gain and retain office have long-range consequences for the evolution of governmental institutions. Representatives who consider themselves responsible for their own electoral fates are less likely to accept government practices and institutions that deny them the means to exercise individual influence than are representatives whose fate lies in the hands of the national party or other higher authority.

In sum, a polity's electoral process, its policy processes, and the finer details of its institutional structure are bound together. If one changes, the others adjust accordingly. Thus, even small features of the electoral process have implications larger than might at first appear.

The Concept of a Personal Vote

The personal vote refers to that portion of a candidate's electoral support which originates in his or her personal qualities, qualifications, activities, and record. The part of the vote that is not personal includes support for the candidate based on his or her partisan affiliation, fixed voter characteristics such as class, religion, and ethnicity, reactions to national conditions such as the state of the economy, and performance evaluations centered on the head of the governing party. These nonpersonal factors account for the lion's share of the variation in election outcomes, especially outside the United States.

Even in the United States the single most important variable affecting the congressional vote remains the voter's partisan identification. Partisan attachments lend stability to the electoral results, although the level of loyalty and its impact on the vote have declined in recent years. Possibly as a consequence, short-term forces now determine electoral outcomes more often than they did a generation ago. Among these various short-term forces, two have to do with programmatic considerations. One force is the incumbent's voting record and position on the issues. Only a minority have any accurate information about these matters, and fewer still know as much about the typical challenger. In contrast, evaluations of executive performance and national issues and conditions make smaller informational demands on the voter. Economic conditions in particular have been salient in recent congressional election campaigns. Even so, the impact of economic conditions on voting for Congress is smaller than popularly assumed, and the precise mechanisms by which it works remain controversial.[15]

Within the set of possible short-term forces only the activities and characteristics of the candidates have increased in significance in recent years. The importance of incumbency has grown dramatically. Incumbents win because they are better known and more favorably evaluated by any of a wide variety of measures. And they are better known and more favorably evaluated because, among other factors, they bombard constituents with missives containing a predominance of favorable material, maintain extensive district office operations to service their constituencies, use modern technology to target groups of constituents with particular policy interests, and vastly outspend their opponents.[16]

Recent electoral trends in Britain are not entirely dissimilar from those in the United States, although qualitatively similar patterns should not obscure the large quantitative differences. Partisan affiliation is an even better predictor of voting choice in the United Kingdom than in the United States, but in Britain too the influence of party loyalty has declined in recent years. Economic conditions have also played a major role in recent British elections, as have such issues as immigration, devolution, and the European Economic Community (EEC). The effects of issues and economic conditions are generally associated with the national parties and their leaders, not the individual members, under the rationale that individual MPs simply do not have the independence to carve out distinctive programmatic identities. In recent years, however, a spate of readoption fights and increasing dissent in the Commons have intensified the differences between individual and party positions.[17] If these trends continue, the voting records and policy stands of MPs could become more of a factor in future elections.

The term "incumbency" rarely figures in discussions of British politics. Generally the characteristics of the candidates for MP are seldom regarded as consequential. Nonetheless, even before the recent upheavals involving the Social Democratic-Liberal Alliance, there were increasing indications of some sort of incumbency effect in the national elections, as illustrated by the passages quoted earlier. As yet, however, there is little systematic research on the subject.

The magnitude of the effect is indeterminate, though generally agreed to be small, and its bases are largely a matter of informed speculation.[18] Indeed, the principal reason for our original decision to study Britain was the belief that it was a single-member district system in which the forces underlying incumbent-oriented voting had been completely checked, although incumbent MPs were known to engage in some of the same kinds of activities as congressmen. Only after the study was underway did it become apparent that we were looking at a significant and possibly growing phenomenon.

The import of the personal vote depends on three interrelated factors: its magnitude, the electoral swings common in the system, and the degree of competition for legislative seats. Other things being equal, a large personal vote has greater implications for legislative behavior and policy making than a small personal vote. But other things may not be equal. The average personal vote in one system might be 5 percent as compared to 10 percent in another, but if the second system often experiences interelection swings of 15 percent, whereas the first seldom sees a swing larger than 3 percent, the smaller personal vote of the first system could be more consequential than the larger personal vote of the second. Similarly, if the districting arrangements mean that most districts in the first system are won by less than 5 percent and most districts in the second are won by more than 15 percent, the smaller personal vote of the first system could motivate the representative more than the larger personal vote of the second.

Although the importance of the personal vote evidently depends on both the magnitude of electoral swings and the value of the swing ratio, or the relationship of seats to votes, the magnitude of the swing ratio is itself affected by the existence of personal votes. As Stokes noted, every interelection swing in the United States can be thought of as composed of three components: a national swing, a state swing, and a district swing, which includes the personal vote. Personal votes may augment favorable swings and depress unfavorable ones, and the effect may not be at all random. For example, those most endangered by swings, marginal incumbents, may work most diligently to construct personal supporting coalitions. If successful, the swings evident in different districts would be composed in different parts of national, state, and local swings. Similarly, if representatives construct personal votes and thereby enhance their margins, this would simultaneously alter the swing ratio, explaining the temporal decline in the U.S. swing ratio and perhaps the recent decline in the British ratio.

There are, in short, many difficulties in moving from studies of representatives' personal votes to studies of their broader implications for the political order. The critical considerations involved are mutually interrelated and difficult to disentangle.

The Personal Vote and
Intralegislative Relations

There is a large personal vote in the United States and a small but possibly growing one in Great Britain. Such electoral support is related to other significant electoral phenomena, such as the decline of party loyalties, electoral volatility, and changes in the nature of campaigns. But of more far-reaching significance, the personal vote also holds implications for the process and substance of policy making.

Consider the matter of intralegislative relations. The internal structures and processes of the American Congress and British Parliament differ greatly. Congress is a decentralized body with legislative labor and power divided among the various committees and subcommittees. Because so much of real political importance takes place in these "little legislatures," rules and practices have developed that allow routine access to and orderly accretion of power within them.[19] The resulting legislative structure is highly sensitive to the wishes and requirements of the ordinary member. In contrast, governing authority in Britain is concentrated in the front benches of the ruling party. There is a division of labor between front and back benches but relatively little division of labor within the back benches. Legislative success depends overwhelmingly on the favor of the front bench of the majority party. Overall, the organization of Parliament shows much less accommodation to the needs of the individual members.

Moreover, the structure of legislative careers differs profoundly between the two systems. The path to power in Britain runs through the party. If leaders are impressed with a new member, they may put him or her on the leadership ladder as a parliamentary private secretary or junior minister. Alternatively, if the aspiring leader fails to impress or alienates the party leaders in some way, he or she risks permanent backbench status. While the life of a backbencher is attractive to some, it is frustrating to those interested in making policy or putting their mark on politics. The contrast with Congress is marked. In Congress there are many ways to exercise influence and thereby to shape a career. Depending upon the representative's place in the committee system, a congressional seat can be used to attain local or regional benefits, build expertise and influence in important policy arenas, or shape the chamber's internal conduct.[20] Moreover, congressmen can use their office as a stepping-stone to a more influential office in the public sector or a more lucrative position in the private sector.

Many of these contrasts between Congress and Parliament stem from explicit constitutional differences. In particular, the American concepts of checks and balances and the separation of powers have no counterparts in Britain. The evolution of strong national party organizations in late nineteenth century Britain is another major factor. For reasons not fully understood, British parties developed in such a way as to establish effective control over access to parliamentary office.[21] By so doing, the parties gained a degree of control over their elected members that is matched only faintly in short periods of American history. At the national level American parties have never been much more than loose confederations of state and local organizations, and even within this confederated structure, state and local leaders generally have not exercised more than a modicum of control over access to Congress. American congressmen represent their districts to the national party; in Britain the reverse is more nearly true.

The nature of the representative's electoral base helps to explain the degree of control that parties and their leaders exercise over individual members of the legislature. To the extent that members achieve a personal hold on their office, they become more difficult for party leaders to coordinate and control. The result may be the kind of "managed" politics found in Britain around 1760, the immobilism of the French Third Republic, or the stalemates between legislative and executive branches common to the United States in the past few decades.[22]

To elaborate, if legislative office is valuable, incumbents will seek to increase their hold on it. They may press for additional resources, such as staff, offices, and other perquisites, or for expanded opportunities to claim credit. Efforts to increase credit-claiming opportunities can take the form of demands for a secure hold on committee seats and ranks, such as the 1910–1911 revolt in the House, or for growth in the number of committee seats, as has been the general trend in Congress since 1946, or for expansion in the role of committees per se in the legislature, as in the recent British select committee reforms. Such pressures may appear unexceptional in many cases, but their cumulative effect can have a structural impact, and party leaders who understand the implications of such demands for legislative coordination resist them. If representatives attain a significant measure of control over their own fates, however, they are likely to bring renewed pressure on legislative leaders to increase the level of resources and opportunities, which will produce still further independence. Thus, party discipline unravels as increased resources and influence interact with electoral independence in a mutually reinforcing fashion. Evolution of the legislative process in this way is entropic. Power devolves to subunits; representatives feel free to defect on party votes; norms of party responsibility crumble; and responsiveness to national electoral verdicts gives way to bargaining among particularistic interests.[23]

Thus, within the institutional context of single-member simple plurality systems, the vigor of legislative discipline and ultimately the possibility of coherent legislative behavior rests on assuring that the maintenance and advancement of individual careers occur through the auspices of party. The party leadership must work to maintain this dependence by restricting access to resources and opportunities that would allow legislative members to build strong personal ties to their constituencies. If the leadership fails to do so, the game is up. Once members can assure their return to office independently of the course of national events and national performance, the parties must rely on shared views and moral suasion—which are better than nothing, but not much to depend on when the chips are down.[24]

Events in the United States have gone very far in these respects. Contemporary congressional leadership is severely constrained by the necessity to accommodate to the needs of the rank and file. Congressmen generally get the committee assignments they request; they rise rapidly to positions of subcommittee leadership without consideration of their loyalty; and they routinely gain floor recognition to offer motions and amendments inimical to party interests.[25] In these and other ways they have numerous opportunities to engage in policy formation as independent actors, subject only to constituency sanction.

By comparison, the differences between backbench and leadership interests are sharply delineated in Britain. Party leaders oppose granting committee powers and staff resources to backbenchers and have only grudgingly made concessions in these areas in recent years. Even so, the period in which these concessions occurred has been one in which members have begun to show greater independence in their parliamentary behavior. Party voting on three line whips has eroded substantially since 1974, and governments have shown less of a proclivity to turn division lobbies into questions of confidence.[26] Common forces underlie these small erosions in the front bench monopoly of power. Anthony King noted the relationship between developments such as the decline of party cohesion, the increasing importance of select committees, and the rising careerism of MPs. Geoffrey Smith, a political journalist, wrote:

> What is beyond doubt is that a more assertive and independent breed of MP is entering the House these days. They are professionals in the sense of devoting their careers to politics, even if they retain another job on the side. They have gone into Parliament not because they believe it to be the best club in Europe but because they want to have a direct influence on public policy. That was always true of a number of members, of course; nowadays it applies to nearly all entrants. It follows that there are therefore a higher proportion of ambitious—and potentially frustrated—backbenchers who are determined to exercise their own judgment on public policy.[27]

In sum, the first potential effect of the personal vote is upon legislative discipline and control. If individual legislative members are independent representatives of distinct geographical areas, legislative discipline must rely relatively more on the carrot and less on the stick. But increasingly independent members will seek to appropriate the carrot after they have eliminated the stick. Thus, policy making evolves toward a system of symmetrical bargaining among near equals. Such a system is inherently limited in the kinds of policies it can develop and the type of representation it can provide its citizens.[28]

The Personal Vote and Executive-Legislative Relations

Where the executive and legislative branches are separate, as in the United States, the personal vote affects relations between the two.

Where formal separation is absent, as in Britain, with the legislative party leaders forming the government, any inability to control back-bench behavior creates difficulties in the coordination of executive and legislative actions.

The formal separation of power makes coordination between the branches of government dependent upon informal institutions and practices. Patronage is one of these practices. If the executive can deliver such services as attractive jobs and contracts to important allies of legislators, then within certain limits legislators may choose to sell their policy support. Historically, patronage has been an important tool of executive leadership in both the United States and Britain. For a variety of reasons, however, it has declined in both importance and acceptability.

Executives and legislators can still engage in explicit exchange. Legislative support can be purchased by modifying the proposal at issue or other unrelated proposals. Logrolling, horse trading, and other colorful metaphors describe such activity. But if the goal is coordination in support of a coherent legislative program, the means and ends are at cross-purposes: coordination is purchased at the expense of coherency. Coordination based on exchange may be an improvement on no coordination at all, but it also contributes to policy failures and frustrated expectations.[29]

Historically, informal electoral practices have provided a significant incentive for legislative-executive cooperation. If presidential coattails are lengthy, for example, many legislators will regard their electoral fates as closely connected with that of the president. If the president fails, the legislators may also. Similarly, if the electorate treats midterm elections as referenda on the performance of the incumbent administration, legislators again have a self-interested reason to concern themselves with the administration's performance. A message of dissatisfaction from the electorate may entail their defeat. When such electoral ties exist, the president can count on some degree of self-interested support from legislators simply because they realize that national conditions and presidential performance are not abstract notions but critical determinants of their own electoral support.

At times presidential-congressional electoral ties have been strong in the United States. For example, the Democrats lost 116 seats in the midterm of 1894, the Republicans lost 75 in the midterm of 1922, the Democrats lost 56 in 1946, and the Republicans lost 49 in 1958. In recent years, however, midterm elections have seemed much less like national referenda. The Carter administration lost only 15 seats in 1978, and the Reagan administration, despite the most serious recession since the 1930s, lost only 26 seats in 1982.

Presidential coattails also appear to have weakened. In 1920 the Cox candidacy cost his fellow Democrats 59 seats, and in 1932 Hoover led the Republicans to a loss of 101 seats. By comparison, the Democrats lost only 12 seats in the McGovern debacle of 1972 and 33 in the Carter repeat of 1980. The connection between presidential and House voting has dropped 75 percent since the New Deal.[30] A dramatic manifestation of this long-term trend appears in the rise in the number of districts that support the presidential candidate of one party and the congressional candidate of another (Table I.1). Whereas a mere 3 percent of the districts split their vote in 1900, the percentage has averaged about a third of the districts since 1964.

Declining party loyalties, weakened coattail effects, and a lessened impact of national conditions on the congressional vote have produced numerous unrelated electoral mandates which members of Congress reasonably attribute more to their personal record than to the president's actions or the party's reputation. This development can only reinforce the parochial outlooks they already possess.

Table I.1. Split results in presidential and congressional elections

Year	Districts
1900	3.4%
1924	11.8
1944	11.2
1964	33.3
1968	32.0
1972	44.1
1976	28.5
1980	32.8
1984	43.7

Source: Norman Ornstein et al., *Vital Statistics on Congress, 1984–85* (Washington, D.C.: American Enterprise Institute, 1984), Table 2-14.

Instead of considering a policy from the perspective of its effect on the national electorate, incumbents place greater weight on the policy's effect on their individual districts. Thus, congressmen assessed many of Carter's economic and energy proposals in terms of how these proposals would differentially help or hurt various geographical interests.[31] In short, the particularism that representatives manifest in their policy outlooks has deep roots in the disjunction of electoral bases. By holding only the president responsible for national conditions, the contemporary electorate undercuts critical incentives which in the past brought some cohesion to an institutionally fragmented national government.

The Personal Vote and Interest Group Bargaining

In all democracies interest groups participate in the formulation of public policies. Some groups have highly particularistic concerns and lobby only for policies that favorably affect their narrow interests. Other groups have broader policy or ideological concerns. The pursuit of their aims, broad or narrow, leads groups to try to influence policy making at any relevant level of government, such as bargaining with bureaucrats at a particular agency or ministry, negotiating with cabinet ministers, dealing with the chairmen of relevant legislative committees, or working through local representatives.

Important differences in interest group bargaining patterns characterize different countries. There are two prototypical cases. The first is the pluralist pattern of interest representation, defined by P. C. Schmitter as one in which groups are organized "into an unspecified number of multiple, voluntary, competitive, non-hierarchically ordered and self-determined (as to type or scope of interest) categories not specially licensed, subsidized, created or otherwise controlled by the state and not exercising a monopoly of representational activity within their respective categories." The second is the corporatist pattern, defined by Schmitter as one in which groups constitute "a limited number of singular, compulsory, non-competitive, hierarchically ordered and functionally differentiated categories, recognized or licensed (if not created) by the state and granted a deliberate representational monopoly within their respective categories in exchange for observing certain controls on their selection of leaders and articulation of demands and supporters."[32]

Consider a system in which individual legislators can personally earn financial or other forms of electoral support by promoting the causes of particular interest groups. Such a system is more likely to facilitate, or at least be more compatible with, a pluralist pattern of interest group bargaining than a corporatist pattern. When individual legislators can benefit from intervening on behalf of interest groups, any one group has greater difficulty in establishing a monopoly on bargaining rights in a given area. Additionally, legislative leaders find it difficult to enforce centrally negotiated agreements upon their erstwhile followers. Thus, by stimulating the development of numerous routes of influence below the leadership level, the personal vote encourages pluralistic bargaining and discourages corporatist.

These patterns are related to the tension between functionalist and territorial bases of representation. Functionalist representation gives a voice to the major social and economic groupings in society without regard for spatial considerations. The central justification for this mode of representation holds that policy should reflect the viewpoint and desires of the great interests in a society. Thus, big business and trade union interests should play a major role in shaping economic policy because their expertise is useful and their cooperation is essential. When these patterns become formalized and particular interests achieve a monopolistic bargaining position, functionalist representation assumes a corporatist pattern.

A territorial basis of representation inevitably introduces particularistic and parochial concerns into the policy-making process. A representative elected with the votes, efforts, and resources of the people of a specific geographic area naturally attaches special importance to their views and requests, out of a sense of obligation as well as self-interest. The exact level of particularism varies with many factors, especially the strength of the party system, but the potential basis for local interest advocacy always exists.[33] Territorial and functional representation are not always and everywhere in conflict. A sponsored union candidate in a heavily union constituency, for example, might feel no conflict about representing union and local interests at the same time. When functional representation assumes a corporatist structure, however, there is likely to be conflict between its national outlook and the particularistic orientation fostered by territorial representation.

Both bases of representation probably can be detected in all political systems, but systems differ in the degree to which representation is territorial or functional, as well as in whether the institutional pattern is de jure or only de facto. The same can be said about the degree of pluralism or corporatism which characterizes interest group bargaining patterns. In both Britain and the United States the dominant pattern is pluralist and territorial. Members of Parliament and of Congress avidly defend local, particularistic interests. In Congress, the power of district interests manifests itself in the ways that committees distribute money and projects, their pork barrel practices. Similarly, MPs champion the causes of groups in their constituencies. By and large MPs do not initiate legislation; hence, interest groups cannot look to them for that favor. Still, interest groups can use MPs to lobby ministers and to publicize their causes. Additionally, the threat of backbench rebellion can persuade the government not to introduce legislation or at least to modify it in some way.[34]

The capacity of a government to establish corporatist arrangements depends in considerable degree upon its control over its component parts.[35] Other factors are relevant, including the structure of the interest groups themselves. Still, the government cannot perform its part in a corporatist arrangement if it cannot control its own members, just as the interest groups must exercise control over their own members and component groups. This connection between member independence and interest group bargaining patterns was evident in the 1930s. For a brief period President Roosevelt struck bargains with interest groups directly, without negotiating with legislative leaders, and still got the legislation through Congress. As the emergency receded, however, policy making moved away from high-level negotiations and returned to the more normal pattern of American politics, namely bargaining with locally oriented congressmen and senators with independent bases of power. More recently the increased weakness of the president vis-à-vis the Congress in domestic policy relates to the growing electoral independence of individual congressmen.[36]

Although backbench MPs are more successfully excluded from the processes of policy formulation than are congressmen, interest groups have similarly used them to force issues onto the parliamentary agenda in the face of indifference or opposition from the government. The Clean Air Act of 1956 and the Deposit of Poisonous Waste Act of 1972 illustrate this role of the backbench MP. The greater discipline of the party system and the smaller personal vote in Britain may account for the fact that governments there can deal

more easily and directly with affected interests than can governments in the United States. Still, MPs eagerly assume the role of
policy "scavengers," a propensity perhaps related to the weakening
of party ties and the increasing assertion of backbench independence.[37]

In sum, by affecting intralegislative relations, coordination between legislature and executive, and the pattern of interest group
bargaining, the personal vote affects the policy-making processes
and ultimately their outcomes. When any element of the complex
changes, the others can be expected to adjust as well. To the degree
that legislative members are able to secure electoral independence,
they are less dependent on executive success, less controlled by
legislative leaders, and more capable of dealing independently with
interest groups. Cumulatively these effects produce a more decentralized policy-making process with greater room for particularistic
considerations.

Institutionally, the electoral strategies of legislators in systems
like the Anglo-American tend to push "reform" in the direction of
more decentralization and less coordination from the top. Thus,
legislators request more staff and perquisites. They look with favor
on the creation of additional committees and with suspicion on the
strengthening of central coordinating mechanisms. They prefer to
control the financing of elections and are wary of measures that
would give the parties such control. And if they could freely choose
the timing of elections, they would schedule legislative and executive elections for different times.

Such institutional developments have an obvious consequence
for policy making: they make it more difficult to formulate decisive,
coherent policy. Decentralized systems generally are characterized
by inconsistency and stalemate in the policy-making process. Where
a corporatist state might formulate and impose a coherent five-year
economic plan, the decentralized pluralist state is more likely to
adopt an internally inconsistent compromise. Strong coherent policy
is not at all times and in all places preferable. There may be significant advantages to giving voice to local, particularistic interests and
even to preventing the imposition of coherent, long-term policies.
Whatever the outcome, the personal vote is highly important in
single-member district systems. Its implications extend to the processes of policy making and ultimately to the nature of the policies
themselves.

Study Design

This study of the United States and Great Britain contrasts a political system in which national representatives are viewed as independent political entrepreneurs with one in which national representatives are viewed as the regimented members of cohesive parties. Within the universe of single-member, simple plurality systems, the United States and Great Britain offer the greatest contrast and the most difficult test for arguments based on the significance of electoral incentives.

The design of the study includes both elite and mass components in each country. A comprehensive study of representational questions must provide information about both representatives and those whom they represent. Surveys of the general public alone cannot show what elites really do, nor can surveys of elites show what the public really thinks. The two levels must be brought together in one study, as in the 1958 Miller-Stokes Survey Research Center (SRC) study of representation and the mid-1960s Butler-Stokes study of political change in Britain.[38]

The data on constituents in the United States come primarily from the 1978 and 1980 National Election Studies carried out by the University of Michigan Center for Political Studies, hereafter referred to as NES/CPS.[39] In 1978 the NES/CPS survey introduced a number of items designed to explore nonpolicy aspects of representative-constituency relationships. The survey sampled constituents in 108 of the 435 congressional districts. In order to examine changes over time, we also use the 1958 SRC study and the 1963–1966 Butler-Stokes study.

The data on congressmen and their offices come from interviews with 102 administrative assistants in the 108 offices whose constituents fell in the mass survey sampling frame. The assistants were chosen for interviews because they generally know more than the congressmen about office activity and organization. Few congressmen get deeply involved personally in the details of office structure and activity. The congressional questionnaire included items on the size and organization of the congressman's office, the kinds of activities it undertakes, its attitude toward various constituency activities, and its perception of the efficacy of constituency service efforts. Because of the presumed importance of the electoral incentive in the United States, the American questionnaire focused less on motives than did the British. And because of the generous staffing and equipping of congressional offices, the American questionnaire focused much more on patterns of resource employment.

The British surveys were designed to parallel those in the United States insofar as practical. The data on constituents were obtained from a postelection poll conducted by the British Gallup organization in May of 1979, using questions adapted from the NES/CPS survey to fit the British context. In most instances this meant only small changes in wording, such as "constituency" for "district," but a few concepts were harder to translate.

The data on British MPs come from interviews with 69 MPs and 32 party agents from 101 of the 133 constituencies included in the Gallup sampling frame.[40] A sample of agents and MPs does not exactly parallel a sample of administrative assistants. Agents are staff of the party, not the MP, and their involvement in constituency service varies greatly. The typical MP's staff consists only of some secretarial support, and MPs themselves are deeply engaged in constituency work. Thus the MP was the primary survey target, with the agent a second choice when the MP was unavailable. Because MPs have so much less than congressmen in the way of staff and other resources, and because their motives for engaging in constituency work are less clear, the British questionnaire focused more heavily on their motives, perceptions, and thinking.

Table I.2. Study design

Data	United States	Great Britain
Members	Administrative assistant interviews $(n = 102)$	MP interviews $(n = 69)$
		Agent interviews $(n = 32)$
Constituents	1978 NES/CPS $(n = 2304)$	1979 Gallup $(n = 2031)$
	1980 NES/CPS $(n = 1408)$	1963, 1964, 1966 Butler-Stokes $(n = 2009, 1769, 1874)$
	1958 SRC $(n = 1450)$	

The design of the study makes it possible to compare the perceptions and behavior of American and British representatives and to compare the perceptions, evaluations, and behavior of the American and British publics (Table I.2). More important, it permits the combination of information within each country so as to associate each constituent with a level of activity undertaken by the member of Congress or Parliament from that district and to associate each member with a distribution of perceptions and evaluations of his or her efforts. The value of the merged data set is that it permits an examination of the relationships between what constituents see and what representatives actually do, thereby avoiding the vulnerability of survey responses to problems of perceptual bias. A relationship between constituent perceptions and constituent evaluations of representatives' activities is not as convincing as a relationship between constituent evaluations and reports by administrative assistants or MPs about their activities.

Part I

CONSTITUENCY
SERVICE

1

Member Visibility
and Member Images

Visibility is the cornerstone of an effective district strategy. Without visibility, representatives cannot have independent standing in the electorate's collective mind, and without independent standing they cannot anticipate personal success in otherwise unfavorable political circumstances.

The conventional wisdom about congressional elections accords candidate visibility an importance second only to party identification. The 1958 SRC election study and the 1978 NES/CPS study show that visibility carries a significant electoral advantage. There are few comparable analyses of MP visibility in Great Britain, though surveys typically show that MPs enjoy a higher level of name recall than congressmen.[1] Several factors may underlie this difference. For one thing, the British ballot is much simpler than the American. Rather than decide on every office from president to prothonotary, with congressmen, judges, and coroners in between, the British voter makes a single choice. Fewer decisions presumably entail less confusion and interference for the British voter than for the American facing a laundry list of choices. In addition to such cognitive explanations, there once was a good institutional reason for higher name recall of MPs. Until a statutory change in 1969, the candidates' parties were not listed with their names on the ballot. Thus, the ability to cast a sensible vote for the national government was predicated on the ability to match proper names with parties. Perhaps such an emphasis on who stands for each party lingers on after its objective basis has disappeared.

Name Recall and Recognition

The visibility of American and British representatives is measured by the recall and recognition of candidates' names (Table 1.1). The figures on recall in both countries were generated from the simple survey questions, "Do you happen to remember the names of the candidates for Congress (Parliament) who ran in this district (constituency) last fall (on May 3)?" Name recognition is harder to measure. The feeling thermometer was used to elicit recognition in the United States, on the assumption that any response other than

Table 1.1. Comparative visibility of congressmen and MPs

	Name	
Status of member	Recall	Recognition
United States[a]		
Incumbents	32%	82%
Democrats	31	81
Republicans	32	83
Challengers	12	43
Democrats	12	43
Republicans	12	43
Great Britain		
Incumbents	65	—
Labour	64	—
Conservative	65	—
Liberal	78	—
Nationalists	67	—
Challengers	48	—
Labour	48	—
Conservative	42	—

a. Averages of 1978 and 1980.

"Don't know anything about this person" is tantamount to recognition. Since budget constraints in Britain prevented use of the feeling thermometer there, no recognition figures were gathered for MPs.

The recall of congressional candidates is less than half as high as recognition. Only about a third of all citizens recall the incumbent candidate, but four-fifths recognize the name when presented with it. The disparity is even greater for challengers, with almost four times as many people recognizing the names of challengers as recalling them. Members of Congress have a wide edge over their challengers by either measure. Republican challengers had recognition levels 10 percent higher than Democrats in 1980 and 10 percent lower in 1978. Jacobson's observations probably account for some part of these differences. The districts surveyed in 1978 had weaker challengers compared to all districts. Moreover, these weaker challengers received less of the sample vote than the totals objectively recorded for them. Of course, the majority of challengers were Republican. In 1980 a well-organized and well-financed Republican effort probably accounted for the higher visibility of Republican challengers.[2]

Name recall in Britain is much higher than in the United States—twice as high for incumbents and four times as high for challengers (where multiple challengers are present in a constituency, the challenger recall figure is that of the one who is best known). There are partisan differences in recall, with MPs of the two major parties trailing Liberals by a significant amount. This difference accords nicely with the Liberals' self-conscious emphasis on grass-roots campaign tactics and diligent service to the constituency.[3]

To promote cross-national comparability, succeeding analyses rely on name recall as the principal measure of visibility. Although recall underestimates visibility, it has the compensating advantage of possessing much more variance than name recognition. Recognition levels among American voters are so high that there is virtually no variation to analyze. Sole reliance on recall would be problematic if it led to conclusions different from those obtained by using name recognition, but in all subsequent analyses use of a recall rather than a recognition measure of visibility makes almost no difference for either coefficient estimates or goodness-of-fit statistics.

Representatives clear the perceptual thresholds of some constituents and not others for a variety of reasons. Individual characteristics predispose citizens to be more or less attentive to politics. Sociodemographic factors, such as education and occupation, and psychological factors, such as political interest and civic concern, influence what and how much particular voters know. In our studies visibility increases dramatically with self-described political attentiveness, a relationship that probably explains a tendency for self-identified independents to have lower recall levels than partisans. While visibility also shows the expected relationship with education and occupation, detailed statistical analysis indicates that the citizen's self-assessed attentiveness to public affairs is the single most important correlate of name recall (Table 1.2). Increases in attentiveness move the probability of recall dramatically upward. With attentiveness taken into account, none of the standard demographic indicators, such as education and occupation, have any independent impact on visibility, although they are themselves associated with attention to public affairs. These findings confirm the conclusions of other studies that demographic characteristics have no significant effects on the visibility of congressmen once the effects of attentiveness or interest are taken into account. One additional finding deserves brief mention. Affiliates of the congressman's party are significantly more likely to recall his or her name in the 1978 NES/CPS data, but a comparable relationship does not emerge in the 1980 NES/CPS data.

The patterns for British recall are similar (Table 1.3). Political attention is strongly connected to recall, though the British measure differs from the American. Partisans of an MP's party are more likely to recall the MP's name than are partisans of another stripe. The expected associations with occupational status and education also emerge, but in contrast to the United States, occupation retains a significant relationship with recall levels even when political attentiveness is controlled.[4]

These patterns comport with other findings on political capacity and interest. No matter how little some representatives do in office, some constituents will recall their names, just as some constituents will forget representatives' names no matter how much they do.

Over and above constituent characteristics, various characteristics of representatives themselves may increase their salience to constituents. Serving as prime minister is an extreme example, but less extreme possibilities are holding committee positions in the United States and serving on the ministerial ladder in Britain. Even

Table 1.2. Correlates of member visibility in United States (probit estimates)

Variables	Name recall 1978[a]	Name recall 1980[b]
Constituent characteristics		
Party identification		
Independent	−.22*	−.53**
Same as member	.23*	−.02
Attention to public affairs		
Low	.37**	.41*
Medium	.47**	.75**
High	.90**	1.11**
Incumbent characteristics		
Committee chair	—	−.16
Subcommittee chair	.09	.02
Year elected	.00	.02**
Incumbent contacts		
Met personally	.19*	.50**
Heard speak	.33**	.21
Talked to staff	.01	.24
Mail	.52**	.39**
Newspaper/magazines	.28**	.39**
Radio	.19*	.10
TV	.17*	.07
Hearsay	.26**	.12
Constant	−1.58**	−3.37**
Chi-square/df	365/15**	246/16**

a. $n = 1483$.　　*$p < .05$.
b. $n = 1022$.　　**$p < .01$.

the representative's tenure in office may have an effect in that past activities and publicity could accumulate and result in currently higher visibility. Additionally, visibility in the United States may be purchased more or less directly by the expenditure of campaign funds.

The findings on each of these possibilities, however, are weak and inconsistent. Newer members are more visible in both countries.

Table 1.3. Correlates of member visibility in
Great Britain (probit estimates)

Variables	Name recall[a]
Constituent characteristics	
Party identification	
None	−.11
Same as MP	.22**
Occupation	
Manual	.30*
White collar	.48**
Attention to campaign	.13**
Incumbent characteristics	
Ministerial ladder	.01
Opposition spokesman	−.03
Year elected	.01*
Incumbent contacts	
Met personally	.49**
Heard speak	.27*
Talked to agent/secretary	.21
Received mail	.44**
Newspaper/magazine	.40**
Radio	.10
TV	.45**
Hearsay	.10
Constant	−1.44**
Chi-square/df	220/16**

a. $n = 1267$.
*$p < .05$.
**$p < .01$.

There is no significant relationship between recall levels and formal
position in either country, although simple cross-tabulations suggest
that subcommittee chairs and holders of party committee positions
are more visible in the United States. Finally, name recall of congressmen increases with campaign spending, but the magnitude of
the relationship is weak and not especially linear.[5]

The most interesting correlates of visibility are those under the
control of the representative: his or her personal activities, behavior,
and allocation of available resources. Representatives can try to influence their level of visibility by spending time in their geographic
districts, providing services for and assuming responsibilities in their

constituencies, and publicizing their activities and accomplishments. Measuring the personal characteristics of constituents and representatives is a relatively straightforward task; measuring the impact of representatives' activities is less so. There are two types of data, each of which presents a partial picture: what constituents report and what representatives report.

A battery of survey questions address the issue of activities. In particular, there is the so-called contact question which reads:

> "There are many ways in which U.S. representatives (MPs) can have contact with the people from their district (constituency). On this page are some of these ways. Think of (name) who has been the U.S. representative (MP) from this district (constituency). Have you come into contact with or learned anything about (him/her) in any of these ways? Which ones?"

Citizens were asked to choose from the list of possibilities (Table 1.4). Despite the MPs' higher level of name recall, they do not have contact levels nearly as high as those reported for congressmen. On almost every count congressmen have figures twice as high as MPs. The exception is personal meetings, which may reflect the much smaller size of British constituencies.[6]

Although the level of reported contacts in Britain is lower than in the United States, the relationship between contacts and visibility is equally strong. The levels of name recall in both countries are

Table 1.4. Citizen contact with incumbent representatives

Type of contact	United States[a]	Great Britain
Met personally	14%	12%
Attended meeting where he/she spoke	12	7
Talked to staffer	9	4
Received mail	54	25
Read about in newspaper or magazine	52	32
Heard on radio	25	7
Saw on TV	43	16
Second-hand[b]	29	15
None whatsoever	21	44

a. Averages of 1978 and 1980.

b. Response to question, "Do you know anyone, any of your family, friends, or people at work, who have had some contact with (name)?"

significantly higher among individuals who report some kind of contact with their representative (Table 1.5). In Britain, a 20 percent gap in recall emerges between those who report any contact with the MP and those who do not. In the United States, the gap is on average close to 30 percent. The associations between contacts and recall are substantively strong and statistically significant (Tables 1.2–1.3). Personal meetings, the receipt of mail, reading about the member in newspapers or magazines, and seeing him or her on TV all relate to recall. In both Britain and the United States radio and staff contact appear to be less efficacious than other means of building visibility, though in Britain few MPs have much that would strike an American as staff.

These findings are consistent with the argument that incumbent behavior affects constituent awareness, although it is curious that

Table 1.5. Association of member visibility with reported contacts

	Recall	
Type of contact	United States[a]	Great Britain
Met member	62%	87%
Not met	30	62
Heard member speak	66	88
Not heard	30	63
Talked to staff	59	92
Not talked	32	64
Received mail	49	82
No mail	17	60
Read about member	48	81
Not read	18	57
Heard on radio	52	84
Not heard	28	63
Saw on TV	47	83
Not seen	25	61
Second-hand	55	79
No second-hand	26	63
No contact at all	8	46

a. 1978.

nearly half of British constituents recall the names of representatives they deny having met, heard, heard about, read about, or seen on TV. Of course, the reported contacts must themselves be explained, and the explanations draw on the same sorts of factors that arose in connection with recall and recognition. In the United States political attentiveness relates most strongly to reported contact, with the relationships stronger for the impersonal or media categories. The same structure of relationships holds for educational level, though the magnitudes of the relationship are weaker. Only reports of hearsay and receipt of mail show significant relationships with occupational status. Self-professed political independents are least likely to report contacts.

In Britain the picture is less clear-cut than in the United States. Reading about the MP is strongly related to education, but five of the eight contact types show no relationship whatsoever with education. The relationships between contacts and attention to the campaign are consistent but not as strong as those for name recall. Finally, constituents with no party identification are the least likely to report contacts, and those sharing the MP's affiliation are the most likely.

As for representatives' characteristics, in the United States reported contacts are marginally related to seniority level: the more senior the congressman, the greater the likelihood of contacts, especially of the secondhand variety. This pattern is the reverse of the negative relation between seniority and name recall. In Britain, however, there is no relationship between tenure in office and reported contacts except that the most senior MPs are most likely to have been heard on the radio and seen on TV, perhaps reflecting their somewhat greater likelihood of holding or having held important positions in the parliamentary party.

Finally, the relationships between position in the Congress and contacts are neither strong nor consistent and thus provide little basis for generalization. Constituents of American subcommittee chairs consistently report a higher level of contact—19 percent higher in the case of TV. Constituents of congressmen who hold Democratic leadership posts are 20 percent more likely to report meeting or hearing their congressmen personally but are no more likely to report the more passive forms of contact. The pattern is the reverse for constituents of Republican leaders. Such relationships are linked to those for seniority; later chapters will attempt to disentangle the common influences. In Britain, parliamentary position bears no discernible relationship with contact levels, consistent with the previous lack of association with name recall.

In short, more educated and more politically attentive constituents are more likely to know their representatives' names, as they are more likely to know many other things about politics and government. But name recall also is strongly related to constituents' reports about the ways in which they have come into contact with their representatives. This suggests that representatives have it within their power to make an impact on constituents by the activities they undertake.

National Expectations

Being known per se is not enough for most incumbents; few would trade obscurity for a widespread but unfavorable image. U.S. congressmen with image problems may have difficulty raising funds or finding campaign volunteers and may attract strong challengers. British MPs with poor images may create morale problems among local activists or provoke a fight over their readoption. Negative images ultimately contribute to electoral defeat. Consequently, representatives who want to stay in office try to create positive images of themselves. Richard Fenno called the array of activities directed at producing these images the representative's "home style."[7]

Home style is in part a unique, individualized response of members to their districts and the natural inclinations of their personalities, but the public also holds stylized perceptions of representatives and their responsibilities, including expectations about how representatives should behave in office. These expectations derive in part from the common wisdom about how a country's political system works but also from the class, ethnic, age, and social-economic background of constituents. To the extent that role expectations differ across districts, representatives will tailor their home styles accordingly. If representatives satisfy constituent expectations, their images will benefit and their electoral bases will be more secure. Conversely, failure to satisfy constituent expectations can adversely affect the representatives' images and weaken their electoral bases.

Conceptions of a representative's duties traditionally arise from conceptions of the state's responsibilities. Thus, the Benthamite representative makes laws that maximize the greatest happiness for the greatest number; the Lockean representative legislates in order to eliminate the inconveniences of property and personal insecurity in the state of nature; and the Hegelian representative represents one of the major interests in civil society.[8] In the real world, legislative duties do not always match so neatly with the state's responsibilities. Part of the representative's job in contemporary British and American government has a direct constitutional source, but other parts have developed as representatives responded to constituent demands. Since representatives may find it advantageous to encourage these demands, the role of the representative can evolve as representatives and their constituents discover complementary interests.

Because perceptions of appropriate legislative roles can affect how constituents evaluate representatives, it is useful to know how the citizens of Great Britain and the United States perceive legislative responsibilities. But creating a survey question that is comparable and yet sensitive to important differences in the American and British political systems is no simple matter. The 1978 NES/CPS survey of American voters showed them a list of "activities that occupy members of the U.S. House of Representatives as part of their job" and asked them to "rank the activities in order of importance." The same procedure was followed as far as possible in the British survey, but it was necessary to change the wording of the alternatives that British voters were asked to rank. The activities listed for the two countries were:

United States	*United Kingdom*
1. Helping people in the district who have personal problems with the government (abbreviated as "helping people").	1. Helping people in the constituency who have personal problems with the government.
2. Making sure the district gets its fair share of government money and projects ("protecting the district").	2. Protecting the interests of the constituency.
3. Keeping track of the way government agencies are carrying out laws passed by Congress ("oversight").	3. Keeping track of civil servants.

United States	*United Kingdom*
4. Keeping in touch with the people about what the government is doing ("keeping in touch").	4. Keeping in touch with the people about what the government is doing.
5. Working in Congress on bills concerning national issues ("policy").	5. Debating and voting in Parliament.

In cross-national surveys the interests of comparability frequently conflict with those of sensitivity to intercountry differences. This conflict is nowhere more evident than in the third activity listed, keeping track of government agencies. Members of Parliament traditionally have not had access to civil servants, nor have committees in Parliament enjoyed the subpoena and investigatory powers of congressional committees. MPs can question a minister who is responsible for a particular department of the civil service, but for the most part investigations of administrative abuse are handled by the national ombudsman. Still, MPs have retained their right to refer cases directly to the ombudsman, and they can use the threat of adverse publicity and hostile questions in the Commons as well as their informal contacts with ministers to put pressure on offending bureaucrats.[9] So while administrative oversight has more meaning in the context of the American system than in the British, it is sufficiently meaningful in Britain to warrant inclusion.

When asked the question, "Which of these activities is the most important," the voters in each country differed in their responses (Table 1.6). Americans ranked these activities from the most important: keeping in touch, policy, protecting the district and oversight (tied), and helping people. British respondents ranked the

Table 1.6. Most important representative role

Role	United States	Great Britain
Helping people	11%	19%
Protecting district	15	26
Oversight	15	4
Keeping in touch	30	24
Policy	19	11
Don't know, all, none	10	16

alternatives in the order: protecting the district, keeping in touch, helping people, policy, and oversight.[10] As anticipated, a major difference between the rankings in the two countries is that oversight is rated a distant last by the British but tied for third among the Americans. It is reassuring to find that mass surveys reflect to a considerable degree objective differences in the operation of political systems.

Institutional differences also undoubtedly underlie the lesser importance of the policy role in Great Britain. The backbench MP is virtually irrelevant to the policy-making process. Individual MPs cannot change legislation in committee—if they are fortunate enough to sit on one—and are severely constrained by the norms of party discipline. Much of the discussion about Parliamentary reform in the 1960s and 1970s centered on how to give backbench MPs a more meaningful role in legislation. Ironically, while MPs have been pushing to increase their policy-making responsibilities, American congressmen have sometimes appeared to be avoiding such responsibilities. Indeed, some have argued that congressmen have accentuated their casework and pork barrel roles precisely because these entail less electoral risk than the advocacy of controversial policies.[11]

The constituency service roles, protecting the district and helping people, were ranked highest by one-quarter of the American respondents and by nearly half of the British. Indeed, protecting the district was the highest-ranking role in Britain. Objectively, the weaker party system and the power of committees make this role more realistic in the United States than in the United Kingdom. In the American context, securing projects and other advantages for the district is the traditional pork barrel function of the congressman, a function that would seem altogether absent in Britain. Most of the MPs, however, mentioned many specific things they did for their constituencies, such as leading a campaign to prevent the closing of a local hospital, urging the government to construct a road, helping to raise funds for the local football team, and helping to organize a job fair in areas of high unemployment. Moreover, the discovery that British constituents regard the protection of constituency interests as very important comports with evidence that selection committees value a candidate with a feel for local concerns.[12]

The helping people or social worker role was ranked by nearly a fifth of the British constituents as the single most important activity

undertaken by an MP. In fact, 40 percent of the British ranked helping people who have personal problems with the government as one
of the two most important activities an MP undertakes. This is
surprising, since the growth of congressmen's casework responsibilities and of the resources to accommodate them have received far
more attention than have the responsibilities and meager resources
of MPs.[13]

Constituents in both countries assign high importance to the simple matter of the representative's keeping in touch. This partly reflects the fact that constituents want their representatives to have
a good sense of their district's particular concerns. But concern for
close contact also relates to such broader concerns as whether people
think their representatives should act as trustees or as delegates for
them.[14] Delegates adopt the views of those who elect them, whereas
trustees exercise their own independent judgment of the best interest of their constituents. In the United States the keeping-in-touch
function and the delegate role are popularly connected. Those Americans who thought that keeping in touch was most important were
inclined to prefer the delegate role to the trustee role, 64 percent to
25 percent. In contrast, those who said that policy making was most
important preferred the delegate role over the trustee role by a less
striking 51 percent to 33 percent. Unfortunately, there is no comparable data in Britain to show whether a relationship exists there
as well.

Group Expectations

Not only are there significant cross-national differences in the rankings of preferred legislator activities but there also are significant
differences among groups within countries. Specifically, there are
discernible educational, class, ethnic, and party variations in the
expectations held by British and American constituents. Such differences in group rankings are more pronounced in the United States
than in Britain. In the United Kingdom there are variations in the
relative percentages of those who think that a given role is most
important, but only a few differences in the actual rankings across
the various groups. In the United States, however, there are marked
differences in group rankings as well as in the relative percentages.
Discussion of these differences relies on multivariate models (Tables
1.7–1.8). In each of these models whether the respondent ranked the

particular role as most important is the judgment we seek to explain.

The better-educated, middle-class individuals in both countries favor a more policy-oriented role for their representatives, whereas the less well educated, working-class individuals favor a more ser-

Table 1.7. Correlates of role importance in United States (probit estimates)[a]

Constituent characteristics	Keeping track of civil servants	Protect district	Helping people	Keeping in touch	Policy
Union	.059	.105†	−.099	−.055	.000
Age	.010*	−.003	.004*	−.011*	.004*
High school	−.076	−.143*	−.067	.002	.330*
Some college	.016	−.328*	−.280*	−.038	.578*
College	−.227*	−.526*	−.245*	−.211*	.987*
Male	−.057	−.076	−.011	−.020	.150*
Middle class	.109†	−.053	.051	−.102†	.108†
Same party as incumbent	−.006	.031	.062	−.038	−.015
Democrat	−.112†	.198*	−.000	−.049	−.004
Republican	−.070	.203*	−.220*	.023	−.005
Black	−.079	.246*	.230*	−.210*	−.173†
Chi-square/df = 11	38**	54**	29**	53**	133*

a. $n = 1944$.   **$p < .01$.   *$p < .05$.   †$p < .10$.

Table 1.8. Correlates of role importance in Great Britain (probit estimates)

Constituent characteristics	Keeping track of civil servants	Protect constituency	Helping people	Keeping in touch	Policy
Union	−.122	.001	−.129	.062	.149
Left school < 14	.270	−.104	.277*	.308*	−.542*
Middle class	−.090	−.052	−.126	.067	.203*
Age < 20	−.262*	−.110	−.032	.198*	.203*
Male	.242*	.020	−.097	−.128*	.205*
Conservative	−.082	.083	−.085	−.150	.251*
Labour	−.114	−.176†	.069	.104	.054
Liberal	−.171	.219*	−.023	−.332*	.212
Same party as incumbent	−.048	.062	.096	−.079	−.087
Constant	−1.760	−.370	−.880	−.840	−1.010
Chi-square/df = 9	13	22**	24**	39**	63**

a. $n = 1703$.   **$p < .01$.   *$p < .05$.   †$p < .10$.

vice-oriented role. The education effect is particularly striking. In the United States 40 percent of the college educated thought that the policy role was the congressman's most important function, whereas only 17 percent of those with less than a high-school education thought so. The college educated ranked policy number one, whereas the high-school educated ranked it third, behind keeping in touch and protecting the interests of the district. The effect is equally strong in Great Britain. Those who left school at the age of fourteen or less ranked policy fourth, whereas those who stayed in school beyond the age of eighteen ranked policy a close second. The least well educated individuals in both countries ranked keeping in touch first and protecting the interests of the district second. Helping people, which most closely proxies the casework role, was also more heavily favored by the least-educated group, although its ranking did not change in either instance.

Over and above education, social class is significantly related to the ranking of policy and service functions. Characteristically, the rankings of the working class and middle class were identical in Britain, but the percentages varied somewhat. Ten percent of the working class indicated that policy was the most important role of the MP, whereas 17 percent of the middle class felt this way. Conversely, 26 percent of the working class felt that helping people was the most important role, whereas 20 percent of the middle class said so. As with education, Americans showed both a percentage and a ranking difference: the middle class ranked policy second, while the working class ranked it tied for third.

Race is a major continuing feature of American politics. Blacks ranked the roles of representatives very differently from the rest of the groups. They regarded policy as the least important activity and considered protecting the interests of the district and helping people as, respectively, second and third most important. As a group, blacks placed a higher priority on helping people than did any other group. To some extent this racial difference arises from educational and class differences, but even when such factors are taken into account, racial differences in representative priorities remain.

Sociodemographic differences like these parallel differences in political knowledge, interest, and participation. A study of political participation in America found that better-educated, higher-income individuals are more likely to participate in all ways, such as voting, particularized contact, community participation, and campaign activity. The gap in participation is smallest, however, with respect to particularized contact or casework.[15]

Other differences in the priorities of groups are less significant. Age differences are stronger in the United States than in the United Kingdom. Younger constituents in both countries seem more inclined to think that keeping in touch is important. Older constituents, however, think that helping people and, in the United States, oversight are more important. Union membership matters more in Great Britain, with union members in both countries emphasizing policy more and helping people less. Finally, there are scattered party effects. Liberals emphasize protecting the interests of the constituency more than do supporters of other parties, which is consistent with the "parish pump politics" image they projected in the 1960s and 1970s. Conservatives place greater emphasis on policy. In the United States, Republicans attach less importance to the helping people role and surprisingly more importance to protecting the district.

The finding of a class, educational, and racial preference for district service reinforces the fact that a representative's home style is influenced by the kind of district he or she represents.[16] The choice of an issue-oriented home style rather than a more service-oriented style is shaped in part by the expectations that constituents hold. Representatives probably can affect the expectations of constituents as well, but a representative who wants to be issue oriented in a working-class, low-education district probably receives less appreciation from his or her constituents than someone who adopts an issue orientation in a middle-class, high-education district.

Party Discipline

Another expectation that influences constituent evaluations of representatives is the extent to which congressmen and MPs adhere to the party line rather than exercise their own judgment when voting on legislation. A priori, one would expect differences in the attitudes of the British and American publics on this question. The postwar British party system has been characterized by high levels of party discipline, particularly when compared to the party system in the United States. Support for the president by members of the administration party in the House of Representatives ranged from 61 percent in 1977–1978 to 72 percent in 1953–1954; by comparison, the percentage of divisions in Parliament witnessing any dissenting votes ranged from less than 1 percent in 1964–1966 to 28 percent in 1974–1979. The situation in Great Britain has thus changed in recent years. Indeed, backbench rebellions have increased to such an extent as to alter traditional notions about motions of confidence and the customs surrounding resignations.[17] In the 1978 NES/CPS and 1979 Gallup studies people were asked whether representatives should "support the position their parties take when something comes up for a vote, or should they make up their own minds regardless of how their parties want them to vote." There were three alternatives from which to choose: "support the party," "it depends," and "make up their own minds." Although the views had significant and predictable cross-national differences, these were not nearly so large as might have been expected. The British were 15 percent less inclined to say that representatives should make up their own mind and 5 percent more inclined to say that representatives should support their party, as is consistent with the character of the British party system. Nonetheless, a majority in both countries felt that representatives should make up their own minds. On its face this finding suggests a surprising lack of public support for parliamentary discipline. Perhaps the unpopularity of recent governments, the trend away from the two major parties, and the growing unhappiness of voters, journalists, and academics with the British political system are reflected in people's desire to see their MPs act more independently. Thus, the new patterns of backbench rebellion appear to be consistent with the public's role expectations.[18]

Various groups view the "party or conscience" question differently in both countries. Again, education is an important factor, although its effect differs in the two countries. Eighty percent of college-educated individuals in the United States said that representatives should make up their own minds, whereas 68 percent of those with less than a high school education said so. In contrast, better-educated individuals in Britain were less likely (49 percent) to say that the representative should make up his or her own mind than were less well educated ones (60 percent). Education seemingly produces a better understanding of the operation of the parliamentary system. Again, surveys mirror institutional realities.

Finally, one might expect class differences in Britain to be significant, especially in light of H. M. Drucker's contention that loyalty is crucial to the working-class, Labour ethos.[19] As it turns out, however, the evidence for this presumption is slight and statistically insignificant. Moreover, it is stronger for Democrats in the United States than for Labour in Britain.

In sum, the public has three expectations of British and American representatives. First, in both countries constituents expect their members to play an active part in constituency affairs. Second, although there are predictable sociodemographic differences, even the most educated middle-class constituents expect their representatives to be accessible, to do casework, and to further the interests of their district. Third, although support for party loyalty is stronger in Britain, a majority in both countries would prefer their representatives to make up their own minds and not simply follow the lead of the parties.

National Evaluations

Incumbents who wish to make their positions more secure need to develop favorable images. But such images can be developed more easily in some types of political systems than in others. Given the important differences between the disciplined and nationalized British party system and the undisciplined and individualized American party system, MPs inevitably differ from congressmen in building favorable evaluations among constituents.

Evidence of this comes from a battery of questions asking British and American constituents whether there is anything in particular that they like about their incumbents. Congressmen have been more successful than their parliamentary counterparts in developing positive images. Whereas 43 percent of Americans claimed that they liked something about the incumbent, only 25 percent of the British said so. And whereas Americans had four times as many good things as bad things to say about their representatives, the British had only twice as many good things to say. Liberal MPs resembled American congressmen in the heavy preponderance of their positive remarks (56 percent) over their negative (15 percent). Perhaps this illustrates the efficacy of the "parish pump" tactics of the Liberal party.

Since MPs are closely associated with their parties, that fewer British respondents make positive comments about their representatives may reflect popular dissatisfaction with the party system (Table 1.9). British respondents were considerably more likely to mention the MP's party or policy views than were respondents in

Table 1.9. Substance of member evaluations

Content of constituent evaluation	United States		Great Britain	
	Positive	Negative	Positive	Negative
Constituency attentiveness	32%	11%	46%	35%
Personal/general	45	59	31	30
Party/policy	15	25	23	35
Other	8	5	—	—

the United States, and more than one-third of the negative references in Britain fell into the party or policy category, as compared to 25 percent in the United States. The greater prominence of party and policy issues in Great Britain is clearly apparent in the responses. Had British constituents made fewer remarks about party or policy, and more about constituency attentiveness and personal qualities, they would have evaluated their MPs relatively more positively.

A more important implication of Table 1.9 is the relatively greater risk of a policy strategy than the risk of constituency strategy. The ratios of positive to negative references for issues of party and policy were lower than those for constituency attentiveness and personal characteristics. In other words, people were more likely to say something bad about policy and party than about the other two categories. As a result, incumbents run fewer risks by emphasizing their personality and constituency service than by touting their views on policies.[20] Incumbents presumably need no advice from political scientists on this point.

The role expectations held by constituents may constitute a frame of reference for constituents if the abstract expectations they hold shape the way that they evaluate their incumbents. Thus people who believe that the policy-making role of the representative is most important could be more inclined to evaluate their incumbents in terms of policy positions, while people who think that the district service role is most important could be more inclined to evaluate their incumbents in terms of their constituency activity. In the United States the relationships are rather weak. Americans made almost twice as many positive references to constituency service as to policy, regardless of their abstract beliefs about the comparative importance of policy and constituency roles. Although the negative references in the constituency realm were too few to analyze, Americans who considered the policy role most important were ever so slightly more likely to make negative references to policy than were those who considered the constituency role most important. The relationships are weak but more consistent in Britain. There were too few positive references to the policy stands of the incumbent MPs to analyze, but negative references to policy were marginally more frequent when the policy-making role was ranked highest. Both positive and negative references to constituency tended to increase when the constituency service roles were rated highest.

Thus, there is slight evidence of a connection between what people consider the most important representative role and their evaluation of representatives. More exact tests would probably reveal a stronger connection. How representatives are judged varies to some degree with the role that their constituents think they should play, and certain activities are more or less politically rewarded in some kinds of districts than in others.

Implications for Member Images

U.S. congressmen present themselves to their constituents in a manner that is consistent with the makeup of their districts and their personalities. The incumbent's "presentation" is based on what he or she says or does in the course of meeting and dealing with district residents. Thus, by their choice of activities, incumbents can to some degree control the images that constituents have of them. In order to establish or improve their images, incumbents try to increase the number of favorable contacts they have with constituents through more personal visits, staff presence, casework solicitation, mailings, media appearances, and whatever else seems appropriate to particular districts.

To say that incumbents have some control over their images through their activities is far from asserting that they have complete control. The ease of communicating a message to constituents varies with education, class, and inherent political interest. Better-educated, middle-class, and highly active individuals assimilate the incumbent's message more quickly than less-educated, working-class, and politically indifferent ones. Moreover, the kind of appeal that succeeds with those who assimilate information quickly may be less appropriate to other constituents. For instance, middle-class, higher-educated whites have a relative preference for policy-oriented representation, whereas working-class, lower-educated minorities prefer service-oriented representation. Even more fundamentally, the message the incumbents try to convey to their constituents is colored by their partisan predispositions. So representatives' control over how they are evaluated is by no means complete.

Caveats aside, incumbents' activities do affect the tendency of constituents to form positive or negative images of them. This issue can be explored in two ways. First, those constituents who report various forms of contact with their representatives are more likely to say something positive or negative about them. Reported contacts of all varieties are significantly related to the formation of incumbent images. For instance, whereas 43 percent of the Americans and 25 percent of the British could mention something they liked about the incumbent, that percentage approximately doubled to 80 percent in the United States and 55 percent in Britain among those who had personally met the incumbent. Similarly, knowing someone else who had had some form of contact with the representative, contacting the representative for help, and knowing someone else who had requested help significantly increased the percentage of those who could say what they liked or disliked about their representative.

Self-reported contact may be biased by existing impressions of the representative. If people like their representatives, they may be more likely to get in contact with them. This would not explain why dislikes also increase with incumbent contact, but the probability of simultaneous causation cannot be casually dismissed. Therefore, a second way to look at the relationship between incumbent activity and images—a way which gets around the issue of a potentially biased contact response—is to see whether constituent opinions favoring or disapproving the incumbent relate to independent estimates of incumbent activity, the subject of Chapters 5 and 6.

In summary, only about a third of the American public and a sixth of the British regard policy making and administrative oversight as the most important jobs a representative should undertake. Constituents in both countries favor a strong district orientation and some degree of party independence from their representatives. There are clear class, educational, and racial differences in these role expectations, suggesting that representatives in different districts are rewarded for different mixes of activities.

Constituents have favorable images of their representatives, though these images are considerably more positive in the United States than in Britain. These images are in some degree related to expectations, particularly in Britain, so that members are not entirely free to cultivate any image they might wish. The effect of contact with the member upon constituent evaluations is quite strong in both countries. Thus, taking an active role in constituency affairs and communicating these efforts widely would appear to be an effective way for representatives to create a favorable image among constituents.

2

The Nature of
Constituency Service

Constituents attach relatively greater importance to service responsiveness and allocation responsiveness than do academics, who traditionally have been preoccupied by policy responsiveness or congruence. To be sure, policy congruence is an important matter, but as Heinz Eulau and Paul Karps noted, "Exclusive emphasis on the policy aspects of responsiveness may give a one-sided view," and as Richard Fenno further noted: "The point is not that policy preferences are not a crucial basis for the representational relationship. They are. The point is that we should not start our studies of representation by assuming they are the only basis for a representational relationship. They are not."[1] The survey data do not suggest that constituents are obsessed by policy congruence. Though they attach great importance to policy congruence in the abstract, only a handful of respondents in the surveys actually evaluate their representative primarily on the basis of national policy or ideological considerations. While it is logically conceivable that representatives reflect constituents' policy preferences so well that policy responsiveness is universal and thus never mentioned as something constituents like about the representative, in a heterogeneous country this possibility seems exceedingly improbable.

Constituents appear to focus on the tangible and the proximal relatively more than academics, who prefer the intangible and the distal. Whereas constituents attach considerable importance to policy making in the abstract, when it comes to *evaluating* their representatives, policy considerations decline sharply, and constituent assistance and district service considerations advance. The only considerations that are slightly more common are the personal qualities of the representatives, and these may depend on the representatives' record in other areas, constituency service being at least as likely a possibility as policy evaluations. It is not that policy and programmatic considerations are irrelevant to representative-constituency relations. Such considerations are by no means absent from other varieties of citizen evaluations of representatives and, more to the point, from citizen voting decisions. But the scholarly literature has underemphasized service responsiveness and allocation responsiveness. For too long political scientists have viewed such aspects of representation as primitive or lower forms of political behavior—belonging to a category ranging from baby kissing to bribery—best kept out of serious academic discussion.

Constituency Perceptions

Fenno provided a working definition of constituency service:

> Many activities can be incorporated under the rubric of "district service," or "constituent service," but the core activity is providing help to individuals, groups, and localities in coping with the federal government. Individuals need someone to intercede with the bureaucracies handling their veterans' benefits, social security checks, military status, civil service pension, immigration proceedings, and the like. Private groups and local governments need assistance in pursuing federal funds for water and sewer projects, highways, dams, buildings, planning, research and development, small business loans, and so forth. Sometimes service benefiting individuals is known as "casework" and service having larger numbers of benefactors is called "project assistance." Sometimes both are lumped together as casework.[2]

To study casework, the 1978 NES/CPS study adapted the following battery of items from the 1958 SRC study:

> Have you (or anyone in your family living here) ever contacted Representative (name) or anyone in his/her office?
> (If yes) Was it to:

Express an opinion?
Seek information?
Seek help on a problem you had?
Did you get a response?
How satisfied were you with the response: very satisfied, some-
what satisfied, not very satisfied, or not at all satisfied?

Constituents then were asked whether they knew of anyone else who had contacted the representative and, if so, whether they had received a response and their degree of satisfaction with the response. No differentiation was made by the three possible purposes of contact—offer an opinion, seek information, seek help. Constituents were asked the following less personal item (also adapted from the 1958 SRC study) designed to tap "allocation responsiveness": "Do you happen to remember anything special that your U.S. representative (name) has done for this district or for the people in this district while (he/she) has been in Congress?" Up to two responses per respondent were recorded. These survey items were modified in the obvious ways for use in Great Britain.

In the United States the 1978 and 1980 figures are very similar (Table 2.1). Roughly 15 percent of the American public reported having gotten in touch with a congressman or with his or her office. These communications were fairly evenly distributed among the three kinds of purpose. In Britain, fewer people reported having contacted their MP, with most of them specifying that the contact involved a request for help.

The citizens of both countries overwhelmingly felt that their requests and communications were handled satisfactorily. Ninety percent or more received a response; nearly half in Great Britain and more than half in the United States were highly satisfied with the response; and only small minorities in both countries were unhappy with the response they received. The slight variations in these figures seem plausible enough. Those who wrote or called to express opinions were the most likely to be ignored in Britain, and in the United States in 1978. Such people were also somewhat more likely to express dissatisfaction with their response in the United States but not in Britain. Representatives would be expected to have most difficulty satisfying those who communicate strong policy disagreements or "crank" positions, and in some cases they might choose to ignore the communication. The flip side of these differences is the relatively higher level of satisfaction expressed by those

Table 2.1. Constituent communications and evaluations of response

Communication or evaluation	United States		Great Britain
	1978	1980	1979
Citizen-initiated contacts	15%	16%	8%
Express opinion	6	6	2
Seek information	6	6	2
Seek help	5	9	5
Response			
None			
Opinion	10	4	17
Information	4	6	5
Help	6	6	9
Very satisfied			
Opinion	52	49	31
Information	61	64	47
Help	65	61	54
Not satisfied[a]			
Opinion	13	20	12
Information	7	8	19
Help	10	16	18
Second-hand contacts	19	20	6
Response			
None	4	3	—
Satisfied	69	62	—
Not satisfied	6	6	—
District service	29	18	13
Particularized	10	9	—
Pork barrel	8	8	—

a. Collapsing of two least positive coding categories.

requesting information or seeking help. In Britain, however, information and help requests resulted in both more satisfied and more dissatisfied constituents than did expressions of opinion. In general, the help and information responses are sufficiently similar to be combined into a single category of casework.

In addition to personal and familial communications, constituents hear about the experiences of others who communicate with representatives. About 20 percent of the Americans but a much smaller proportion of the British had such second-hand experiences. These experiences too were highly positive.[3] Second-hand communications are not differentiated by purpose, but constituents would probably hear more about the aid representatives have provided their friends and co-workers than about expressions of opinion. Thus, we treat the second-hand citizen-initiated contact data as second-hand casework data, though this may overestimate casework somewhat.

Finally, a fifth or more of the Americans and an eighth of the British claimed to recall something special that the incumbent had done for the district. About half these individuals in the United States mentioned a particularized benefit of some sort, with slightly fewer specifically mentioning a local project or program. In Britain, most of those recalling some district service mentioned a clearly local matter.

While only small minorities of constituents have personally received assistance from their representatives, the proportions were larger among voters, especially in the United States. Also in the United States, though not in Britain, the probability of voting increased with the satisfaction of the casework experience. The direction of causality is unclear. Possibly those more "connected" to political affairs are more likely both to vote and to contact their representative, or alternatively the communication may stimulate participation, or both processes may be operating.[4]

Moreover, the sheer number of constituents who have personally received assistance from their representative may not be the crucial consideration. Because of differences in their sociodemographic composition, some constituencies may have a much greater basic demand for assistance than others, but constituents without current need might still believe that, should the need arise, their representative would be there to help. According to Fenno, congressmen attempt to create the general belief that they are accessible to constituents, that they would be helpful in appropriate situations, that they should be *trusted* by constituents. The 1978 NES/CPS survey included an item intended to tap this kind of relationship. Dubbed the expectation of access or expectation of helpfulness, it read: "If you had a problem that Representative [your MP] could do something about, do you think he/she would be very helpful, somewhat helpful, or not very helpful to you?" This question refers to an expectation rather than an experience, and the expectation presumably would be a function of the *reputation* of the representative. That reputation, in turn, would naturally reflect the efforts of the representative on behalf of his or her constituents but would also have the potential to affect the behavior of numerous constituents who had not had personal dealings with the member of Congress or Parliament. As it turns out, about a quarter of both British and American constituents expected their member to be "very helpful" if a problem arose, and only about a tenth expected that the member would not be helpful. The distribution is quite similar in the two countries, the only difference being a slightly higher percentage who volunteer an "it depends" answer in Britain.

Evaluative questions like the expectation of helpfulness item raise suspicions. Perhaps constituents simply expect incumbents of their party to be helpful and those of another party not to be. Or perhaps constituents are naturally prone to optimism and respond in a positive manner but one not systematically related to other interesting variables. Such disturbing possibilities cannot be completely dismissed, but statistical analyses provide some indication that expectations have real content and are neither purely random nor purely rationalization. The figures in Table 2.2 derive from statistical models in which expectations of access are related to a number of predictor variables. The models incorporate the hypotheses that incumbent reputations depend positively on visibility and on the actual provision of assistance to constituents. The models also test for the possibility that constituents have more positive expectations about an incumbent who shares their party affiliation. On the other side of the ledger, a visible challenger might dim the luster of the incumbent, given that the challenger may attack the incumbent's record, person, and so forth as part of his or her campaign.

The British and American results are similar. MPs get more political mileage out of personal contacts than congressmen, and congressmen perhaps get more out of second-hand contacts, contacts with friends, relatives, and co-workers about whom the constituent has heard.[5] After taking contacts into account, name recall had little or no effect in Great Britain or in the United States in 1980, but it had a significant effect in the United States in 1978. Partisanship was somewhat more important, *ceteris paribus*, in Britain, where minor party identifiers were even less likely to evidence positive expectations than identifiers with national parties different from the

Table 2.2. Expectation of access equations[a]

Variable	United States		Great Britain[d]
	1978[b]	1980[c]	
Contact			
Personal	.13*	.36**	.56**
Media	.36**	.39**	.23**
Second-hand	.32**	.24*	−.02
Casework			
Very satisfied	.90**	1.07**	.92**
Somewhat satisfied	−.32*	.17**	−.60*
Not satisfied	−1.18**	−1.22**	−1.39**
Second-hand casework			.57**
Satisfied	.36**	.66**	
Somewhat satisfied	.40*	.02	
Not satisfied	−1.22	−.67*	
District service	.53**	.38**	.55**
Party identification			
Independent	.04	.02	—
Minor party	—	—	−.44*
No party	—	—	.24*
Same party	.30**	.19*	.41**
Recall incumbent	.30**	.16†	.05
Recall challenger	−.49**	−.05	−.02
Year elected	.01*	−.01*	.01
Constant	−.26	1.25**	.14
Chi-square/df	311/15**	239/15**	179/14**

a. Positive coefficients indicate more positive expectations.
b. $n = 1135$.
c. $n = 811$.
d. $n = 821$.
*$p < .05$.
**$p < .01$.
†$p < .10$.

incumbent's (the latter constitute the omitted reference category in the set of dummy variables). Those who identified with the incumbent's party were naturally the most optimistic about the likelihood that the incumbent would help in a pinch. Finally, in the United States tenure in office yielded inconsistent results. In 1978 new incumbents were expected to be more helpful than more senior ones, but in 1980 the relationship was just the opposite. No relationship at all was apparent in Britain.

The variables that have the largest effect on expectation of help-fulness, however, are those that measure the incumbent's previous efforts. Satisfied constituents are highly positive about the member's future potential, and dissatisfied constituents, though rare, are highly negative (the omitted reference category for these dummy variables is comprised of those who report no casework experience).[6] Those who claim to recall something already done for the constituency are likewise very positive. These figures indicate that incumbent representatives can behave in a manner calculated to enhance their constituents' images of them, and this holds for MPs as much as for congressmen.

To be sure, these conclusions rely exclusively on mass survey data which are potentially subject to rationalization and misreporting. Thus, we will preview data of a more objective nature to be reported in later chapters. Respondents in different congressional and parliamentary districts show considerable variation in their expectations, from more than 75 percent very helpful to none very helpful. Such cross-district variation relates positively and significantly to independently obtained reports of incumbent activities and allocation of resources. Some amount of rationalization may still underly the relationships reported in Table 2.2, but the additional analyses indicate that these relationships reflect reality as well as rationalization.

The Demand for Service

The crucial component of constituency service is casework, which is defined as the provision of information and assistance to constituents who have problems. Although this definition remains very general, the range of matters that constituents bring to the attention of members of Congress or Parliament is enormous, encompassing both egregious injustices and trivial inconveniences. Sometimes even the representatives are surprised by what they are asked to do. Consider the experience of one MP: "My wife was going through some old correspondence the other day and she came across a letter that said: 'Dear Mr. Tuck, I want to thank you for all the help you have given me the past few weeks. My toaster has never worked better.' I can't for the life of me remember the details of the case, but I must have helped her get her appliance fixed." More typically, however, cases arise from disagreements between the constituent and some governmental body. Consider this example from the United States:

A shipyard worker had been severely crippled in an on-the-job accident. Because of technicalities in his former employment status, he had been three times ruled ineligible for disability compensation. A "Catch 22" interpretation also made welfare unavailable. By the time the constituent sought help at his Congressman's field office the situation was desperate. He had been unable to work for several years, medical and other bills had piled up, the family budget was in shambles, home utilities were about to be shut off, the family car had been repossessed and a bank was about to foreclose on the home mortgage.

Resolving this case required several months and more than a hundred caseworker manhours. Eventually the shipyard (federal agency) was persuaded to reclassify the former employee. That enabled the constituent to qualify (following more appeals by the caseworker) for disability compensation (state agency) as well as for welfare (county agency—more appeals). Meanwhile, the caseworker and the AA used their patron's good offices to persuade the constituent's banker (private), automobile credit agency (private), hospital (county) and utility company (city) to accept delayed debt-repayment schedules. Finally, the caseworker went to the constituent's home to give advice on home economics and family budgeting.[7]

Another example involves a young MP:

For five years—ever since he was first elected to represent Walsall South—Bruce George had campaigned to get the barriers for people whose lives were made miserable by the din of six lanes of motorway traffic roaring past day and night. The trouble was that some civil service types had said that only motorways built after a certain date could have barriers. This led to the ridiculous situation where the M6 south of Bescot junction could have noise barriers, but north of the junction it could not.

But just a few weeks ago, Bruce's patient years of campaigning paid off. It was announced that the so-called cut-off date for noise barriers had been scrapped—meaning that barriers can be installed wherever motorways pass close to housing.[8]

As these cases demonstrate, casework frequently provides an opportunity for elected representatives to help constituents challenge the decisions of bureaucrats. This ability is reflected in the kinds of cases that members of Congress and Parliament typically receive. In the United States the two most frequently reported types of cases are social security and military or veteran's benefits problems, followed by immigration, unemployment benefits, disputes with the

Internal Revenue Service, health care problems, civil service issues, housing, and black lung cases. Like their American counterparts, British MPs also receive cases that concern pensions and social security, taxes, immigration, health care, and military problems. There are notable cross-national differences, however. In Britain more requests deal with education, planning permits, and various public utilities. Moreover, the most common type of case in Britain involves housing, a type that is minor in the United States. Such differences mirror differences in the kinds of services offered by the two governments. For example, the large size of the public housing stock in Great Britain partly explains the many hours that MPs spend investigating unrepaired windows or acts of vandalism and expediting housing transfers. As British local councils have assumed the role of landlord, MPs in effect have become the tenants' defenders.

As illustrated by the shipyard worker, handling cases often means that representatives and their staff must work with officials at several levels of government. A complex case in the United States might involve federal, state, and local agencies as well as the private sector. British MPs too must work with borough, county, and national civil service officials. But even when the cases are not complex, they often fall outside what could reasonably be assumed to be the natural jurisdiction of a congressman or MP. This presents a dilemma. Rejecting a constituent's request for assistance can alienate a potential vote, but at the same time representatives and their staffs often feel uncomfortable about non-national cases. Housing in Great Britain is illustrative since it concerns the local borough council and not the national government. Complaints about the waiting list for houses or the lack of repairs in council flats really should be referred to the local housing officer in the first instance, and then to the local councillor. In fact, many constituents take their housing complaints directly to the MP in the not unfounded belief that the MP's greater influence will increase the chances of successful resolution. Different MPs handle housing cases in different ways. Some discourage housing cases and routinely refer them to local councillors, while others handle all or a large number of them directly. But on the whole, MPs are somewhat less likely to observe local versus national distinctions than their congressional counterparts. Whereas 54 percent of congressional offices regularly refer state or local cases to the appropriate state or local authority, only 17 percent of the MPs decline local authority cases. Even so, a third of the MPs assisted on local cases reluctantly. As one MP put it, "There are actually two levels of government, but people don't understand this. For many people, the MP is the only one they know. People see us as the way to deal with the system. You have to help them." Another MP complained that "periodically I tell people that housing is local councillor responsibility, but they persist. I am no more effective than a local councillor in dealing with housing: in fact I take care not to be more effective."

One reason MPs feel it necessary to handle local cases outside their natural jurisdiction is that Britain has fewer elected officials who can provide such services. In the United States assemblymen, state senators, mayors, and a variety of elected county and city officials have their own offices and staff to deal with citizen complaints. By comparison, British local councillors are less visible, have fewer resources, and are not usually career officials. Thus, MPs often explain their involvement in local affairs by the twin facts that councillors cannot be trusted to do the job right and that mishandled complaints can reflect negatively on the MP.

Although the nature of constituent work is fairly similar in both countries, the resources available to members certainly are not.[9] This simple fact helps to explain a number of cross-national differences in constituency service practices. Above all, there is a crucial difference in the amount of staff support. As compared to congressmen, MPs get very little assistance. In addition to their administrative and legislative aides, research assistants, receptionists, community representatives, and project workers, congressmen have an average of between four and five full-time caseworkers who work exclusively on constituent service problems. Seventy-five percent of these caseworkers work in the district offices. Twelve percent of the congressional offices even bring their services to the district by means of a mobile van.

District offices play an important role in the casework process. Many representatives maintain more than one district office in order to maximize the accessibility of their staff to constituents: 60 percent have at least two district offices and 27 percent have three or more. Typically, these offices are open five days a week; in a few instances, they are open every day. Usually the district offices are administered by a district representative (47 percent) or by an administrative assistant in Washington (24 percent), but sometimes the authority is completely decentralized (17 percent). Only rarely do congressmen (5 percent) administer the district offices themselves. In most cases there is a great deal of coordination between the district and Washington offices: in only 10 percent of the offices is there little or no daily contact between the two. The distribution of the casework burden varies widely. One-third of the Washington offices handle 10 percent or less of the cases, and at the other extreme, 10 percent of the Washington offices handle all of the cases. Most offices fall between these extremes, with the number of Washington offices which handle more cases than the district office being less $(n = 40)$ than the number which handle more $(n = 51)$. About a quarter of the administrative assistants thought that cases were generally handled better in Washington, but most felt that it depended on the kind of case under consideration. For example, some viewed the Washington office as being better able to handle complex and delicate cases. Others felt that military and immigration problems were better handled in Washington, whereas social security and veteran's benefits were better handled in district offices, which are generally closer to regional social security and veteran's department offices. By the nature of things, the Washington offices tend to deal with constituents in a less personalized manner than the district offices. District offices rely more on personal contact and phone calls when handling casework, whereas the Washington office handles casework primarily by mail.

Although the pattern of working relationships between the Washington and district offices varies from congressman to congressman, one feature seems to be fairly constant across all the offices: casework in the United States is primarily a staff activity. In sharp contrast, MPs labor with almost no assistance from staff and have a more direct hand in their constituent affairs. Most MPs have a part-time secretary to assist them with their constituent work, but almost three-quarters of the secretaries do no more than handle the clerical work associated with casework, such as typing letters and answering phone calls. Even so, a few MPs proudly claimed to answer many letters in longhand. When questioned about the amount of autonomy their secretaries had in dealing with cases, half the MPs insisted that they directly supervise each case themselves and that their secretaries have no autonomy in such matters. A third of the MPs claimed that their secretaries sometimes handle cases without their direct supervision, and less than 10 percent claimed that their secretaries deal with cases autonomously.

In addition to secretarial support, MPs sometimes receive help from the local party agent. Although the agent's primary tasks are to maintain the organization of the local party and to assist in the running of constituency election campaigns, some are also responsible for screening cases during the week and arranging appointments for the weekend surgery, the designated time when the MP meets with constituents to hear complaints. Agents of ministers, in particular, tend to feel that they have to do more screening than do agents of backbenchers. In any case the amount of the agent's casework involvement often depends upon his or her personal relationship with the MP since the duty is not a formal one: agents are technically employees of the party, not of the members. About half have no casework responsibility whatsoever.

All things considered, the substantial personal involvement of the MP differs greatly from the more bureaucratic approach of most congressional offices. When asked to estimate the amount of time the congressman personally spends on casework, 47 percent of the administrative assistants said that the Congressman rarely spends any time on casework, and only 9 percent said that the Congressman spends more than 10 percent of his or her time on casework. In contrast, 37 percent of the MPs said that they spend between 50 and 60 percent of their time on constituency service, and another 10 percent gave no specific estimate but said "most" or "a good deal" of their time. Only 5 percent said that they spend 10 percent or less of their time on constituent affairs.

One consequence of the bureaucratized approach of congressional offices toward casework is that there is less correspondence in the United States than in Britain between the importance that congressmen assign to casework and their personal involvement. Most congressmen and MPs take casework very seriously: about 75 percent of the representatives in both countries rated casework as "very important." Thirty percent of the congressional offices even said that casework is their top priority. Yet it is not unusual to get comments from them like: "It matters a lot for staff, but not much personally. That is, the congressman himself spends little time on casework, but he thinks that it's important and wants his staff to do it well." Or, "It matters a lot. Nothing hurts him more than when people come to him because the staff couldn't help them. Then we have failed in our job." Thus, the key to congressmen's casework commitment is the effectiveness of their organization; the key to the MPs' casework commitment is the personal time and effort they are willing to devote to constituency service.

Not surprisingly, some MPs are concerned about the strain that casework puts upon their time and energies. In fact, two-thirds felt that it is important that MPs be given larger staff allotments. Fifteen percent, usually older MPs and Conservatives, wanted the staff for legislative purposes only, but 43 percent, especially younger MPs and Labour members, wanted the staff to lessen their casework burden. Those who opposed the expansion of the MP's staff offered several reasons for their position. By far the most common was that Britain is a small country lacking the resources and wealth of the United States and that it is therefore not reasonable for the MPs to have staff support comparable to their congressional counterparts. MPs also noted that British constituencies are about a fifth the size of congressional districts. Some MPs, especially ministers and Conservatives, felt that adding staff would only further the professionalization of the MP's role, ruining the personal touch and adding to the growth of the government sector. As they perceived it, the library adequately provides basic information. If MPs were given staff for legislative purposes, it would make it easier for them to avoid thinking about issues and to shirk their policy responsibilities.

Solicitation of Cases

The investment of staff resources and personal time are not merely passive responses to exogenously arising demands. Representatives may work actively to stimulate demand, inasmuch as an image of helpfulness can be fostered by the aggressive solicitation of new cases, whereas a more passive approach can signal indifference or remoteness from the affairs of constituents. Although complaints will come to representatives even when their services are not advertised at all, advertising can raise the caseload level and thereby increase contacts with individual citizens.

Sixty-four percent of MPs and 85 percent of congressmen advertise their casework services in some way.[10] The exceptions offer two main reasons for not advertising. A few claim that they have enough cases already. This does not imply that they are inattentive to their constituents' problems. Older representatives with high visibility and an established reputation for constituency service, for instance, may not feel that they have to remind voters of their services, particularly if there is a high rate of repeat business. Others do not advertise because they find casework distasteful. One congressional office even puts out a comprehensive listing of government services in a special newsletter in order "to tell people where to go so that they wouldn't come to their Congressman." This is an example of negative advertising designed to discourage the flow of casework. Such examples are certainly not typical.

In the United States the methods of casework advertisement are diverse. By far the most common (44 percent) is the newsletter or district mailing. The district mailing often describes the services available and lists the phone number of the office and the hours in which the staff are on call. Sometimes, it also includes examples of cases so that people can get a better idea of what is offered. Some offices add supplementary mailings and questionnaires. Rarely used methods are to put an advertisement in the papers (4 percent), mention the office's casework services in the congressman's weekly column (3 percent), and advertise casework through the local radio and TV stations (2 percent). Finally, there are the more personal methods, such as sending the staff out "shopping for cases" or tying casework into the congressman's regular district tours (9 percent). A few congressmen even hold formal "workshops" or "town halls" where cases are taken personally in the manner of the British surgery. In many instances, just having good relationships with key groups in the district fosters cases. One office reported making a point of keeping up good ties with senior citizen organizations because "they will recommend to us people with social security and Veteran's Administration problems."

In Britain advertising casework often involves highly personalized methods, such as touring neighborhoods, picking up cases at political and social functions, getting referrals through local party activists, and even knocking on doors to call on constituents individually. A good, if slightly extreme, example of the personal efforts of some young MPs to promote casework is that of Mr. G.:

> Mr. G. is deeply involved in all sorts of community affairs. He holds surgeries every week at two locations for two hours each. He actively solicits cases by advertising his surgeries in the local paper and by walking through the town on weekends and letting people approach him on the street with their problems. As Mr. G. explains, this serves the dual purpose of picking up cases from people who could not attend the surgery as well as making him

visible to his constituents. As we walked through the town market and through the complexes of council homes, people would come up to Mr. G. to tell him their problems. Mr. G. recorded the person's request in a notebook and promised to get back to them shortly. Some of the people we saw invited Mr. G. in to have a quick cup of coffee while they complained about the vandalism of neighborhood kids or the neglect the local council had shown towards the repair of their homes . . . The immigration cases are a very important bridge to the immigrant community for Mr. G. He has no trouble developing ties with the white, working class community, but the immigrants tend to maintain separate religious and cultural ties. Thus, Mr. G. took us to a local immigrant bar-brothel where he nonchalantly collected cases and heard complaints while we looked on in slightly embarrassed discomfort.[11]

Approximately 70 percent of the MPs advertised their surgeries, often in the newspapers, or sent out "circulars" about their casework services, which many referred to as their "may I help you" letters. MPs commonly concentrate their mailings on eighteen-year-olds just entering the electorate and on areas of "new estates" where many constituents do not yet know their MP and his or her agent or assistant. In addition, 27 percent of MPs solicited cases by knocking on doors or by directly writing to a constituent when they read or hear about a problem that the constituent has. As one MP remarked, "The process of electioneering is seeking out cases. I wrote letters to people seeking cases. I carried a notebook and went to see people at their own homes when I was campaigning." Other casework practices seem to be uniquely British. Several MPs advertised their services through local council publications or enlisted the aid of local councillors in drumming up new problems. Again this is less likely to occur in the United States, where many of the state and local elected officials handle cases themselves. Many candidates for seats also take up residence in the constituency upon adoption as the party's candidate and begin to do casework before the election. The usual explanation is that some constituents feel uncomfortable about bringing their problems to an incumbent from the "other party." This practice also gives challengers a chance to show their commitment to interests of the constituency.

One peculiarly British institution for generating cases is the surgery, so named because it resembles a doctor's office hours. The surgery provides an opportunity for citizens to meet with the MP personally to discuss their problems and complaints. Usually, the

MPs are assisted by an agent, party volunteer, or secretary who takes the names of those who are waiting and determines the order in which the MPs will see them. Sometimes the MPs write down the details of the case themselves, and in other instances the MPs circulate around the room while those assisting them take down the necessary information. Many of those who show up have attended before, not infrequently about the same matter.

The use of surgeries is not a wholly reliable indicator of an MP's constituency effort. MPs in rural constituencies maintain that surgeries are more useful in densely populated areas than in sparsely populated areas because of the greater difficulty that constituents experience in getting to a designated area. Rural MPs may be just as dedicated to their constituency as their urban counterparts and yet hold fewer surgeries. One must keep such caveats in mind when reviewing the frequency with which MPs hold surgeries. Less than 10 percent of the MPs said that they hold no surgeries or hold surgeries only irregularly and infrequently. Almost 90 percent of the MPs hold surgeries at least every month, and nearly 60 percent of them hold surgeries every two weeks or more. These figures contrast sharply with those reported by R. E. Dowse in 1963, based on a mail survey of 69 MPs.[12] More than a third of the earlier MPs claimed to hold no regular surgery, a number that dwindles to almost nothing in recent times. At the other extreme, only one-third of the earlier MPs held surgery at least every two weeks, as opposed to well over one-half of current MPs. Over the span of two decades surgery has apparently become a much larger part of the MP's professional life.

Resolution of Cases

The first component of an aggressive casework strategy is the generation of cases. Representatives who wish to increase the number of contacts they have with constituents will advertise widely and take the initiative to "drum up business." There is no point in soliciting cases, however, if they are not handled well. Thus, the second component of an aggressive strategy is the expeditious handling of cases. This means two things: taking quick action to deal with cases and achieving a satisfactory result.

With respect to taking quick action, some congressmen and MPs regularly refer cases outside their national jurisdiction to local and state officials. Nevertheless, nearly all representatives in both countries felt that it is important to give a prompt and courteous answer to every request that comes to them whether the case was referred or not. It was common for them to say that "I always try to give a sympathetic reply," "I always listen to them," or "we try to handle all calls courteously." Inevitably, however, some proportion of the cases are hopeless or fabricated, so problems naturally arise. A few representatives bravely inform their constituents that the case is unworthy of attention. Said one retiring MP, "I tried to let it be known that I would handle good cases only." Most, however, will go through the motions of handling the case anyway. As one lamented, "I tried to explain early in my career that I couldn't help people on certain matters. But I decided that I couldn't afford the appearance of indifference and now I go through the formalities in all cases." Several of those interviewed in both countries suggested that they had developed an informal signaling system with the officials they had to deal with most frequently; in a subtle way they would indicate a case was important or that all that was required was a formal reply to show the constituent. As one put it, "we pursue some cases more vigorously than others." The important thing is to show the constituent that the representative cares about the problem and has acted on his or her behalf. If there is nothing to be done, there may still be credit to claim if it can be shown that the effort was sincere. Consider the case of one MP, Sir H.:

> As he explains it, the very fact that a man of his stature in the community takes the time to listen to some average fellow's problems in itself creates good will and electoral reward. To illustrate his point, he gave us the example of some fellow in a pub complaining about a problem he has with the government. His friends tell him that he has been wronged and suggest that he see Sir H. So the fellow calls or writes Sir H. who dutifully sends off a letter to the constituent informing him of his actions and one to the relevant minister to please enquire into the matter. The minister writes back a reply—in many cases, unable to help—and Sir H. sends a photocopy of the minister's letter to the constituent. The constituent's problem often does not get solved, says Sir H., but at least the constituent can take the letter with him to the pub "happy in the knowledge his case has received attention at the highest levels." Sir H. in return acquires the reputation of being a good constituency man who cares about his constituents.[13]

Sympathy and courtesy are all well and good, but the clearest example of a successful case is one resolved in the constituent's favor. Estimates of the cases that are resolved successfully in this sense are very disparate. In the United States, where administrative assistants were willing to give a numerical estimate, the figures range from 10 to 90 percent, but a majority felt that cases are successfully resolved more often than not: 44 of the 64 assistants who gave percentage estimates thought that the results are favorable in 50 percent or more of the instances. Of those 20 assistants who did not want to give numerical estimates, 15 said the results are favorable in most of the cases, and one said in all cases. Few MPs ventured to give numerical estimates of successful cases, but when they did, these figures too are usually over the 50 percent level.[14] Several MPs maintained that the success rate is really lower and that their colleagues are deluding themselves about their impact on the outcome. Much appears to depend on the nature of the case. For instance, when MPs try to get repairs for council property, they are extremely effective, but they have much less success when people ask them to assist in getting housing transfers because the housing lists are set by a uniform point system.

Legislators may also be claiming credit for actions that would have occurred—albeit at a later date—had they not interceded. Most members felt, though, that their intervention forces bureaucrats to give a case special attention. As an administrative assistant put it about one constituent, "He was merely a statistic in some bureaucrat's in-basket without our help. Once we started making inquiries he became a 'problem' for the agencies. By the time we were through, he had become an individual person—instead of a statistic or problem."[15] British civil servants themselves confirmed such judgments:

> We asked several local officials why, and in what ways, they paid attention to the Member's requests. The Housing director told us that a complaint from an MP did not get special attention per se: if the complaint was unjustified, there would be no special circumstances applied to it. However, the MP's enquiry was usually given a higher priority in the sense that where the normal time for a reply was about four months, the department would handle the MP's request in a matter of days.
>
> As for why the MP's request received a higher priority, there were two responses. One was that while it was not a "duty" or "right," the MP was entitled to a prompt reply as a matter of "courtesy." But in addition, it was based on a wariness of the consequences of not responding properly. As one official frankly admitted, an MP's letter was viewed with apprehension since in

most cases, if the letter got that far, it indicated that the complaint was important. When asked what would happen if they did not respond, we were told that the MP could cause a great deal of trouble by giving the department bad publicity. The fear of a messy, public row formed a strong incentive to comply. Thus, the MP's influence in these matters derives both from the courtesy of good working relations with permanent officials and from the implicit threat of public exposure of departmental or individual incompetence.[16]

Still, some cases are not resolved successfully, and one wonders whether these failures hurt representatives in some way. A majority (60 percent) in the United States felt that unsuccessful cases do not hurt them so long as the office acts promptly and can demonstrate effort. Only about 10 percent felt that unsuccessful cases hurt the representative no matter what. The British representatives also felt that much depends on how the cases are handled. Most (63 of 68) emphasized the importance of promptness and competence and the need to prevent overly high expectations: their rule was never to promise more than can be delivered. A small number (5 of 68) felt that some bad feelings are inevitable because of the nature of the constituent's problems, the fact that bad or unwinnable cases do not get properly screened, or simply the fact that the publicity surrounding the case backfires. In sum, representatives and staff in both countries think that casework can be politically beneficial whatever the outcome so long as it is handled properly. This corresponds with the finding that most citizens who contact their representative for help or information tend to find the incumbent's response satisfactory and evaluate the incumbent positively.

Publicizing Casework

Solicitation and resolution are the first two elements of an aggressive casework strategy, but these may contribute little to the representative's reputation if a third element is not present: publicity. To some extent, incumbents can count on word of mouth to inform people of what they have done for constituents who contacted them. In addition, attention from the media may occur as a matter of course. Some incumbents, however, may wish to speed up the process of reputation building by publicizing their casework accomplishments. Almost all MPs and congressmen try to get publicity for projects that benefit the constituency as a whole or some significant segment of it, but an entrepreneurial representative may extend his or her credit by claiming success in individual cases as well. Many representatives, however, feel that publicizing individual cases is unnecessary and improper. Sixty-eight percent of the congressmen and 51 percent of the MPs took this position. Some of those who did publicize cases in the United States (11 of 27) tried to preserve the anonymity of the person helped unless they had secured that person's permission to use his or her name. Moreover, all but a handful restricted their casework publicity to newsletters. In contrast, the British tend to use the newspapers to publicize their casework. Many MPs write their own press releases, and if the local press is not hostile, they may regularly place stories in the local paper about individual or constituency wide causes they have assisted.

About a third of the MPs did not bother to advertise their surgeries or publicize their casework services in any way whatsoever. Some felt that doing so is undignified. One MP said, "You shouldn't thrust yourself upon your constituents." Others said that just making themselves available is enough, since "success breeds success" and "people tell their friends" when a case gets resolved successfully. A few, however, expressed fears of possibly negative consequences that might stem from an overly aggressive approach to casework, particularly cases involving local officials. One young MP remarked that older members had warned him not "to step on the toes of local officials." A study of the relationship between an MP who did a lot of local casework and the public officials in his community suggests that there may indeed be a real basis for such fears: when interviewed, some local officials in fact complained about the MP and felt that he was excessively quick to try to embarrass them with adverse publicity to facilitate a case.[17]

Volume of Casework

The number of actual ongoing cases must be distinguished from the number of pieces of mail received by a representative in a given week since the mail per se could contain either multiple letters on the same case or expressions of constituent opinion as opposed to requests for assistance. Not all representatives were willing or able to give numerical estimates of their case volume, either because they really did not know or for some reason did not want to say. But in absolute numbers congressmen and their staffs have much larger caseloads than do MPs. The average number of reported cases per week was 71 in the United States and 36 in Britain.[18] A smaller percentage of congressmen than MPs fall into the under 20 category, and many more fall into the over 80 category. Yet in per capita terms the caseload of the MP is higher, given that the average parliamentary constituency is approximately one-fifth the size of the average congressional district. The comparison is all the more remarkable when one considers that the MP labors largely without the benefit of staff support.

Project Work

Although constituency service primarily involves casework it also includes other kinds of service. Particularly in the United States project work makes up another important aspect of district service. Cases that involve large numbers of constituents, extraordinary amounts of public attention, federal grants, or construction projects are called projects. In many instances, the dividing line between casework and project work is blurred. Individual casework involves handling the complaints of individual constituents. Closely related to the individual case is the constituency- or district-wide case, sometimes referred to as high-level casework, which concerns the interests of a group of constituents. Distinct from both of these types of district service is project work, defined as helping businesses, groups, and governments in the district to secure government facilities, public works, grants, and contracts.

High-level casework is qualitatively similar to individual casework in that it can be a defensive action against the perceived arbitrariness of public officials, but more often it is a way in which representatives attempt to ensure that their districts get a fair share of government largesse. The notion that congressmen defend the parochial interests of their districts is ingrained in the lore of American political science; the analogous notion that MPs also look out for the interests of their constituencies is not. And yet many MPs, when asked to describe the things they do for their constituencies, mentioned such chores as "protecting the local interests," helping the constituency "fight for its share of the national cake," and "acting as an intermediary" for the local council with the national government. Almost every MP had a story about how he or she helped to protect constituency interests. For example, several MPs mentioned that they took the lead in negotiations with the government over noise and pollution problems related to lorries in their area. One MP claimed that he helped to persuade a minister to build a bypass that the government was dragging its feet on due to cost considerations. The same MP also claimed that he helped to secure the location of a national museum in his constituency. Another MP said that he played a major role in delaying the closing of a local shipyard in his constituency. Numerous MPs claimed that they helped to prevent the closing of a hospital in their area or that they led the campaign to stop the construction of a road through their district.

To be sure, MPs claim credit for events that would have occurred anyway, but the same can be said of congressmen and their staffs. According to a study of congressional influence over the allocation of agency expenditures, congressmen and their staffs spend a great deal of time creating the impression that they have helped groups secure money from the government; and "even when Congressmen perform none of these services, they frequently attempt to take credit for favorable decisions. Virtually all Congressmen announce with great fanfare the awarding of grants and contracts to groups in their constituencies, and few forget to have their own names mentioned at the same time."[19] MPs too wish to claim credit when they can.

An important difference between congressmen and MPs is that for MPs "projects" are really cases. MPs cannot change the allocation decisions of government departments, but sometimes they can protect constituency interests from particular rulings made by civil servants. As one MP commented, he could not really get projects, but he could "sometimes stop things from being closed." The way MPs prevent bureaucratic decisions from being carried out highlights another important difference from their American counterparts. MPs act as lobbyists and community leaders: they focus media attention on the problem, arrange meetings between the interested parties, and use whatever personal influence they have with ministers and local officials. Consider the efforts described by an MP: "The government has wanted to close down two schools in my constituency for several years now. But I just keep making a fuss in the papers, arousing my constituents, and writing letters, and I have held it up even though the Tory local council wants them closed too. Eventually, I think, we will compromise and close one of them.

The important thing is to be tenacious and not to let go." The tools of personal casework service are the tools of high-level casework also. Unlike congressmen, MPs cannot use a position on a committee or the threat of budget cuts to influence government decisions, so in this crucial sense they cannot protect their local interests as do congressmen.[20]

Although a few MPs provide their local councils and industries with information about government grants, in the strict sense project work applies almost exclusively to congressmen. Most congressional offices assign the task of overseeing project work to particular staff members. Almost half the offices employed a full-time project specialist. In other offices the administrative assistant most often had principal responsibility for project work, but legislative assistants, district representatives, and caseworkers were also involved. Three-quarters of the offices did their project work in Washington where they had the best access to the agencies.

Project work consists of two components: solicitation and influence. Solicitation means helping local groups learn about and prepare applications for grants, arranging meetings between the groups and the agencies, checking on the status of grants, and even helping with appeals. The advent of computer technology facilitates the solicitation role somewhat: FAPPERS and SCORPIO are computerized grant-indexing systems that allow congressional offices to keep track of available money. Some offices eschew modern technology and rely on traditional documents, such as the Domestic Assistance Catalogue and the Federal Register. Of the offices surveyed, 15 used FAPPERS, 33 did not actively search out grants for their district, and the rest relied on other sources.

Congressional offices have developed various methods of apprising constituents about project money. One office, for instance, holds regular seminars attended by local officials and agency representatives. A few send out packages of information to those on special mailing lists, and another phones interested constituents directly upon learning of grant possibilities. Some offices feel that it is harder to interest rural constituents in applying for grants. "Cities get most of the money," complained one, and "it's hard to compile a mailing list for constituents interested in federal programs in a rural district," said another. Other offices feel that a tradition of project work in the district is a major factor. One administrative assistant suggested that his office had a hard time building up project work because the previous congressman had done so little of it, and another pointed out that people in his district had become accustomed to sending their requests for assistance to one of the senators. Conversely, one administrative assistant felt that his office owed the high volume of project demand to the success and reputation of the previous congressman. Even local politics affects grant seeking. One Republican office complained that "Democratic mayors don't want to ask a Republican representative for any help on projects." Thus, staff efforts are only one aspect of the involvement of the congressional office with projects.

Apart from their role in the solicitation of projects, members of Congress can attempt to exert influence over project decisions. The extent of congressional influence in the allocation of agency money is a matter of debate.[21] Two points, however, are worth noting here. First, congressmen and their staff pay attention to the intensity of constituents' concerns when they decide whether to involve themselves in a project. As one administrative assistant put it, the congressman "usually reserves his influence for situations where a local business interest has a lot at stake." Second, congressmen are more likely to get involved and be successful with grants related to committees on which they serve. One administrative assistant remarked that his congressman was "only helpful on a project if he is on the right committee . . . and holds a funding threat over the agency." Another reported that the office had little success at first because the congressman's committees did not match up well with the kinds of projects his constituents wanted. When his committee assignments changed, his success with projects increased. Membership on the Appropriations Committee can be particularly helpful. One staffer observed that since his congressman "is on the Appropriations Committee, once or twice a year, if he can't get something through an agency, he'll put it specifically in the appropriations bill and literally legislate the project. Then the agency *has* to do it."

The success of congressional staff efforts varies. With respect to helping constituent groups apply for grants, most staffs thought that they provide a useful service. Said one staffer, "constituents usually use the wrong procedure, and the office can be of help in straightening them out." Aside from providing accurate information, the staffs also felt that they are helpful in "cutting red tape." But over and above such high-level casework, they are also successful with respect to the actual procurement of grants and projects. Of those who ventured a percentage guess, 6 offices reported a success rate of one-third or less, 17 reported between one-third and one-half, 19 reported between one-half and three-quarters, and 6 said above three-quarters. Their qualitative evaluations were similar. Six said "a few" were successful, 11 said "some," 17 said "most" and 3 said "all." A few thought that it is harder to be successful today than it was in the past: "Today we're just letting agencies know. The bureaucracy has hardened itself to political pressure." As is true of casework, some amount of grant solicitation is simply for political show. "An agency does what it wants to," one staffer explained, "and pays little attention to letters from congressmen.The effort is for political purposes." Also like casework, the success of project work often depends on factors that are outside the congressman's hands. Even the staffer of one of the most successful project-oriented representatives complained, "Success depends on factors we can't control. So much money is distributed by specific standards." The growth in formula programs has probably changed the nature of project work.[22] Rather than intervening in a specific allocation decision after the law is on the books, congressmen now must intervene at the time the formula is being written into law. After that stage the congressional office plays more of an informational and facilitating function.

A third of congressmen did not actively solicit projects for their districts. Some conservative members of Congress claimed to oppose such solicitation on ideological grounds. They maintained either "we're not here to hand out money" or "It is inconsistent with his voting pattern." Other offices felt that potential political liabilities accompany project work. One administrative assistant warned, "Intervention often gets the congressman involved in a dangerous local squabble where he can't win." Another advised that the best strategy is to wait for a local initiative, allow for local differences to settle down before wading in, and then send a regional officer to advise the local groups, because "You don't want something that people think some politician rammed down their throats."

The surveys suggest several tentative conclusions. First, constituent problems are generally similar in the United States and Great Britain, with specific differences in types of cases reflecting the nature of state services in the two countries. Second, MPs have only a small fraction of the support services of congressmen, but they devote a greater proportion of their personal time and effort to constituent service than do congressmen. Third, in both countries representatives encourage demand for their services by various means. Fourth, in both countries representatives feel they are quite successful in handling the cases that come to them. And finally, the level of casework is higher in absolute terms in the United States and in per capita terms in Britain.

3

Incentives for Serving
the Constituency

Constituency service in the United States and Great Britain exhibits considerable variation both in the level of involvement and in the specific practices adopted by members of Congress and Parliament. Some members service their constituencies more actively than others, and some members adopt practices that are different from others. The sources of this variation lie in the differing circumstances in which members find themselves and in the differing motivations held by members. Motivation is the subject of this chapter. We approach this difficult subject first by looking directly at the testimony of the members and their staffs and then by employing the less direct but more objective method of statistical inference. Our inquiry begins with an examination of the perceptions and beliefs of MPs and congressmen.

Electoral Motivations

This book rests on the hypothesis that members hope to profit electorally from their activities. In the United States, this presumption is widely, if not universally, accepted. In Britain this assumption is more controversial. National forces such as party loyalty and executive performance play a much larger role in British than in American voting; the personal characteristics and efforts of the candidates for MP simply do not have the latitude to affect behavior that they do in the United States. This is not to deny, of course, that such factors have any effect. Moreover, even if MPs have less personal control over their electoral fates, there is no reason to assume that they have less concern over the little control they do have. Indeed, the opposite could be true: the few personal weapons at the disposal of MPs might be of more psychic importance to them than any of the many weapons in the arsenal of congressmen.

The reader should bear in mind three related but distinct and often confused questions. First, one may ask whether members *believe* constituency service has electoral payoffs. This is a matter of subjective perceptions that may or may not comport with reality. Second, one may ask whether the hope of electoral payoff is the prime *motive* for constituency service efforts. This is a much more difficult question inasmuch as individuals themselves often cannot identify or explain their motivations. Third, one may ask whether constituency service *has* an electoral payoff, regardless of member beliefs and member motivations. Like the first question, this third one permits a more or less objective answer, though methodological problems make the process of answering it difficult. This chapter focuses primarily on the first and second questions. The third will be dealt with later. The second question will be dealt with largely in an indirect, statistical manner: if members believe that constituency service has an electoral impact and engage in such activity in the hope of achieving that impact, particular statistical relationships should be evident.

On the first of these three questions, it is well known that congressmen believe in the electoral efficacy of their service activities. When congressmen's administrative assistants were asked whether their congressman thought that constituency service enhanced his or her election possibilities, only two of 102 replied that service had no significant electoral effect, and three more asserted that the slight effect it had was generally overrated. For the most part the assistants expressed no doubt about the electoral value of their offices' district service efforts. The common view was unequivocally positive: "definitely," "certainly," "undeniably," "absolutely," or "of course." Some elaborated:

> My God, that's why we're here. We're the only office on the Hill with 24-hour turnaround. ——— was defeated because of a six-month turnaround.

Yes. In our first election we had a majority of only (less than 500) votes. This year we had a 70 percent majority, which is reflective of service to the district.

You're elected to be a legislator, but casework and projects keep you elected. People in the district expect you to represent them in their dealings with the bureaucracy. Our prime responsibility is to see them and attend to their problems.

People don't know about legislative performance, but they do know if the sewers work.

Being here depends on casework.

As a freshman, constituency service is more important than legislation because he has no power and he needs to get reelected.

Not all staffers, however, were quite so certain. Some wondered about the reality underlying their beliefs:

I'm sure it does! But how much impact could three or four employees have in a district of 500,000 people?

Others drew distinctions among the various things they did for the district:

Projects yes, casework no.

Casework less than newsletters.

A large project effort, yes, if proper press. Doing casework doesn't help you. Not doing it does hurt you.

A number of administrative assistants opined that tangible efforts mattered less than the not so tangible perceptions they could produce:

Individual social security cases won't determine an election, but over time the congressman gets good PR and a reputation for accessibility and attention. Media coverage for large projects helps.

Indirectly, you get a reputation for responding. Hopefully it will permeate and give you a good name.

Yes, although what really matters is not how much you do but how much you publicize it.

Finally, several administrative assistants explicitly rejected the implication that electoral considerations motivated constituency service, whatever its actual effect:

> No question about it—not that we do it for that reason.

> I suppose that's true and it has helped. But he's not one who does nothing but casework. He doesn't try to win elections that way.

And in a vein reminiscent of Fenno's discussion of the potentially constraining effects of established home styles, two assistants complained:

> A dominant factor. Very important. But we should have gotten this over with in the first four years. Now he's sure of re-election so we should maybe concentrate more on legislation. The problem is that we don't want to cut services.

> Currently he couldn't disengage, it's part of his service. People now expect it. The number of people served must constitute only a small proportion, but a disappointed person can cause a lot of problems.

In sum, whatever the reality, denizens of Capitol Hill unequivocally believe that their district service activities have salutary electoral consequences.

According to the conventional wisdom, electoral considerations have almost no part in the motivations of members of Parliament. The scanty research on this question has produced mixed results. In a 1963 survey by Robert Dowse, which asked MPs "whether they thought that surgery work won them votes," only 27 percent (17 of 62) responded flatly yes, whereas 44 percent (27 of 62) answered flatly no. In 1970, however, a survey by Anthony Barker and Michael Rush found that MPs universally believed that their personal activities and reputations had some impact on the vote.[1]

The findings of our MP survey come much closer to the Barker and Rush study. When asked whether casework activities had any impact on the vote, 83 percent (57 of 69) of the MPs answered definitely yes; another 16 percent (11 of 69) thought that a limited effect existed; and only one flatly denied any effect. The discrepancies in these findings may be accounted for by the fact that the Dowse study referred exclusively to surgeries, whereas the Barker and Rush study and ours dealt with constituency and casework activities generally. Alternatively, there may have been a major behavioral shift during the 1960s.

Whatever the reason, people are reluctant to believe that MPs are motivated to any significant extent by mundane electoral considerations. Consider the interviews conducted by Anthony King and

Anne Sloman for the BBC. These nicely reflect the prevailing consensus. One conversation took place with Shirley Williams, then a member of the Labour shadow cabinet:

> *King*: If it takes up so much time, if MPs have to write so many letters, if they sometimes find the work depressing, why do almost all members of Parliament hold surgeries? The cynic would say "in order to win votes, of course." But the cynic would be wrong. There is no evidence that this sort of careful individual constituency work makes any substantial difference at the time of a general election, and MPs know it . . .
>
> *Williams*: I don't think that it makes much difference. All you can say is that perhaps you gradually build up a reputation as a conscientious or reasonably hard-working MP, and that is of some advantage. But with the individual cases I suspect there's almost no influence at all.
>
> *King*: How much advantage—hundreds of votes, thousands?
>
> *Williams*: At most, hundreds.

A similar colloquy took place with Roy Hattersley, then a Labour front bencher:

> *King*: But in the end doesn't all this constituency work, doesn't the writing of all these letters, the holding of surgeries and advisory sessions, boil down to an effort to win votes, to make sure of getting in next time? . . . How much help . . . do you think your constituency work is going to help towards your re-election when the time comes?
>
> *Hattersley*: Very little indeed. My re-election when the time comes depends on the standing of the two parties. I hope I shall poll about nineteen or twenty thousand votes. If two or three hundred of those are the result of my constituency work, I shall have done rather well.
>
> *King*: Why, then, . . . do the work?
>
> *Hattersley*: I do the constituency work, not for a political bonus, because there isn't a political bonus in it. I do it because it's part of the job.
>
> *King*: Part of an MP's job. The non-partisan, non-speech-making, little-publicized part that goes on week in and week out, even when Parliament is in recess.[2]

The views expressed here are not shared by most of those in our MP study. Perhaps our sample was unrepresentative, or perhaps they took the question in a different manner from the way we intended it. But then again, perhaps constituency work is a more important concern of backbenchers, who are seldom interviewed, than of front benchers, who receive more scholarly attention. Perhaps, too, prominent politicians are loathe to announce over the BBC that their actions stem from anything but the highest of motives. At any rate, when asked privately and confidentially whether they believed that their casework had any relation to the vote, MPs responded unhesitatingly:

> Oh, I would have thought so. I only suffered a 3.1 percent swing against a regional swing of 8 percent.

> Oh yes. There's a close correlation between size of majority and amount of constituency work.

> Yes. There is a personal vote. It can be substantial—about 2000 votes. It's not just the people you help; they tell their friends.

> Undoubtedly. If you're a good member, you can gain 1000–2000 votes. In a marginal seat it may make the difference.

> I can't tell, since I've only stood once. But when I was a councillor, it certainly did. I drove my vote from 500 to 7000 with casework. It's vital that you have a reputation as a good caseworker.

> Yes, massive. My seat is marginal, and I have a pretty big personal vote—more than 1500 votes easily.

> I'm sure. There's a consensus of opinion: "Whether the qualities of the MP are good or bad, this only affects the result marginally." But the MP personally affects 3000 votes and *can* swim against the tide.

> Yes. Most of the Liberal seats are won by hard work. I only held on by casework, but my majority went down.

> Yes. I disagree with Butler about the 500 vote figure.

> Definitely. A successful case is worth 10 votes.

> Certainly. 2 percent at the moment.

Many MPs not only believe that their efforts produce a personal vote but have definite ideas as well about the precise magnitude of that vote. This feature contrasts with the vague opinions of the American administrative assistants. The British news media give more play to the results of academic studies (such as the appendices to the Nuffield election studies) than do the American media, and this may explain some of the difference. But many of the MPs clearly were making their own estimates of the influence of casework on the vote. One casually suggested that his agent could provide an estimate based on the recent election. Another made reference to a quasi-experimental design:

> Yes, no doubt. It takes a long time to build. If you build up a general reputation as an active helper, this could be of substantial help—it could be as large as 5000 votes. In ——— there were local elections at the same time as the general. I won by 5000, while Labour won by 400 at the local elections.

By and large, MPs agreed upon the approximate number of votes that could be won by constituency efforts, even when they attached differential importance to them. In contrast to the "massive" personal vote of 1500 mentioned by one MP, another MP commented:

> Yes. It's well known that the personal vote is small—maybe 2000 votes. But people who get out of contact with local activists or the local people make themselves vulnerable. It's important to defend the locality, important for people to see that you are active.

A number of MPs called attention to the indirect importance of constituency work through the link of firing up the local activists:

> A member is expected to act as a welfare officer. If one didn't do this, it would have its consequences. My plurality has been increasing, and casework makes your own people feel that you are doing a good job. That's where it does work. It gets them to work harder.

The MPs seemed somewhat more concerned about the possibility of negative consequences of casework than were the American administrative assistants. Two commented:

> Yes. If you foul up a case, you lose 100 votes. A good case won't yield that much.

> If you have a bad reputation, you can lose a seat. My predecessor went from a 25,000-vote margin to 6000, and then the party chucked him out.

One of the more skeptical evaluations of constituency service came from one of the MPs who suffered electoral defeat. He seemed unreconciled to the decision of his constituency and observed:

> Not much—maybe 50 votes or so. It is dwarfed by other things. MPs delude themselves. I guess it keeps them going.

Yet another defeated MP looked at the bright side:

> Undoubtedly. The cases I did had a lot to do with losing by *only* 5000 votes.

As in the United States, a number of MPs were cynics, feeling that their work mattered less than how it was publicized. And the lone unbeliever, a sponsored Labour MP, commented in full:

> No. You could put a monkey up, and he'd get in if he was Labour.

In sum, most MPs indeed believe that their personal efforts have electoral consequences. This is not to say that such consequences are the sole motivation for such efforts; as in the United States, a number of MPs explicitly denied that suggestion. Nor is it to say that an objective reality underlies the subjective perception. In addition, there is a major caveat to keep in mind. Although the American and British views regarding electoral effects are virtually identical, the frame of reference is very different. To the MP, an unequivocal "Yes, it matters substantially" means perhaps 2000 votes, a number which some congressmen might consider beneath notice. Whatever representatives in the two countries view as important is relative to the context of their own electoral system.

To a much greater extent than the British, Americans view the entire electorate as up for grabs. In Britain most MPs take most of the electorate as a foregone conclusion. Thus, the British are considerably more likely to treat the personal vote as a specific, identifiable quantity, one of real concern to members of Parliament from marginal districts. MPs from a safe seat, however, have little concern for the personal vote, though they obviously cannot behave so badly as to cost the party 19,000 votes, as in the instance claimed in one of the preceding quotations. For members from a safe seat, constituency activity may be something of a formality—a show of solidarity with the locals, a stirring example to the activists. Perhaps a few votes are gained as a by-product, but they are not of major concern. Americans are much less likely to adopt such views. Seats are safe because of incumbent efforts, they believe, and can be lost if such efforts falter. "Safe" congressmen may be somewhat less motivated than their colleagues who live in fear for their electoral lives, but the variation is more continuous than it appears in Britain.

Nonelectoral Motivations

Whereas representatives in both countries believe in the electoral efficacy of constituency service, only the most hardened cynic maintains that winning votes is the sole motivation for service. Representatives have other motives as well. Winning over marginal votes through diligent service may matter a great deal to the electorally insecure, but other factors must account for the representatives in safe seats who also provide a substantial amount of constituency service.

Unfortunately it is sometimes difficult to say where narrow political motivations leave off and higher motivations begin. This is especially true for one of the most commonly expressed motives in both countries, that representatives engage in constituency service because it is expected of them. It is part of the job. In the words of the congressional staffers:

> He's conscious of the fact that he's there to take care of people.

> He feels that he is strictly a liaison between constituents and federal agencies and will do anything to make sure that the casework is handled well.

> Casework has nothing to do with being in Congress, but members are expected to do it.

> They put him here to help.

This same refrain appears in comments made by MPs and their agents:

> It's an important part of the MP's job.

> If I did not do it, people would think that I was neglecting my responsibilities.

> It's the most important thing that I do. We don't have the freedom to vote as we wish, so I regard myself as a constituency MP. I have no political ambitions. I am just trying to do a job for my constituents.

> It's sort of a matter of duty.

Such remarks reflect the general notion that elected officials have duties associated with their positions, which they fulfill as a matter of obligation. For some representatives such a sense of duty can be a higher motive, one abstracted from expectations of reward or punishment.[3] But many other representatives have something less ethereal in mind. It might be called a negative political incentive, as expressed in the comment, "If I do not perform these services, my constituents will think that I am not doing my job properly, and I will acquire a bad reputation." How constituents evaluate a representative depends in part upon how they view the representative's role. If constituents expect a significant amount of constituency service, representatives must adjust their home styles accordingly or see their images suffer. Whether a bad image in the district ultimately undoes the representative depends upon many factors, such as the availability of a good challenger, the partisan composition of the district, the compensatory value of the representatives' other activities, and their relations with activists; but most representatives, being averse to risks, prefer to avoid bad images and the vulnerability they bring. Thus, the notion that constituency service is a duty sometimes shades into another electoral incentive, one which emphasizes the negative consequences of neglect rather than the positive consequences of attention.

In addition to duty, representatives often have another reason for doing constituency service, one that is more general than but not divorced from electoral considerations. This is the claim that doing casework buys the legislator a measure of policy freedom. Illustrative remarks from United States congressmen are:

> It is very important from the standpoint of establishing firm credibility with people back home. People will understand and support you even if you vote wrong.

> You never get yourself reelected on legislation. They'll always remember you got their social security check.

Here are similar statements from British MPs:

> My constituency is small enough that if you're active, the word spreads. It makes your base firm. The stronger my reputation is with the constituency association, the more I can get away with on policy.

> Casework helps me buy some independence from the leftward drift of the party machine.

> If the constituency party feels that the MP is neglectful, it can be very damaging. A good reputation can buy forgiveness for anything.

> When the flak flies, as it will for this government, people will say, "but of course ——— is our man, and he's a good man." You can get away from the party thing.

Some representatives in each country believe that diligent constituency work establishes a fund of personal credit which they can draw on when taking unpopular policy positions. There is one significant difference, however, between the two countries. Americans seem to have individual voters in mind, or at least that stratum of voters who pay enough attention to politics to know how their representative has voted in Congress. The British are generally thinking not of individual voters but rather of the activists in their constituency parties.

In Britain the nominating procedures and structure of the major parties give activists more power than in the United States. Contrary to popular misconceptions, the power of selecting candidates to stand for Parliament rests securely in the hands of local party members. National party influence over the selection process is more nominal than real. In theory, for instance, local Conservative parties are supposed to choose their candidates from an approved list kept by the Standing Advisory Committee on Candidates and the Vice-Chairman of Party Organization. In practice, it is possible to consider a specific candidate before he or she is included on the central list.[4]

At the beginning of the postwar period, constituency parties rebelled against their MPs infrequently, often to ensure that they followed the party whip. In recent years, however, challenges by constituency parties to incumbents have become more frequent in the Labour party, and in a departure from the previous pattern, MPs have been dislodged for adhering to the party whip. This problem is especially acute in local parties dominated by the Militant Tendency. In the early 1970s a number of moderate Labour MPs, including Dick Taverne and Reg Prentice, were challenged by their local parties for their views on issues like Britain's membership in the EEC.[5]

Pressures to make Labour MPs act more like local party delegates led at the 1978 Labour Party Conference to a re-examination of the policy of automatic reselection (the routine readoption of Parliamentary incumbents). In 1981 the party changed its rules to require that each MP must be reselected by his or her party within three years of the previous election. In the first round of reselections under this new policy, only eight Labour incumbents were dropped by their parties, but the number would have been greater had a number of moderate MPs not defected to the Social Democratic Party first.[6] Although our MP study was completed before mandatory reselection was implemented, the policy was being considered at the time, and disputes between moderate Labour MPs and their activists received much publicity.

As the local pressures on MPs have mounted, good relations with activists have become more essential than ever. Some MPs who had trouble with activists over policies also tended to have bad personal relationships with them. The two problems actually reinforce one another. In a common pattern, they suggested, MPs disagree with their activists over a policy issue, causing them to withdraw from the affairs of the constituency and to become less accessible. This in turn widens the differences and worsens the animosities between them. But MPs who maintain good relations with the constituency party can cross-pressure their critics and blunt attempts to damage their reputation, and conscientious constituency service is a major means of fostering good relations.

Representatives in both countries gave another major reason for serving their constituencies. Some suggested that service has grown in importance because the world has become more complex and government activities more comprehensive. This could be called a "demand" side reason. Examples from both countries are:

> There is a sense of frustration by the people. They look to their congressman to get them through.

> We live in a red tape era in which a lot of people can't get through the bureaucracy.

> It's a beneficial safety valve in a society that is quite closely regulated by the government.

> The stronger the government, the greater the danger of injustice.

Ombudsman services are important in part because there is a real need for the representative's services. People genuinely need assistance in dealing with the complexities of modern government.

Constituency service is not the only avenue for redressing grievances against the bureaucracy. In Britain, for instance, there exist a number of other avenues of appeal for citizens with complaints against the government. Administrative tribunals, established during the period of Liberal legislation at the turn of the century, were intended as a quicker, cheaper, and more expert alternative to the British court system.[7] The most common kind of tribunal deals with benefit entitlements, but others concern such subjects as industrial disputes, rents charged by private landlords, and tax assessments.

Not all areas are covered by tribunals, and consequently since 1967 Britain has also had an ombudsman empowered to investigate cases of maladministration by the national government. Because MPs feared that the ombudsman might impinge on their traditional casework role, the establishing act required that cases be routed through the MP.[8] In 1973 the ombudsman was also given the job of health service commissioner, dealing with complaints about the Health Service, and in 1974, as part of local government reorganization, Britain established a network of local government ombudsmen. All these institutions are testimony to the fact that citizens in modern states need to be protected against maladministration and bureaucratic injustice. Constituency service by representatives thus is yet another natural reflection of a real need.

Some conservative representatives in both countries feel personal conflict in having to be "welfare officers." Should those who have opposed the development of the welfare state go to great lengths to help their constituents get as much as they can from the government? Somewhat impertinently, we posed this question to several of those we interviewed. Some felt that there was a contradiction:

> Members of Congress ought not to be spending all this government money on helping people who ought to be taking care of themselves.

> In the past, people did things for themselves. We've gone soft as hell.

> It's become very important. Whether that's correct constitutionally, I don't know.

Others rationalized their welfare officer role as making the best of a bad situation: the government services should not be provided, but if they have to be, it is the representatives' role to make sure that their constituents get what they deserve. Still others said that it is quite consistent with conservative ideology to fight the bureaucracy and that casework provides representatives with the opportunity to do this. A few let the issue pass without comment.

Some representatives felt that there are ancillary benefits to constituency service. One of the most important, particularly in Britain, was that it allows the representatives to witness the effects of legislation and to see how the laws they pass are being implemented in practice.

> It is a means of assessing how legislation is working out. Sometimes legislation works out differently in practice than what you thought. It also forms 'the basis of raising questions about the performance of agencies.

> It helps you understand how policy works in practice and shows you where you need change.

> Casework shows the reality of the impact of government on the ordinary person—where the shoe pinches.

Ironically, although MPs were more likely than congressmen to cite this as a side benefit of doing constituent service, they were also less able to change the law when they saw the need. Only a handful could recall an instance when a case caused the successful passage of either a government bill or a private member's bill. British governments tightly control their legislative agendas, and successful private member's bills are extremely rare.[9]

Reflecting the different institutional structures in which they operate, MPs gave two additional explanations for the importance they attach to constituency service. First, people judge an MP's effectiveness by his or her constituency service, because in a parliamentary system that is the only way he or she really can be judged:

> When someone has a problem, you can help him when he needs it most. Without casework, you are nothing as the MP. Constituents judge how able you are by your accessibility.

> If I were the minister of transportation, I would still be judged in my constituency by how concerned I was with their problems. The people's perception of an MP's effectiveness is based upon how active a constituency man he is.

> Framing policy is more important, but from the point of view of the constituent, casework is more important. My reputation is based on casework. You give people very tangible things. If you consider your effectiveness as an MP, it's the cases on which you are most effective. On legislation, you can effect a change once a year. On cases, you can effect a change several times a week.

Naturally enough, backbenchers were most likely to feel this way.

The second explanation relates to the importance of party activists in British politics. Not only does constituency service buy the MP some measure of policy independence, but it also improves the general morale of the local party:

Casework pleases the activists.

If you do a good job, it inspires them.

It gives my activists a sense of having influence over Westminster. They like the regular contact with me.

They like to hear people say that I work hard.

If people see that the MP is industrious, they feel more obliged to work for him.

They want to be able to say, "Go to the MP," and know that it will work.

The thing that motivates them is national issues, but it helps if they think they have a good constituency man.

The association pays, after all, to support my office in the constituency, and they would be unhappy if I didn't do some casework.

Some MPs were more skeptical of the party-related benefits of service. Said one, "I don't think it has much relation to the party, because it's pretty invisible." Complained another, "Most do not know what I am doing." Whether diligent service carries party-related rewards or, conversely, whether lackadaisical service carries party-related costs may depend on how active the local association is, how closely they monitor the MP's activities, and what they think is important.

Finally, a few MPs reported simply that they enjoyed casework:

It's the part of politics that I like best. You can't win them all, but you get an enormous satisfaction if something works. My campaign style is door-to-door canvassing: 'Here I am, your MP.' Sometimes a problem comes up right there. It's great fun. It's immensely satisfying.

Congressmen, in contrast, seldom get personally involved in individual casework.

Ultimately, the MPs' heavy personal involvement in constituency service means that they pay a high price in terms of personal time invested. Thus, some MPs questioned whether the casework demands currently made on them have become too large and now interfere with what they were really elected to do:

Casework has increased too much and ought to be reduced.

It's sizable. Most of it should not be handled by me. It's not a good

use of my time, but it does help me keep in touch with my constituents.

Casework takes too much time. Some sort of balance is needed.

Being a welfare officer is part of the job. Up to a point it's a good
thing, but it shouldn't overwhelm you. It's gone too far.

The volume has increased over the years. MPs have kept up with
the increasing work load, but at the expense of their sanity and
domestic peace.

I sought election to Parliament to participate in government, not
to be a welfare officer.

More than a few MPs had serious doubts about the value of their
casework activity. They realized that their constituents appreciate
their services, but they sensed that they are being drawn away from
the traditional debating and voting functions of Parliament. Many
of them were proud of their activities and comfortable with their
welfare officer role, but others felt trapped by demands they could
not control and did not enjoy fulfilling. With less ability to determine
their own home style, some British MPs feel constrained and frustrated in their role as representative.

Testing the Electoral Motivation

The interviews of members of both Congress and Parliament suggest
that the electoral incentive operates as an important stimulus for
constituency service in both the United States and Britain. But people are not always good judges of their own motives, though the
most obvious source of self-delusion, social acceptability, hardly
seems operative in this case. At any rate, the motivational question
is susceptible to a more objective test. If the electoral incentive is
at work, certain regularities in behavior should be apparent.

For one, if all members believe that constituency-oriented activity
is electorally efficacious, and if there is little variation in the value
of the activity for other purposes, resource allocation ought to be
directly related to electoral vulnerability. If the electoral incentive
is real, then the amount of resources devoted to this effort, personal
or staff, should depend on the congressman's or MP's electoral situation. Those in marginal seats should feel more insecure about
their positions and consequently more anxious to do what they can
to make them safer. Conversely, those in safe seats should value
the electoral benefits of constituency work relatively less and judge

the opportunity costs as relatively higher. Although incumbents' perceptions of closeness of elections may not correspond with actual circumstances, individuals holding seats with small majorities are presumably more likely to regard their seats as marginal than those holding seats with large majorities. Thus, a defensible, though imperfect, measure of vulnerability is the closeness of the previous election. Those who won close races in the previous election should be more likely to view their seat as unsafe and undertake measures to consolidate their position than those who won by larger margins.

Other considerations suggest that the relationship between length of service and constituency activities should be negative. If the development of trust and reputation in the district is viewed metaphorically as a stock of capital, then representatives with large existing stocks should invest less additional resources in their district activities than other representatives. Assuming further that the more recently elected have had less time and opportunity to build up their reputation in the district, then the level of constituency effort should relate negatively to years of incumbency.[10]

The impact of marginality and seniority follows logically from arguments about rational office-seeking. But a proper test should take into account additional factors to ensure that the results are not unintentionally biased. One factor is the congressman's or MP's party. Although many Conservative and Republican representatives see nothing inherently contradictory in casework activities, they still might be less inclined to help their constituents take advantage of the welfare state than Labour MPs or Democratic congressmen. Moreover, the natural constituencies of the left and the right may place different demands upon their representatives. Working-class individuals, for instance, may need ombudsman services more than middle-class individuals. Either of these considerations would suggest a disproportionate presence of constituency entrepreneurs among Democrats or Labour than among Republicans or Conservatives.[11]

Other potentially relevant variables include whether the MP is a backbencher or minister, whether the congressman chairs a committee or subcommittee, whether the MP has experience in local government, and a number of sociodemographic characteristics of the constituency, such as age and percent immigrant, which could indicate the underlying demand for casework services. None of these variables emerged as statistically significant predictors of casework activity, so they will receive no further discussion.[12]

There are several ways to measure the level of casework effort.

One is to examine the various separate activities and allocations of resources and see how each relates to the three predictors. The problem with this method is that indicators of casework effort may be differentially valid. Surgeries and district offices, for example, may not indicate the same effort in a sparsely populated rural district as in a densely populated urban one. Although the separate activities are indicators of the casework effort, different levels of the separate activities could coexist with similar cumulative levels of effort.

Thus, a second approach to measuring casework also is advisable. Assume there is a general orientation to constituency effort which cannot be directly observed. At one end of the continuum of effort are the industrious constituency entrepreneurs who leave no stone unturned; at the other end are the members who neglect constituency work completely. Although the member's orientation cannot be observed directly, one can observe specific manifestations of it, such as whether the member solicits cases and whether he or she holds surgeries more than twice a month. There may be differences in the specific mix of activities undertaken in different constituencies, but the underlying orientations toward casework effort are presumably comparable and determined by similar considerations.

The simplest way to build a scale of constituency effort is to sum a number of individual activities. If each individual activity or resource allocation is measured as a binary (yes = 1, no = 0) variable, then the index of constituency effort for a specific member is the sum of these numbers. The common sense assumption behind this procedure is that more activities undertaken signify greater effort. Four activities constitute the index in the United States: whether the congressman's office solicits cases from constituents, whether it publicizes successful cases, whether it handles cases involving local or state government, and whether it has an especially large number of caseworkers (defined as a number in the top third of the sample). The British index of casework effort includes whether the MP solicits additional casework from constituents, publicizes successful cases, handles local cases, and holds surgeries more frequently than twice a month.

There are more complicated ways to measure the hypothesized unobserved constituency orientation. One is to assume the familiar factor analytic model in which one observes the casework activities of the legislators and estimates their relation to the hypothesized underlying orientation. The result of a factor analysis is one underlying dimension for both countries. The relationships between scores on this dimension and the three predictor variables are similar to those obtained from use of the simpler additive procedure, but the factor analytic results do confirm the hypothesis of an underlying general orientation toward casework effort.[13]

A final approach to measuring casework effort is the traditional Guttman scaling method which assumes a cumulative ordering of the activities such that if members undertake an activity high on the scale, then they will also undertake every activity lower on the scale. Hence, if the activities are ordered by the procedure as x,y,z,w, an individual who undertakes z will also have undertaken x and y. Efforts to scale the casework activities proved fruitless, however, for both the American and British casework activities, consistent with the notion that activities have different significance in different constituencies.[14]

The relation of the additive index of casework effort to the three predictor variables, party, previous electoral margin, and year elected appears in Table 3.1. The party variable assumes a value of 1 if the incumbent belonged to the Democratic or Labour parties. The year elected is simply the last two digits of the year the incumbent was elected. Previous margin is the percentage amount by which the member won in the preceding election.[15]

In both countries, incumbents in the party of the left are somewhat higher on the scale of casework orientation than incumbents in the party of the right, though the American estimate is not significant at conventional levels. More important, members who were more recently elected and those who represent marginal seats indeed

Table 3.1. Correlates of constituency effort in Great Britain and the United States (probit estimates)

Variables	United States[a]	Great Britain[b]
Previous margin	−.022**	−.023**
Party	.350	.410*
Year elected	.036**	.023**
Constant	.465	.181
Chi-square/df	15/3**	17/3**

a. $n = 102$.　　*$p < .05$.
b. $n = 101$.　　**$p < .01$.

have a greater casework orientation.[16] Thus, evidence consistent with electoral motivation appears in patterns of observed behavior.

In summary, constituency service consumes significant amounts of a member's time in Britain and resources in the United States. Members and their staff are quite aware of the electoral and political significance of their activities. They also feel that constituency service is expected of them, that it can purchase freedom in the policy arena, and that it is necessary in an era of interventionist government.

Members' beliefs are reflected in their actual behavior. Constituency work in both countries shows understandable patterns. In particular, the level of casework effort is related to the representative's perceived vulnerability as measured by the margin of victory in the previous election. In addition, because personal support is a stock of political credit built up over time, there are identifiable career cycles. The relationship between these considerations and casework activities is somewhat stronger in Great Britain than in the United States. One possible explanation is that in Britain service activities are not mediated by large staffs and other perquisites, so that individual MPs pay a higher personal price, in terms of opportunity costs, to build up their stock of political credit. All other things being equal, those who face higher resource costs will naturally take more care in their allocation.

4

Temporal Change in Constituency Service

Today constituency service is important to American and British voters and representatives alike. Probably this has always been true, but there is reason to believe that representative-constituency relations have become more important in the postwar decades. On the American side, there is the puzzle of the increased incumbency advantage: during the 1960s congressional incumbents became more insulated from national forces, possibly as a consequence of increased constituency service.[1] Today's voters have high constituency service expectations, and congressmen work hard to meet those expectations. But are they working harder than they did in the fifties, and if so, does this explain the increasing insularity of congressional races?

On the British side, electoral behavior has changed in important ways. Party ties have become less meaningful to both voters and MPs, and the importance of class has lessened.[2] The precise shape of this altered electoral environment is not completely clear—it may still be changing. But if voters are relying somewhat less on partisan ideological and programmatic cues, they may be weighing parochial constituency concerns more heavily now than before. And if the major parties have alienated large numbers of voters, contemporary MPs may work harder than before in an effort to insulate themselves from adverse national electoral tides.

Changes in the representative-constituency relationship can take any or all of several forms. Voters might have more contact with or information about their representatives. The nature of their contacts and information may be different. Or, if the level or nature of representative-constituent interaction has not changed, voters may value the interaction more highly than they did before. Such possibilities are difficult to examine, since relevant data are scarce. Some fragmentary evidence about member behavior in earlier periods is available, and limited comparisons of changes in popular attitudes are possible by utilizing the 1958 SRC American election study and the 1963 and 1966 Butler-Stokes British studies, in conjunction with the late 1970s studies that supply the bulk of our data. Comparing data drawn from different surveys is a risky enterprise. Even when the wording of questions remains constant over time, shifts in the social or political context may change the way in which citizens respond.[3] When question wording varies, the difficulties and dangers are compounded. Consequently, it is not possible to reach definitive conclusions about temporal changes. It is only possible to piece together a suggestive picture of how the behavior of voters and members in both countries has changed during the past three decades.

The American Picture

One explanation for the increased advantage of incumbency is the theory that incumbency had become a voting cue.[4] If House elections are low-information, party-line contests, as previously believed, and party identification had declined, then an increasing number of voters would be casting about for an alternative rule of thumb for voting. Because incumbency is easily ascertained, it could serve as a readily available cue for voters no longer reliant on party identification.

Casting an automatic vote for incumbents seems like a simple-minded way to vote, and it conflicts with some explanations for the declining role of party identification—an electorate becoming more rather than less sophisticated. In addition, as shown by public opinion polls, citizens were becoming increasingly cynical and distrustful of people in government. Would such people cast more or less automatic votes for incumbents? Moreover, increases in the advantage of incumbency vary systematically across House cohorts, suggesting that incumbent behavior itself accounts for some of the observed change.[5] Still, the decline in party identification may constitute part of a more complicated explanation even if not the whole story by itself. Incumbents can behave in ways calculated to take advantage of weakened party ties, or even in ways calculated to weaken those ties further. One indicator of the increasing self-reliance of congressmen is the trend in the growth of staff resources over the past two decades.

In 1959 a congressman could employ up to eight people. That number was increased to nine in 1961, ten in 1964, twelve in 1966, fifteen in 1971, sixteen in 1972, and eighteen in 1975. Congressmen have made ample use of this growing resource. The mean number of personal staff actually employed rose from 5.3 to 13.9 during this period. The trend since 1963 has been fairly steady and shows no significant partisan differences.

District staff has grown even more rapidly. In 1959, the mean number of district staff members was less than .8, but by 1979 the figure was 5.5—a seven-fold increase. Once again, partisan differences are slight. Whereas Democrats on average have always employed more district staff than Republicans, these differences are small relative to the variation across districts and over time.

Incoming congressmen tend to have larger staffs than those they replace. A third or more of the year-to-year increase can be accounted for by the replacement of older members of Congress with newer members.[6] Among the departing members, those who retire tend to have fewer staff than those who run for higher office. Newer members also are more likely to place staff in their district than in their Washington office. This could reflect greater electoral insecurity or simply fewer demands in Washington. Those whom they replace, especially retirees, have fewer district staff for the opposite reasons.

Though newer members of Congress on average hire larger district staffs than departing members, those who return also increase their district staff allocations. Thus, replacement by itself is not the whole story. The only time that replacement explained more than half the total change was 1971, when continuing members actually decreased their average number of district staff members. Hence, there seems to be a general trend toward allocating staff resources to the district. This accords with a variety of other changes indicating that incumbents have become more solicitous of their constituents during the postwar period. Congressional use of the frank skyrocketed during the mid-1960s. Authorizations for travel and offices have increased greatly since 1958. And campaign expenditures have clearly increased, although reliable data are available only for the 1970s.[7]

Such evidence leaves little doubt that the availability and use of tangible resources by House incumbents increased greatly between 1958 and 1978. Are such increases related to the increasing advantage of incumbency? One possibility is that incumbents have used their greater resources to become better known than they were in the past. Increased advertising by congressmen has produced greater product recognition and increased brand name loyalty.[8] A second possibility is that congressmen have managed to communicate different information; even if no better known, what constituents know has changed. In particular, if today's constituents are more likely to know about noncontroversial, nonprogrammatic constituency service than about controversial stands on issues, then congressmen's images may be more positive than in the past.

Information Levels in 1958 and 1978

The level of constituent information about congressmen did not change significantly between 1958 and 1978 (Table 4.1). Name recall was actually lower in 1978 than in 1958, marginally so for incumbents, greatly so for challengers. The lower level of incumbent recall is partly explained by the heavy retirement rates of the mid-1970s. In 1978, 40 percent of House incumbents had entered the institution since Nixon's resignation; lower name recall partly reflects the lower visibility of these relatively junior incumbents. There appear to be methodological reasons for the lower challenger recall. The 1978 NES/CPS sampling frame included a poorer, less well known set of challengers than those who actually ran across the nation.[9]

Another indicator of information is the question asked in 1958, "We're interested in knowing what sorts of persons these candidates are. Have you read or heard anything about Mr. (name of Republican/name of Democrat)?" This question was asked after those citizens who could not recall the candidates' names were provided with their names. Incumbents had a two-to-one edge over their challengers according to this question. The 1978 survey did not repeat the 1958 question, instead asking a series of questions known as the contact battery. Citizens were asked whether they had come into contact or gained information about the candidates by meeting them personally, attending a meeting where the candidates appeared, talking to a staffer, receiving mail, reading about them in a newspaper or magazine, hearing them on the radio, and seeing them on TV. This question appears comparable to the 1958 question in that it explicitly mentions most of the ways a citizen might hear or read something about the candidates, but the distribution of responses is greatly different. The two-to-one informational advantage of incumbents also appeared in 1978, but the absolute levels for both incumbents and challengers were twice as high as in 1958. It is hard to say how much of the increase is simply due to differences in question wording.[10]

Yet another indicator of information levels is the percentage of citizens correctly identifying the incumbent after receiving the names of the candidates. Nearly identical questions appeared in both the 1958 and 1978 surveys. About ten percent more citizens could correctly identify the incumbent in 1978 than in 1958.[11]

In sum, comparisons of information levels between 1958 and 1978 are inconclusive. Name recall actually suggests a decline in information levels. Two other indicators suggest an increase, but in these cases differences in survey questions and their sequence reduce confidence in the resulting figures. The comparisons thus provide no convincing support for a change in information levels over time. The simple increase in incumbent advertising probably is not a major explanation for the enhanced advantage of incumbency.

Constituency Relations in 1958 and 1978

Increased visibility is the simplest and most obvious link between expanding incumbent resources and a growing electoral advantage, but it is not the only imaginable link. Even if the sheer amount of information possessed by constituents has not changed, the content of the information may have.[12] An expanded federal presence may have increased the importance of two traditional roles of House members: the role of ombudsman for constituents and groups unhappy with bureaucratic decisions, and the role of broker between federal agencies and constituents desirous of procuring a share of the largesse those agencies dispense. The casework loads of House offices have grown, and the number of federal programs for which some local group or government might be eligible has increased. If House members increasingly emphasize their ombudsman and broker roles, constituents might gradually substitute nonpartisan, nonprogrammatic, nonideological perceptions for more partisan, programmatic, and ideological ones. In a nutshell, less controversial information would replace more controversial information in the memories of those having any information at all. Thus, increased support for incumbents would stem from an increase in the positivity of constituent information rather than in the absolute level of information.

The 1958 SRC study asked questions that are relevant to this argument, but their use is problematic because the questions were asked of only a portion of the sample. For example, the study asked whether constituents had had a casework experience and whether they recalled anything special the incumbent had done for the district. These items were asked, however, only of those constituents who could correctly identify the incumbent. Although it might seem logical that constituents who could not identify the incumbent would report no recollections of casework or district service, any experienced analyst of survey data would hesitate to make such an assumption. In order to maximize comparability of the data, we attempt to isolate subsamples of the 1978 survey sample that correspond to the subsamples of the 1958 survey who were asked the pertinent questions.[13]

In 1958, 88 percent of the sample lived in districts with incumbents running for reelection—exactly the same as in 1978. Ten percent more of the sample could identify the incumbent in 1958 than in 1978 (Table 4.1). Thus, using ability to identify the incumbent to filter out uninformed constituents nets a marginally larger proportion of the 1978 sample than of the 1958 sample. Both surveys included a nearly identical question, "Can you remember anything special (the incumbent) has done for this district or for the people in this district?" In each year two responses were recorded by the survey organization and categorized according to an identical scheme. The similar filter and the similar survey item permit a relatively clean comparison of recollections of district service. Both samples also were asked about casework experiences, but here the items differed. The 1958 sample was asked: "Has he ever helped you or done anything personally for you or your family?" Up to two responses were recorded. We defined casework as "personal favors and services" and "information and publicity," omitting from the latter category those who specified receipt of unsolicited promotional materials. In 1978 constituents were asked whether they or a family member had ever contacted the incumbent and, if so, whether it

Table 4.1. Basic facts about contested races with incumbents running[a]

	All respondents		Voters only	
Information	1958	1978	1958	1978
Name recall				
Incumbent	43%	34%	57%	49%
Challenger	26	11	34	17
Read or heard about incumbent	38	—	49	—
Read or heard about challenger	19	—	25	—
Some contact with incumbent	—	79	—	89
Some contact with challenger	—	37	—	44
Know which candidate is incumbent	59	67	71	82
Vote for incumbent				
Sample	—	—	60	79
Actual	—	—	58	67

a. 1958 figures do not include at-large races in Connecticut and New Mexico, which were in addition to district races.

Table 4.2. Casework experiences and district service recollections among citizens who could correctly identify House incumbent

	All respondents		Voters only	
Constituent reports	1958	1978	1958	1978
Total casework	4.5%	14.9%	5.6%	17.2%
Personal help	3.5	9.9	4.1	10.8
Information	1.1	7.7	1.5	9.8
District service	33.2	29.0	37.2	34.3

was to express an opinion, seek help with a problem, or request information. The last two categories were defined as casework. While the questions differ in the two years, the 1978 questions were more difficult. The constituents in 1978 were asked whether they had taken the initiative and contacted the incumbent, whereas constituents in 1958 were asked only if some contact had ever occurred. Thus, finding an increase in casework between 1958 and 1978 is likely to underestimate any true increase.

Casework reports have tripled over the two decades 1958–1978 (Table 4.2). Such an increase is consistent with the growth in personal staffs and district office operations. In contrast, recollections of special services to the district were more widespread in 1958 than in 1978, even though federal programs proliferated between 1958 and 1978, and congressmen have developed credit claiming to a fine art. A breakdown of the responses to the district service item sheds some light on this puzzling finding (Table 4.3). Constituents take the question very broadly, but as would be expected, the number of constituents who mention local problems and projects has risen considerably—by more than 25 percent. Volunteered *negative* responses to the district service item virtually disappeared over the twenty-year period.

Thus, over the course of the past few decades there appears to be an increase in the proportion of constituents who associate their representative with particularistic benefits, both in the personal sense of casework and in the broader sense of local problems and projects. Although the comparisons are not as clean as one would prefer, they are considerably more conclusive than those involving information levels. Real change appears to have taken place in the area of constituent recollections of particularized benefits.

One final comparison concerns the representative's actions in the policy arena rather than the service arena, but it is relevant to this discussion in that it explores the question of a parochial versus a more general perspective. In both 1958 and 1978 all constituents were given a version of the classic delegate-trustee dilemma: "Sometimes voters want their United States representative to do some-

Table 4.3. Nature of district service recalled

Service recalled	1958	1978
General competence	8%	7%
Provides access to government	4	7
Communicates with constituents	7	4
National legislation, policy	22	22
Local problems/projects	30	42
Good party member	2	—
Group references	14	15
Negative comments	5	1
Other/miscellaneous	8	2
Total comments (n)	(419)	(435)

thing the representative disagrees with. When this happens, do you think the representative should do what the voters think best, or should the representative do what he or she thinks best?"[14] In 1958 a plurality of Americans opted for the trustee pole of the classic dichotomy, preferring that representatives do what they think best. By 1978, however, a solid majority of Americans were unwilling to grant their representatives such personal discretion, preferring that they follow the wishes of their constituents. The shift may well be connected to declining levels of trust and confidence in government officials, a question beyond the scope of this book. Whatever the cause, there appears to be an increased willingness to impose particularistic standards on representatives' policy decisions. The assiduous polling and other means of information gathering utilized by contemporary representatives may have a real basis in the attitudes of their constituents.

Candidate Images in 1958 and 1978

Both the 1958 and 1978 surveys contain open-ended questions designed to explore the content of citizen evaluations of House candidates. Such questions permit respondents to express their attitudes in their own words. Thus, assuming that respondents offer their most central or salient attitudes, these questions provide the most accurate information on constituent images of candidates. Unfortunately, there are various difficulties with comparing the answers to these questions at different times. In increasing order of seriousness, the difficulties are: the responses were categorized in different ways in 1958 and 1978; the filter used in the 1958 study does not appear in the 1978 study; and the format, wording, and sequencing of the survey questions differs between the two years.

Coding differences create no insuperable difficulties.[15] Appendix A contains the codes underlying the broad categories presented in the tables which follow. Separating out comparable subsamples from the 1958 and 1978 samples poses a more serious problem. The open-ended questions in 1958 were asked only of respondents who stated that they had "heard or read" something about the candidate. Since the "heard or read" item does not appear in the 1978 study, we use the contact battery as the filter for 1978.[16] Question wording creates by far the greatest difficulties for a temporal comparison of candidate images. For reasons elaborated in Appendix B, it is not possible to compare the overall positivity of incumbent images in 1958 and 1978, because the 1958 question wording created a "positivity bias" in the responses and thus precludes a temporal comparison.

The content of candidate images can be compared with more confidence, because the positivity bias of the 1958 question does not preclude comparing the substance of constituent views in 1958 with those in 1978 (Table 4.4). Apparently the content of incumbent images changed in only one major respect between 1958 and 1978: the proportion of comments about the incumbent's attentiveness to constituents and the district more than doubled. Again, if incumbents' increasing use of resources like staff, mail, and district offices has any effect, such a change in the distribution of responses is no more than should be expected.

As for other minor changes in the distribution of incumbent images, there is a marginal increase in the policy and ideological con-

Table 4.4. Breakdown of positive evaluations of incumbent

Positive evaluation	1958	1978
General, good man	11%	7%
Experience and record	20	15
Personal attributes	30	30
Qualities and characteristics relevant to serving	(17)	(4)
Personality	(13)	(26)
Constituency attentiveness	11	25
Helps with problems	—	(6)
Understands district, keeps in touch	(5)	(7)
Keeps constituents informed	—	(7)
Listens, is accessible	(4)	(6)
Local issues, projects	(2)	(2)
Philosophy, ideology, general approach to government	2	7
Domestic issues/policy	3	5
Foreign policy	0[a]	1
Group references	6	5
Party affiliations/connections	5	1
Personal considerations	8	—
Other	4	4
Total comments (n)	(942)	(1475)

a. Less than 0.5%.

tent of the 1978 responses. Party-related aspects of the image have virtually disappeared, a decline that is probably underestimated in view of the explicit deemphasis of party considerations in the 1958 items.[17] Over the same period, negative views of the incumbent's personal attributes increased somewhat—probably an artifact of the more elaborate 1978 coding scheme absorbing the large "other" category which existed in 1958. All other differences were small, though again party connections are fewer in 1978 than in 1958.

In sum, changes in the images of congressmen across the twenty-year period of the two studies are generally marginal. The principal area of change is consistent with the greater level of constituency effort shown by contemporary congressmen: incumbent images were founded on perceptions of constituency attentiveness more in 1978 than in 1958.

The British Picture

Although there has been a noticeable disruption in the heretofore uniform swing and although some incumbents have managed to hold down the swing against them by their constituency efforts, MPs do not enjoy a substantial incumbency advantage. And although too many incumbents may seem to be safely ensconced in disproportionately Labour or Conservative seats, the constituency efforts of British incumbents are not so successful that they have weakened electoral competition.[18] Still, the landscape of British politics has changed dramatically since the 1960s, so it is reasonable to suppose that the incentives and opportunities faced by MPs may also have changed.

One political development that could have affected MP incentives is the dealignment of Britain's strong, class-based, two-party system. The party system of the 1950s and 1960s left little room for maneuvering by incumbents; the party label was simply too strong for the activities of individual members to matter much. But from the mid-sixties to the mid-seventies, the percentage of those identifying with either the Labour or the Conservative parties declined from 81 percent to 76 percent. Even more dramatically, the number of strong major party identifiers dropped from 71 percent to 61 percent. Additionally, class-related issues and appeals grew less attractive to British voters through these years. As a consequence of these trends, the uniform national swing developed north-south and urban-rural variations.[19] This electoral change and its attendant uncertainty should have increased the incentives for MPs to establish a personal vote.

A related change has been the declining performance of the British economy since the late 1950s. Economic evaluations have a strong role in British voting. But over and above the direct effect of a government's bad economic performance, there is the indirect effect of the British public's suspicion that the economy is deliberately stimulated before an election and its inevitable disappointment following the hyperbolic election-day economic predictions, which have contributed to its mistrust of government.[20] Consequently, MPs in the governing party possibly have had greater need in recent years than in the earlier period of postwar prosperity to buffer themselves against the electorate's retrospective judgment.

Adding to national incentives to create a personal vote are political changes at the local level, such as the end to automatic reselection in the Labour party. The first round of reselections did little to increase constituency service pressures and much to tighten the grip of left-wing elements over their MPs. Still, left-wing elements apparently control only 50–60 Labour constituencies; local pressures in the other constituencies are more likely to be parochial and nonideological.[21]

Reselection is not the only new local pressure that MPs have faced. One by-product of local government reform in the early 1970s has been the creation of a new breed of more partisan and politically ambitious local councillors. Prior to the Redcliffe-Maud report of 1969 and the Local Government Act of 1972, rural county councils had a long tradition of nonpartisan, independent representation. But the integration of rural counties with the urban district councils and the cession to the counties of control over the politically controversial areas of education and social services led to the demise of the independent councillor tradition.[22] Increasingly council office has become a training ground for the House of Commons, and increasingly MPs must worry about the potential challenge from ambitious local officeholders.

Finally, the level of constituency service in Britain has increased simply because of the growth in the opportunities for intervention. The expansion of government services is one aspect of the greater demand for casework. Equally important is the publicity that surrounded the debate, which began in the 1950s, over the adequacy of existing grievance procedures. The Crichel Downs case, a dispute over the government's compulsory purchase of land for use as a bombing site and its subsequent refusal to return the land to the private owners, raised serious questions about how well citizen rights were being protected under the existing system of reliance on ministerial responsibility. The Franks Commission on Administrative Tribunals and Enquiries stimulated a broader interest in the maladministration issue and ultimately the establishment of the parliamentary commissioner for administration, or ombudsman, in 1967. Efforts undertaken in 1977 to publicize the ombudsman's services may have added further to casework demand.

Opportunities for intervention at the local level also increased as a result of the local government reforms of the early 1970s. Local government cases, especially, involving housing and education, constitute a major portion of the MP's postbag. The establishment of the chief executive's office and the imposition of a more rational local bureaucratic structure made local intervention easier for the MP. MPs now tend to take their local cases to the chief executive or occasionally to one or two chairmen of powerful council committees. Prior to these reforms, local governmental authority was fragmented, conflicting, and exercised by individuals who were neither elected nor accountable to elected officials.[23] Having a few key officials who are accountable to the council has facilitated intervention by both the councillors and the MP.

The delicate balance of local-central government relations under the 1972 reorganization may have also increased the number of "brokering" opportunities for members. Local governments derive their revenue partly from central government grants. The central government's power of the purse, combined with its rights to make senior appointments at the local level, give it significant leverage over local authorities. When central and local government goals conflict, opportunities for mediation arise. Many MPs are eager to help local authorities prevent the central government from closing a school or hospital.

In sum, electoral, institutional, and societal changes in Britain over the past two decades have increased the demand and opportunity for constituency service. And MPs have responded to the changing structure of demands and opportunities, as suggested by interviews in 1978 with fourteen retiring MPs. Some of them, like Michael Stewart and David Weitzman, had been in Parliament throughout the postwar period and consequently had a unique vantage point for detecting trends. Though not asked specifically to comment on whether the welfare officer demands had increased in recent years, they were asked to comment on casework demands per se, and in that context the subject of change frequently arose. Of the fourteen, five made no remarks about change one way or the other. Seven of the remaining nine said that casework demands had increased in recent years, although one of these, Michael Stewart, said that the highest period of demand was immediately after the Second World War when returning veterans were claiming benefits for the first time. Two of the retirees thought that demands had not increased, but in both instances they had resented the welfare officer role and during their later years in office had cut back on casework activities.

Those who perceived a rise in constituent demands cited the expansion of the welfare state, the failure of local councillors to do their job properly, pressure from the local party, and the entrepreneurial approach of new MPs. G. Burnaby Drayson, the Conservative MP from Skipton since 1945, felt that there had recently been an increase in casework demands. He argued that while the expansion of the welfare state per se had "increased the number of areas where intervention by the MP was necessary," political pressures were also at work. The present surge was induced "in great part by electoral considerations." He noticed "increasing pressure in the rural constituencies like my own from ambitious young officials in farmers' unions and the like for seats in Parliament." This caused "an excessive local orientation on the part of new members." These pressures "were getting unpleasant." He suggested that the demise of automatic adoption would exacerbate these tendencies.

David Weitzman, the retiring Labour Member for Hackney North and Stoke Newington, shared the perception that there had been "an increase in the constituency load placed upon the MP in the last thirty years." He pointed not only to the expansion of the welfare state but also to the recent influx of immigrants who needed help in dealing with the Home Office on such matters as dependent immigration and extension of visas. Weitzman found it ironic that his load had increased despite the proliferation of administrative tribunals, legal aid, and other alternative avenues of redress. He concluded that "people prefer the intervention of the MP," who is "only too willing to oblige."

There is additional evidence to show that contemporary MPs are more involved with their constituencies than were those of an earlier generation. For example, MPs use their secretaries to help with their constituency mail. Some of them even delegate casework to their secretaries, particularly local cases when the secretary resides in the district. The 1967 survey of British MPs by Barker and Rush inquired about secretarial support.[24] Since the question asked—"What secretarial assistance do you have?"—was quite general, it is not clear whether the MPs were referring to secretarial support from all sources, including business secretaries, whom many MPs use for constituency assistance, or only to support paid for by the official allotment. If business secretaries are included, there was by 1979 a ten-fold increase in the number of MPs who had more than one secretary helping them. If business secretaries are omitted, there was a doubling.

Apart from the question of resource changes, there is the question of effort per se. In 1967 the deliberate generation of mail was rare. In comparison, by 1979 many MPs solicited cases by various means, ranging from door-to-door visits to public advertisement. Moreover, in 1967 only one MP in each main party among over 111 MPs interviewed had deliberately generated constituency mail in an attempt to bolster his electoral position.[25] By 1979, not only was the propensity to solicit cases greater among the most electorally insecure—those in marginal seats and the newly elected—but many members also openly discussed the electoral importance of casework. No matter which group of MPs is examined—new, continuing, or retiring—over 80 percent indicated that casework had electoral benefits. The crucial difference between the two studies is that the later one specifically asked about the electoral benefits, whereas the earlier one replied on the open-ended question, "What do you think about spending this amount of your parliamentary time in this way?" to which the most frequent response was that casework gave the MP "great personal satisfaction" and was part of the job. The later study got similar responses to a similar question about casework, but when it was followed up with the question, "Do you think that these activities have any relationship to the vote?" MPs were quite open about the electoral consequences.

There are other signs that the level of constituency activity has increased in the last twenty years. The amount of time devoted to constituency mail has increased, in spite of the fact that MPs have more secretarial support now than they did earlier. More MPs spend between one and two hours on their mail, and fewer spend less than one hour per day. Another indicator of constituency service is the frequency of surgeries. In this instance the three points of comparison are the mail survey by Dowse in 1963, the 1967 Barker and Rush study and the 1979 MP study (Table 4.5).[26] Curiously, the 1967 estimates are far closer to the 1979 estimates than to the 1963 ones. Barker and Rush attributed the 1963–1967 difference to sampling problems, arguing that their estimates were upwardly biased by the fact that their sample excluded front benchers. The 1979 study, however, never found ministerial status to be a significant predictor of surgery frequency. Hence, the jump between 1963 and 1967 may well have been real. There had been two intervening elections and a fair amount of turnover in membership. Also, the early 1960s saw the first of the Liberal revivals. Some MPs suggested that the Liberals' grass roots strategy forced candidates, especially Conservatives, to devote more attention to constituency affairs. In any event, there was not only a sharp increase in the frequency of surgeries between 1963 and 1967 but also a continued increase between 1967 and 1979. In particular, MPs in 1979 were more inclined to hold at least two or three surgeries per month.

The trend in MP behavior has been in the direction of greater constituency effort. Those who have served in Parliament for many years suggest informally that constituency demands have increased over this period and that new MPs are escalating the level of expectations about constituency service. Objective data confirm their

Table 4.5. Comparison of frequency of surgeries

Frequency of surgeries	Dowse (1963)	Barker & Rush (1967)	CFF (1979)
None	17%	2%	4%
Ad hoc	20	7	3
Yes	63	91	93
Weekly or more	(12)	(16)	(15)
2 or 3 per month	(22)	(30)	(43)
Every 3 weeks	(6)	(14)	(6)
Monthly	(23)	(30)	(25)
Less often	—	(10)	(11)
Total responses (n)	(65)	(111)	(100)

impressions. MPs are spending more time on their constituency mail, holding more surgeries, and soliciting cases more aggressively than before.

Changing Perceptions of MPs

As shown by the American experience, increased investment of resources in constituency service may produce one or more of several effects. First, greater constituency effort may alter incumbent visibility. Second, even if visibility levels are unchanged, greater effort may change the substance of representatives' images. The same possibilities exist in Britain.

To test the effect of increased activity on MP visibility, a series of name recall figures were constructed going back to 1964. The specific question asked in the Butler-Stokes study, the source of the figures for 1964–1970, was, "Do you happen to remember the name of the candidate who was elected to Parliament for this constituency?" This wording differs slightly from the one in 1979 when constituents were asked, "Do you happen to remember the names of the candidates who ran in this constituency on May 3rd?" Far from experiencing an increase in name recall, MPs were less well known in 1979 than in the 1960s. Whereas 85 percent of constituents could name their MP in 1964, only 61 percent could do so in 1979. In short, despite other trends in their behavior, MPs are now less well known.

One likely explanation is the 1969 ballot reform. Before the 1970 election, only the candidates' names were printed on the ballot. This placed a premium on name recognition in that a sensible vote required the voter to match names with parties. Beginning with the 1970 election, the party labels of the candidates were printed on the ballot, and this may have had the predictable effect of lessening the salience of the candidates' names. Another relevant factor is the lowering of the age qualification for voting in 1969, which may have added less knowledgeable voters to the electorate. In any event, the trend toward more active MP participation in constituency affairs has not increased MP visibility. This finding parallels that in the United States.

Increased levels of MP constituency activity have produced detectable changes in the images of MPs, as in the United States. In 1963 and 1966 the Butler and Stokes study asked a question which serves to measure district service, "Do you happen to remember anything that (name of MP) has done for the people of this constituency?" This question was asked only of those who answered yes to the query, "Have you read or heard anything about (name of MP before the election)?" The analogous question in the 1979 study was, "Do you happen to remember anything special your MP (name) has done for the people in this constituency while (he/she) has been in Parliament?" For purposes of comparison, as with the American data we followed the strategy of retaining only the responses of those who reported contact with the MP in one of the ways specified in the contact battery.

The level of personal service contacts can also be compared over time. The question asked in 1963 and 1966 was, "Has he/she ever done anything for you or your family personally?" In 1979, the question was, "Have you or anyone in your family living here ever contacted (name of MP) or anyone in his/her office?" Contacts with the incumbent to "seek information" and to "seek help on a problem" were combined into a positive response. Like the district service questions in 1963 and 1966, the personal service questions were asked only of those who had read or heard about the incumbent. Thus, as in the American analysis, the contact battery was again applied to filter the 1979 personal service responses.

Curiously, the British situation exactly parallels the American. Reports of personal service by the MP show the expected increase, from 8 percent to 12 percent, but recollection of district service is highest in 1963 and falls 15 percent by 1979. The 20 percent figure for 1979 is almost identical to the figure of 19 percent uncovered by a 1972 survey for Granada TV, so it is unlikely to be a statistical aberration.[27] The rise in personal service contacts is consistent with all the other findings, but the decline in those who are able to mention the incumbent's district service is puzzling. Following the strategy employed with the American information, the responses to the open-ended question about district service were examined for changes in substance over time, although this procedure is necessarily less conclusive in the British case because Butler-Stokes and Gallup did not utilize the same coding schemes.

The great preponderance of 1979 constituents mentioned the MP's role in local issues and campaigns, whereas in the 1960s the question apparently captured a more symbolic component of the MP's behavior, unless Butler and Stokes adhered to a very broad concept of "ceremonial" (Table 4.6). British citizens' notion of district service over the course of two decades appears to have become somewhat more weighted toward the instrumental and less toward the symbolic.

Thus, the higher levels of personal contact and the increased efforts of MPs on behalf of local causes are reflected in the perceptions of constituents. But have these changed perceptions changed the popular image of the MP? Unfortunately, the Butler-Stokes study did not include the same questions as the 1979 American study. The Butler-Stokes study includes a job rating item. Respondents were asked, "On the whole, do you feel that (name of MP) is doing a good job as a member of Parliament, a fair job or only a poor one?" Then they were asked, "Why do you feel that way?" and their first response was coded. Like other items in the study, this one was asked only of individuals who indicated that they had read or heard about the MP.

Although the 1979 study asked constituents to rate their representatives, no follow-up probe was included. Thus, to compare the substance of member images in 1979 with those in the mid-1960s, we utilize the familiar likes/dislikes question: "was there anything in particular that you liked (disliked) about [name], the MP from this constituency?" Constituents were allowed up to four responses for both likes and dislikes, but in fact they rarely made more than two. Because the job rating item allowed only one mention of why the respondent thought that the MP was doing a good or bad job,

Table 4.6. Comparison of open-ended responses to district service questions

Service recollection	1963	1966	1979
Constituency service	4%	15%	19%
Local issues	19	15	70
Transportation	(10)	(7)	—
Employment/local industry	(7)	(5)	(15)
Housing/hospitals	(2)	(2)	(10)
Local causes	—	—	(31)
Local works	—	—	(13)
General interest	77	70	11
Availability	(35)	(32)	—
Ceremonial	(41)	(39)	—

Table 4.7. Comparison of MP evaluations

Content of constituent evaluation	Job rating		Likes/dislikes
	1963[a]	1966[b]	1979[c]
Positive			
Party	4%	4%	13%
Policy	1	2	10
Constituency	33	27	46
Other (personal characteristics, etc.)	62	68	31
Negative			
Party	7	4	12
Policy	6	2	23
Constituency	24	27	35
Other	63	67	30

a. $n = 356$ positive, 81 negative.
b. $n = 505$ positive, 74 negative.
c. $n = 605$ positive, 212 negative.

we report only the first response to the like/dislike question. In practice, not much is lost because the distribution of responses does not vary much when the first comment is compared to all comments. The things that people reported liking or not liking about the MP were assigned to the four categories of party, policy, constituency, and "other" for comparison with the responses to the job rating question.

There are numerous differences between the past and present responses (Table 4.7). Positive comments about party, policy, and constituency are all up, while positive comments about personal attributes are down. The same is true about negative comments, especially about policy. The proportion of negative references to constituency service is much higher than in the United States. Most such comments reveal constituent disappointment with the MP's commitment, as in "the MP is not a local man," "he never visits the constituency," and "he is not accessible to his constituents." Because the 1979 questions and the Butler-Stokes question are not the same, the apparent temporal differences may be artifacts of different wordings, but they are obviously consistent with the data already presented.

On the whole, there are similar changes over time in the United States and Great Britain. In neither country does greater constituency effort create higher name recall, but in both countries incumbents have successfully altered the substance of what people think about them. In the contemporary period constituents are more likely to evaluate their representatives on the basis of some constituency relevant consideration, that is, something under the heading of district service activities. Constituents are now more likely to seek personal assistance from their member and more likely to remember some local project, program, or other matter in which their representative has taken the lead. Although the data cannot establish that member images have consequently become more positive (see Appendix B), the increasing constituency component of these images would have that effect.

Part II
CONSTITUENT RESPONSE

5

Unraveling a Paradox

In a review of research based on the 1978 NES/CPS survey, Timothy Cook observes that "voters in general may point to personal qualifications of incumbents, remember being contacted, recall 'something special' done for the district, or expect helpful responses from the staff. Members of Congress in general may spend time communicating a personal image to constituents, intervening with bureaucracies, and protecting district interests. But it remains unclear how closely connected individual incumbents' activities are to their constituents' evaluations, and decisions."[1] Since Cook's review additional studies have appeared, but their conclusions are consistent with his. There appears to be little or no evidence that the activities and resource allocations of congressional offices have any effect on the perceptions, evaluations, and voting decisions of their constituents. Consider the following roll call of recent findings:

On campaign spending
The more incumbents spend, the worse they do (Jacobson).[2]

On travel
Incumbent electoral success is unrelated to visits home (Fenno).[3]

On staff
Incumbent electoral success is unrelated to district staff presence (Fenno).[4]

On casework
"Using returns from the 1978 Congressional elections, we estimate the effects of three strategies that incumbents may use to increase their vote totals ... we find that casework has no statistically significant effect and further find that a substantively important effect is unlikely, given our estimates" (Johannes and McAdams).[5]

On federal spending
"All in all, we found *no* evidence that obtaining local federal spending for his district or protecting against spending cutbacks is a useful way for a congressman to pursue reelection" (Feldman and Jondrow).[6]

On legislative activity
Incumbent electoral success is unrelated to bill sponsorship and committee position (Ragsdale and Cook).[7]

On campaign communications
"Voters' knowledge of candidates' personality characteristics is not increased (even among those voters who are most likely to pay attention to political communications) when candidates emphasize their personality in their campaign communications ... Indeed, the findings presented here suggest that when politicians talk, nobody is listening" (Raymond).[8]

On resources in general
"Of paramount interest, incumbent resources, including representative activities and campaign money, do not significantly affect the district vote" (Ragsdale and Cook).[9]

"As for the ultimate question—how to explain the incumbency effect and the diminishing marginals—we cannot claim to know the final answer. Casework, it seems, is not part of the answer. Neither, apparently, are many elements of the incumbent's 'home style'—trips home, allocating staff resources to the home district, and the like" (Johannes and McAdams).[10]

Does incumbent behavior affect voter perceptions and behavior in more subtle ways, such as by attracting campaign contributions or discouraging strong challenges? Apparently not:

"Generally, the evidence does not support the hypothesis that bringing government spending or employment to his district is a good way for an incumbent to raise campaign funds or to avoid a serious challenge."[11]

"Incumbents' use of the 'perks' available for 'advertising and casework,' on the other hand, is not related to any indicator of challenger quality . . . the use of these 'perks' does not discourage campaign contributors nor politically experienced opponents once the effects of ideological discrepancy and partisan vulnerability have been taken into account [perks include district offices, total staff, percentage of staff in district, and percentage of staff designated as caseworkers]."[12]

When viewed in combination, these findings are troubling.[13] An intelligent layman perusing the political science literature could arrive at the remarkable conclusion that House incumbents can close their district offices, fire their staffs, stop doing casework, abandon the quest for federal money, give up their district residences, choose committees purely on the basis of personal interest, tell the political action committees where to put their money, and still get as many votes—perhaps more—than if they continued to behave as incumbents presently do. No doubt politicians in general and incumbent congressmen (and their challengers) in particular would regard this conclusion as preposterous. Indeed, we are sure that with the possible exception of Johannes and McAdams none of the researchers cited would accept the stark implication of their combined findings, though they accept their individual findings considered in isolation. Only Fenno and Jacobson hesitate to take their findings at face value.

When research results conflict with theory, common sense, or even political folklore, scholars should entertain the possibility that something could be wrong with the research.[14] In the present context, rather than blithely concluding that high-level politicians have no contact with reality, scholars should pause and wonder whether something might be wrong with the data and/or methods. In the course of our research we have encountered scores of nonrelationships and even a few perverse negative relationships between incumbent efforts and constituent perceptions or evaluations. This repeated confounding of expectations has at least three bases. The first simply involves the crude and imprecise nature of the data. The second involves problems of simultaneous causation which render suspect ordinary statistical procedures. The third reason seems obvious in retrospect but has been overlooked heretofore. It involves problems of cross-level inference. We illustrate the arguments with congressional data because the prevailing doubts arise from analysis of such data, but the arguments apply equally to the British case and indeed to any studies that attempt to determine the response of the citizenry to the behavior of political leaders.

Problems in Relating Member Behavior
to Constituent Reports

Problems of conceptualization and measurement pervade attempts
to link incumbent behavior to constituent perceptions and evaluations, and lead directly to problems of specification in statistical
analyses. Some variables are easy to measure—the number of district
offices and campaign expenditures, for example. Others present greater
difficulties. Anyone who has asked congressional staff how many
cases their offices handle in a month, how many grant applications
they monitor, what percentage of time the member devotes to constituent service, and so forth is well aware of the uncertainty attending responses to such questions. Estimates are data and better
than nothing, but it is dangerous to treat them with the confidence
we might treat something like dollars of expenditure. Attempts to
relate the quantitative information supplied by staff to reports by
constituents often come to naught. For example, the bivariate relationship between number of cases handled per week by a congressional office and constituent evaluations of the congressman's
constituency attentiveness is essentially zero. When "caseload" is
included in a multivariate equation, the coefficient is often tiny and
statistically insignificant. Yet recoding the variable in a manner that
places less weight on small differences in caseload levels produces
a different finding. Table 5.1 provides a vehicle for some extended
discussion. The third column of the table differs from the second
only in the inclusion of some individual level variables, a matter
not addressed until later. For now, simply compare column one with
two.

The dependent variable is the individual response to the survey
item, "Do you happen to remember anything special that your U.S.
representative (name) has done for this district or for the people in
this district while he/she has been in Congress?" Some of the district
level variables relate to the individual responses in the expected
way. For instance, constituent recollections are significantly higher
in districts whose offices report an active effort to get grants, whose
congressmen come home frequently (weekly or more often), and
whose congressmen are Democrats. Constituent recollections are
significantly lower the more junior the congressman. This is a reasonable finding if constituents in fact remember achievements from
longer ago than the very recent past. Caseloads, however, do not

Table 5.1. Correlates of district service recollections (probit estimates)[a]

Variable	(1)	(2)	(3)
Frequent visits	.318**	.344**	.371**
Democratic incumbent	.217**	.211*	.281**
No. of district offices	−.068†	−.020	.003
Office seeks grants	.258**	.225**	.188**
Year elected	−.025**	−.022**	−.018**
Cases per week	.000	—	—
Medium caseload	—	−.043	−.050
Heavy caseload	—	.143†	.204*
No. of staff members	.022	—	—
Medium staff	—	−.128	.133
Large staff	—	.353*	.273†
Impersonal contact	—	—	.966**
Second-hand contact	—	—	.724**
Constant	.369	.356	−1.040*
Chi-square/df	62/7**	75/9**	271/11**

a. $n = 1591$. **$p < .01$.
*$p < .05$. †$p < .10$.

seem to matter in Equation 1. The coefficient suggests not the faintest trace of a relationship. But consider Equation 2, where caseload is specified not as a continuous variable but by dummy variables representing low (up to 30), medium (31–90) and high (over 90) levels. Low and medium levels are indistinguishable, whereas high caseload levels relate significantly to high recollections of district service. Here the substantive conclusion hinges on a specification decision.

Social scientists are loath to throw away information in the data, but the contrast between the first and second columns of the table may indicate that the data contain less information than meets the eye. Possibly the caseload estimates are better used to separate legislators into broad groupings rather than to distinguish small differences among them. With estimated caseloads so uncertain, the definition of a case not constant from office to office, and the mix of cases (such as individual versus high level) unmeasured, should we really expect one office's figure of 50 to be associated with a constituency response significantly different from another office's figure of 60? Probably not. But such an expectation might be more reasonable when comparing figures of 30 and 100.

On the other hand, the coefficients of the staff variable suggest additional possibilities.[15] Administrative assistants would be expected to provide a more accurate report of the full-time equivalents in their office than of their weekly caseload, but the coefficient of the continuous measure of staff (Equation 1) is small and insignificant, whereas a discrete classification (Equation 2) produces a stronger relationship, as again, only offices with larger than normal staffs can be differentiated from the other categories. The raw data show a clumping of offices in the range of 8–11 staff members; of 87 offices whose congressmen sought re-election, only 13 had fewer than 8 staff members, and only 8 had more than 11. There is no discernible relationship in the large middle category, but there is a discernible one on the extremes, namely, a doubling in various reports and evaluations as one moves across the three categories (Table 5.2). Large staffs are associated with the effect for district service recollections and expectations of helpfulness, whereas small staffs are associated with the effect for positive comments about the member's constituency attentiveness. Multivariate analyses analogous to those in Table 5.1 confirm these bivariate impressions.

The estimates for staff possibly indicate the inappropriateness of a linear specification. Alternatively, the results may reflect no more than noisy data, as with caseloads. At first glance, measuring staff is relatively easy: count the bodies. But staffs are more or less efficient, and more or less geared to district service. Considerations like these may muddy the import of the precise figures, whereas broad categorizations may separate offices into meaningful categories.

The general point is not that categorical representations of incumbent resources and activities are superior in any ultimate sense

Table 5.2. Size of Washington staff and constituent responses

	No. of staff members		
Constituent response	0–7	8–11	12+
Remembers district service	16%	20%	31%
Incumbent would be very helpful if problem arose	22	27	42
Positive mention of incumbent attentiveness to constituency	8	14	16

to the continuous measures.[16] Rather the point is that caution is needed. If conclusions are contingent on the precise mode of representing the variable of interest, then no analysis can be considered conclusive until there is a consensus on the most appropriate measure and specification.

Many researchers act as if such a consensus were at hand. For example, almost every relevant analysis thus far published or presented has assumed that the effects of incumbent resources and activities are linear. Thus, the typical regression analysis requires that the estimated effect of 20 trips home is $20b_i$, of 35 trips $35b_i$, of 50 trips $50b_i$, and so forth. Such linearity assumptions are untenable in a wide variety of circumstances. Consider representative A in the protectionist career stage gliding along with election victories of 70 percent.[17] The possible electoral benefit of any particular activity is limited by the existing electoral base since anyone who would ever consider voting for the representative already may be a supporter. In contrast, consider representative B, a young member in the expansionist stage trying to make a marginal seat safe. This representative might get considerable mileage out of behavior which would only keep representative A in a steady state. The positions of some members leave room for their activities and allocations to have larger effects than those allowed by the positions of other members. The use of logit and probit methods goes some way toward incorporating such considerations because these methods presume diminishing effects of the independent variables as the probability of the dependent behavior approaches unity.

Congressmen in the same electoral circumstances may have constituencies that differ in other relevant respects. For example, representative C's caseload consists largely of individual requests from socially marginal people, such as the elderly poor, disabled veterans, and immigrants, who vote at low levels, give little money, and remain outside of the established social networks. In contrast, representative D has a smaller caseload, but it contains more requests from businesses and organized groups whose members vote, contribute, and communicate with other political actors. The prosperous constituents of representative E ignore the announcement of $500,000 in federal funds, whereas the less fortunate constituents of representative F rejoice at the announcement of a grant of $300,000. Representative G, a busy subcommittee chair, cannot get home as often as representative H, a freshman with few pressing Washington responsibilities, but G compensates by means unavailable to H and unmeasured by us.

In short, the effects of incumbent activities and resource allocations are naturally conditional upon various features of the representative's district and political circumstances. It would be convenient if every variable of political interest worked in simple, additive, unconditional fashion, but it is unlikely that they do. The problem for researchers is that representatives themselves are much more likely to understand the true forms of the relationships and the elements that condition those relationships. Choices that are perfectly comprehensible to them pose a complicated problem for analysis. Because this problem does not yield to the simplest attempted solution, however, does not mean that its structure is purely random.

Problems of Simultaneous Causation

The problems discussed thus far can be addressed by renewed efforts at data gathering, hypothesis formulation, and statistical analysis. While labor intensive, such problems are less intractable than problems of simultaneous causation. To illustrate, consider Table 5.1 once again. Note that the district offices variable takes on a negative sign twice, and in one case achieves statistical significance. As the number of district offices goes up, recollections of district service, positive comments about incumbents, expectations of helpfulness, and overall job ratings go down. In multivariate estimations *significant* negative relationships occur with some regularity. Thus, to Jacobson's strange observation that "the more incumbents spend, the worse they do," we can add the equally odd observation that the more district offices incumbents have, the less their constituents like them.

Understandably surprised by his finding, Jacobson went on to explore its basis. The results are now well known. Incumbent spending is principally defensive; it is highly responsive to challenger spending. Incumbents do worse when they spend more precisely because spending more usually indicates that they face a strong challenge which makes them do worse.[18] This circularity lies at the root of the statistical problem. Let us examine the district offices anomaly more closely. Table 5.3 presents data on the most striking example: as the number of district offices goes up, expectations of helpfulness decline in close to a negative linear fashion.

Table 5.3. Confusing causal linkages: an illustration using district offices

No. of district offices	Very helpful	Don't know how helpful	No. of respondents
1	35%	18%	774
2	27	26	716
3	20	27	428
4	15	32	104
5	9	30	23

Year elected	Very helpful	Don't know how helpful	Avg. no. of district offices	Avg. 1976 vote
1964	29%	20%	1.6	62.4%
1964–1972	29	21	1.9	64.2
1974	26	25	2.2	58.8
1976	22	35	2.4	59.9

A larger number of offices is strongly associated with lower expectations of helpfulness. In addition, the more district offices representatives have, the higher the proportion of their constituents who do not know how helpful they would be. The bottom panel of the table contains some additional information. Less senior members have more district offices; they also have a less secure electoral base than more senior members and a less well-formed reputation in their constituencies. Thus, a second hypothesis emerges. New members of Congress who are less well known, less positively evaluated, and less electorally secure establish more district offices in order to improve their political standing. Their efforts may well have the expected positive effect, but that effect may be overwhelmed in cross-sectional data by the initial weakness (relatively speaking) of newer members.[19]

If a relationship is composed of two partially offsetting components, one would like to break down the relationship into the separate components. In essence, two-stage estimation procedures using instrumental variables attempt to do just that. By substituting an instrument for the problem variable on the right-hand side, one attempts to obtain an estimate of the one-way effect of the right-hand side variable on the left-hand side variable. In practice, difficulties often arise because of the requirement that the variables comprising the instrument be related to the right-hand side variable but not the left-hand side variable. Previous electoral margin, for example, relates significantly to number of district offices, but it also relates to most of the variables one would use district offices to predict, so it is not appropriate to include margin in an instrument. Thus, in attempting to "purge" a right-hand side variable of its troublesome variation, one may end up purging it of all its systematic variation. After reading earlier versions of Johannes and McAdams and Feldman and Jondrow, one of us raised in each case the likelihood of simultaneous causation.[20] Johannes and McAdams responded with a two-stage analysis that supported their simpler analyses. Unfortunately, the instrument for caseload explains about 5 percent of the variance in the original caseload variable, so it is essentially a different variable, or more likely, sheer noise. We have constructed an instrument for district offices using the regression:

$$Y = .053 \text{ year elected } - .012 \text{ city } - .011 \text{ suburb}$$
$$- .456 \text{ Democrat } + .456 \text{ subcommittee chair}$$
$$- .146 \text{ party leadership } - .138 \text{ college } - .805, \qquad R^2 = .29$$

When substituted in the equations, the coefficient on the instrument is almost always insignificant ($-.043$, s.e. $= .089$ in Equation 1 of Table 5.1), but rarely positive, and never positive and significant. This may indicate either that the number of district offices truly has no positive impact on constituents' perceptions and evaluations or that the instrument poorly represents the true effects of district offices.

In early stages of research, analysts may hesitate to get involved with full-blown simultaneous equations structural systems and the time, effort, and money they entail. But they should realize that their analyses are "first cuts" which do not provide findings so definitive as to call into question the behavior of politicians who have achieved the highest levels of elective office. In an uncertain world some aspects of political behavior may well reflect superstitution more than reality. But the faith put in simple statistical methods does not appear to be altogether divorced from superstition.

Overlooked Difficulties in Cross-Level Analysis

Imagine a hypothetical society in which there is a perfect one-to-one relationship between the efforts of representatives and the responses of their constituents. To be exact, if a representative devotes x percent of his or her time to constituency service, x percent of his or her constituents respond with a favorable rating or expectation. Thus, by definition, the aggregate regression for the population shows a constant of 0, a slope of 1.0, and an R^2 of 1.0.

Suppose that political scientists now take a survey of this society. If they are both very careful and very lucky and draw perfect samples within a legislative district sampling frame, each district sample will mirror the district. To provide some numbers for analysis, assume that the total sample consists of 9 district samples having 10 constituents each (Table 5.4).

If the district average rating is regressed on percentage of legislator time, the estimates remain as before—constant of 0, slope of 1.0 (both with standard errors of 0), and an R^2 of 1.0. Generally, analysts do not aggregate survey data, however, preferring to make use of the larger number of individual observations. In the example, if the 90 individual observations are entered rather than the 10 aggregated district observations, the resulting regression is:

$$\text{Percentage of approval} = .00 + 1.00 \text{ (percentage of time)}, \qquad R^2 = .27$$
$$(.18)$$

The regression parameters have not changed, but the switch to individual level analysis has resulted in a drastically lowered estimate of explained variance, and a positive standard error for the coefficient of percentage of time. The reason is that the regression equation makes only 9 distinct predictions, one per district: .1, .2, .3, .4, .5,

Table 5.4. Hypothetical data set

| | Constituent approval | | |
District	Yes ($= 1$)	No ($= 0$)	Legislator time
1	1	9	10%
2	2	8	20
3	3	7	30
4	4	6	40
5	5	5	50
6	6	4	60
7	7	3	70
8	8	2	80
9	9	1	90

.6, .7, .8, .9. Thus, *everyone* in a given district is predicted to have the same value. Moreover, since all constituents actually have values of either 0 or 1, *no one* is correctly predicted by the estimated value for those in their district. The important feature of this example is that 27 percent is the *maximum* variance that any district level variable can explain even though, by construction, the district level relationship is perfect.

Recall the "fundamental identity" of analysis of variance: total variation equals between-group variation plus within-group variation. In the hypothetical example only 27 percent of the variation is between-district, and the district level variable explains all of it. Fortunately, there is still a large, significant coefficient on percentage of time, which indicates the importance of the variable, but conditions need not be so ideal as the example so far presumes. Suppose that political scientists were not quite so lucky and picked up a 10 percent error in their approval ratings through the vagaries of the data collection process.[21] Using a table of random numbers, the approval rating of one constituent of the ten in each district is reversed. The regression now becomes:

$$\text{Percentage of approval} = .18 + .70 \text{ (percentage of time)}, \qquad R^2 = .12$$
$$(.19)$$

and the estimated importance of percent time has dropped 30 percent. Measurement error in the right-hand side variables of a regression equation biases the coefficient estimates, with the bias taking the form of underestimation in the one variable case.[22] Thus, studies of the effects of member activities and resource allocations using rough estimates of caseloads and crude proxies like number of staff generally will misrepresent the effects of those activities and allocations. And while important, that is not the only point of the example.

Refer back to Table 5.1. The estimated equation reported in column three differs from those in columns 1 and 2 by the addition of two powerful individual level right-hand side variables. As shown, constituents who report contact with their congressman through newspapers or magazines, TV, radio, or mail are significantly more likely to remember something special the congressman has done, as are those who have heard about some friend's or relative's contact. Notice the veritable explosion in the chi-square statistic between columns 2 and 3. The individual level variables obviously make a huge contribution to the explanatory power of the equation. This should come as no surprise. The 1500 people in this analysis fall in only 70 districts; on average, 23 people *are assigned the same value for any given district level variable.* Any variation among that score of constituents is completely beyond the explanatory reach of the district level variable. Given the relative similarity of resource usage among congressmen, such as staff size, within-district variation should normally far exceed between-district variation. Since restricting the variance of the right-hand side variables inflates the estimates of their standard errors, analysis of member activities and allocations using crude measures, taken from a limited sample of districts, encounters a kind of statistical "double whammy" that biases coefficient estimates while simultaneously inflating their standard errors.[23]

But if within-district variation dwarfs between-district variation, isn't that an important finding, and doesn't it show that what members do and decide actually does have only minimal consequences for their reputations in the district? For a number of reasons this negative implication is unwarranted. In the first place, the analysis of variance analogy breaks down, since this is not an experimental situation. In an ideal world the congressional offices in the sampling frame would be divided into two groups, and one group would close down all its district offices, reduce its staff to a secretary and receptionist, and quit seeking grants, while the second group would expand its offices, staff, and activities to the legal maximum.[24] This experimental design would legitimately test for the existence and magnitude of treatment effects. But as matters actually stand, few incumbents are either very much lower or very much higher than the rest, as shown by the size of the staffs in Washington. Thus, even if member activities have a large potential for affecting their constituents' perceptions, the observable effects are not likely to be large if members do not differ greatly in what they do.

There is still another reason why the relative magnitudes of within-district and between-district variance can be misleading. The comparison would be important if the following model were the correct one:

member/office variables

constituent variables ⟶ constituent evaluations

Here, the member and constituent variables are theoretically and statistically independent, and given comparable measurement quality, if the latter explain the lion's share of the variance in constituent evaluations, one might reasonably conclude that the former are of little significance. But how would member activities and decisions have effects except *through* constituent variables? How would high caseloads, big staffs, grant seeking, and frequent visits produce positive evaluations if constituents did not read or hear about the congressman, see him or her on TV, get something in the mail, or recognize the name? Thus, the model most researchers implicitly have in mind is

In this case it would not be surprising if member activities made no contribution to explanations of constituent evaluations, since the hypothesized effect is indirect, *through* other constituent variables. From this standpoint the estimations in column 3 of Table 5.1 are somewhat puzzling. Why do frequent visits, high caseloads, large staffs, grant seeking, and Democratic incumbency remain significant when contact variables are added to the analysis? Though the wording of the latter appears comprehensive, they apparently do not fully capture the ways in which incumbent activities affect constituent evaluations.

The point of this chapter is not to attack the usefulness of statistical methods. Rather, the point is to identify a number of reasons why simple applications of common methods may go astray. If a simple tabular presentation or parsimonious regression strikingly bears out a hypothesis, that may be sufficient, though analysis should not necessarily stop there. But if simple methods do not bear out what logic, common sense, previous findings, traditional wisdom, or plausible theories predict, analysis should certainly not stop there. Although data themselves are neutral, every data analysis implicitly makes a host of assumptions about the structure of the data and the relationships among them. If those assumptions are misconceived, the conclusions based on the data may be correspondingly misconceived.

6

Member Behavior and Constituent Response

Electoral incentives will motivate representatives to invest scarce time and resources in constituency service only if voters notice and value the service activities of their representatives. To be sure, elected officials could believe that constituency service affected their standing with voters even though it did not, but aside from such "false consciousness," the failure of voters to appreciate member activities would undercut the electoral incentive for constituency service. Although representatives might still decide to allocate effort and resources to service, variations in their home styles would reflect differences in personal taste, ideology, and tradition.

The analyses in this chapter examine three measures of constituent perceptions and evaluations of the constituency service activities of MPs and congressmen. First is the district service question. About a fifth of the Americans and an eighth of the British claimed to recall something special their incumbent had done for the district. The second measure is the expectation of access. About 25 percent of the constituents in both countries believed the incumbent would be very helpful with a problem. The third measure is constructed from a question that asks constituents what they liked and disliked about their representatives. About an eighth of the citizenry in each country mentioned something that was categorized as constituency attentiveness.[1] These three measures capture somewhat different aspects of a representative's reputation for constituency service. The first focuses on the district at large, the second focuses on individual assistance, and the third encompasses both. Thus, the three measures do not relate to member activities and allocations of resources in precisely the same way.

Reputation for Constituency Service

Only one measure of resource allocation, the number of employees in the Washington office, bears a consistent and common-sense relationship to consistent evaluations of their congressman (Table 6.1). Most of the offices employ from 8 to 11 staff members with no discernible variation in constituent perceptions in this middle range. Representatives whose offices are relatively understaffed, however, do a bit worse than those in the middle range, and representatives whose Washington staffs are larger than the ordinary do more than a bit better than their colleagues with normal-sized staffs. Constituents of generously staffed offices differ from those of sparsely staffed offices by almost a factor of two in offering favorable evaluations of MCs.

In contrast, there is no apparent relationship between the number of district staff that congressmen employ and constituent evaluations. Nor does any relationship emerge for specific types of staff, such as the number of caseworkers, project specialists, and district representatives. The relationship between number of district offices and congressional reputations runs precisely counter to expectations. Most striking, in the district blessed by 5 offices not a single one of the 23 constituents interviewed mentioned something positive about the incumbent's constituency attentiveness.

For Britain, there is little staff variation to examine. The number of paid employees attached to the constituencies is not even a good measure because it includes party agents and other party personnel, not just the MP's personal secretary or assistant. Whatever the reason, restricted variance, a bad measure, or no relationship, MP reputations do not vary systematically with staff size.

The activities of congressmen and MPs provide more meaningful

Table 6.1. Relationship of constituency service evaluations to member resource allocations

Resource	District service	Very helpful	Constituency attentiveness
	United States		
Washington staff			
0–7	17%	25%	9%
8–11	19	26	15
12+	32	40	18
District staff			
0–4	20	27	12
5–8	21	30	18
9+	19	24	12
Project workers			
None	20	27	15
1 or more	20	28	14
District offices			
1	27	34	20
2	17	27	13
3	17	22	13
4	12	15	6
5	9	9	0
All	20	27	13
	Great Britain		
Paid employees			
0–2	14	24	13
3–4	10	29	13
All	12	28	13

comparisons than their resources. Several constituency activities display noticeable relationships with representatives' reputations (Tables 6.2–6.3).

1. Members who handle larger numbers of cases are more positively evaluated by constituents.

2. Members who publicize their casework are marginally more positively evaluated by constituents.

3. Congressmen who spend a relatively large proportion, from one-quarter to one-half, of their time on casework receive some

Table 6.2. Relationship of constituency service evaluations to member activities in Great Britain

Activities	District service	Very helpful	Constituency attentiveness
Visits			
< Weekly	7%	24%	12%
≥ Weekly	16	27	15
Surgeries			
≤ Monthly	10	23	14
> Monthly	11	27	13
Weekly	32	28	16
Cases			
25 per week	11	27	13
25–50	12	24	15
> 50	23	35	19
MP time on constituency affairs			
≤ 33%	8	25	16
34–50	13	30	15
> 50	17	24	13
Solicits casework			
No	10	30	16
Only at elections	5	18	18
Yes	14	25	13
Publicizes casework			
No	8	25	9
Yes	13	26	15
Handles local casework			
No	8	25	12
Reluctantly	15	28	15
Yes	12	25	14

credit, but MPs who spend 75 percent or more of their time on casework show no higher level of constituent approval on two of three measures.

4. Congressional offices that seek out grants and publicize their successes earn the appreciation of constituents.

5. MPs who hold more frequent surgeries have more favorable reputations.

6. Members who return to their districts more frequently, including those who live there, are marginally more positively evaluated by constituents.

Although these relationships generally comport with common-sense expectations, they do not reveal a strong linkage between member activities and constituent responses.

Simple (technically, bivariate) relationships can be deceptive, especially if one fails to consider the ways that various incumbent activities are related to each other. Representatives with more district offices naturally have more district staff. Members who en-

Table 6.3. Relationship of constituency service evaluations to incumbent activities in United States

Activities	District service	Very helpful	Constituency attentiveness
Visits			
≤ Monthly	19%	32%	16%
> Monthly	17	25	12
≥ Weekly	24	30	18
Cases			
≤ 30 per week	18	28	12
31–90	19	27	15
90+	26	33	18
Congressman time on casework			
0	21	30	16
Up to 25%	19	24	15
26–50%	28	34	18
Solicits casework			
No	22	28	16
Yes	20	27	14
Publicizes casework			
No	18	26	13
Yes	24	30	17
Handles local casework			
No	20	27	14
Some	12	22	13
All	22	28	16
Seeks grants			
No	16	22	12
Yes	23	30	17
Publicizes grants			
No	14	23	9
Yes	20	27	15

courage cases tend to do more cases and to publicize casework. Such possibilities can produce spurious relationships, on the one hand, but may also conceal the existence of true relationships, on the other. The effect that incumbent activities have on constituent perceptions cannot be measured properly unless all relevant activities and resource allocations are examined together and in combination with other important considerations such as constituency characteristics and the political characteristics of the member.

A more comprehensive (technically, multivariate) analysis substantially strengthens the weak preliminary picture of the relationship between member activities and their reputations (Tables 6.4 and 6.5).[2] Heavy caseloads, for example, produce more favorable reputations by all three measures in the United States, and by two of the three measures in Britain. In America, grant solicitation and publicization exert an important positive effect on the reputation of congressmen. In Britain, holding frequent surgeries and publiciz-

Table 6.4. Relationship of incumbent activities and allocations to constituent evaluations in United States

Variable	District service[a]	Very helpful[b]	Constituency attentiveness[c]
Daily visits	.264**	.101	.207*
Medium caseload	−.091	−.055	.116
Heavy caseload	.210*	.142†	.251*
Medium staff	−.066	−.019	.198†
Large staff	.103	.278†	.217
Seeks grants	.186*	.256**	.144†
Publicizes grants	.277*	.126	.410*
Democratic incumbent	.140†	.018	.009
Year elected	−.020*	−.001	−.009
District offices[d]	−.011	−.181*	−.322**
Constant	.036	−.568	−.680
Chi-square/df	36/10*	29/10*	38/10*

a. $n = 1478$.   *$p < .05$.
b. $n = 1465$.   **$p < .01$.
c. $n = 1483$.   †$p < .10$.
d. Instrument.

Table 6.5. Relationship of constituency service evaluations to member activities in Great Britain

Variable	District service[a]	Very helpful[b]	Constituency attentiveness[c]
Solicits cases	.474**	—	—
Weekly visits	.191†	—	.202†
Surgeries			
> Monthly	−.113	.195*	−.140
Weekly	.428*	.203	−.096
Medium caseload	.115	.064	−.080
Heavy caseload	.463**	.237*	−.038
Publicizes cases	—	—	.250†
Handles local cases	—	—	—
Backbench	.291*	−.141	−.043
Labor MP	.088	—	—
Liberal MP	.649*	.227	.684*
Year elected	.000	.009	.019
Constant	−2.015*	.276	−2.613**
Chi-square/df	66/10**	16/7*	17/9*

a. $n = 902$.   *$p < .05$.
b. $n = 586$.   **$p < .01$.
c. $n = 677$.   †$p < .10$.

ing successful cases favorably affects one or more measures of reputation. In some instances the relationship between activities and reputation weakens when other factors are taken into consideration. For example, the positive effect of large Washington staff on congressional reputation diminishes in the presence of other variables. Frequent visits by congressmen to the district have a more selective impact than was first apparent. Congressmen who make weekly visits score higher in district service and constituency attentiveness recollections but do not enjoy more favorable expectations of helpfulness. The British pattern is precisely the same. Finally, the number of district offices continues to show a perplexing negative effect on congressional reputations for constituency service.[3]

There are also a few important partisan differences in the constituency reputations of MPs. Liberal MPs are more favorably evaluated by constituents, though Labour and Conservative MPs do not differ significantly. There are few partisan differences of significance in the United States, although Democratic incumbents enjoy more positive reputations, other things being equal.

Finally, the effects of seniority, represented by year of first election, are inconsistent, sometimes positive, sometimes negative, sometimes significant, sometimes not. For example, constituents are less likely to recollect some special district service by younger members than by more senior members, but there is no relationship for the other two measures of reputation. Seniority has figured so prominently in discussions of congressional behavior that it is important to decipher its effects.

The expected effects of seniority on an incumbent's reputation in the constituency depend on how one thinks about seniority. Traditionally seniority has served as the precondition for attaining a leadership position in the Congress. If a representative could survive long enough, actuarially and politically, a committee leadership position would inevitably follow as the night the day, assuming that the representative was not part of a permanent minority party, the unlucky fate that befell Republicans during the past generation. In the contemporary Congress seniority is no longer an automatic route to power. Nevertheless, it still constitutes a principal criterion by which the majority party allocates committee chairs and the more numerous subcommittee chairs. In addition, there are a variety of party positions that experienced congressmen are more likely to fill than less experienced congressmen.[4] Seniority is thus an imperfect proxy for a leadership position in the legislature. As a result, tenure in office should have a positive relationship with constituency reputation: incumbents with longer tenure are more likely to occupy institutional power positions that enable them to do things for constituents, such as secure projects for the district. Thus, if indicators of institutional position are added to the analysis, these should show positive effects on constituency reputations and the effect of tenure in office per se should weaken or vanish.

According to a broader conception of seniority, long tenure correlates with attainment of formal positions in the institution, but in addition it correlates with a variety of less tangible sources of influence. In particular, seniority is associated with the intangible "capital stock" of credit that members of Congress build up with their colleagues, their constituents, Washington bureaucrats, interest groups, the media, and other actors whom they can use and by whom they can be used. These intangibles compliment the congressmen's formal institutional position but exist independently of it. Thus, indicators of formal position, such as holding a committee or subcommittee chair, should not eliminate the effects of seniority because they are only one component of the legislative resources for which seniority acts as a proxy.

In addition to being associated with increases in tangible and intangible resources, seniority is also related to differences in the behavior of differing generations or cohorts of congressmen. Beginning in the mid-1960s, new members of Congress began to place increased emphasis on constituency service activities, making greater use of available resources and building up their political bases by appearing to their constituents as nonpartisan, nonideological ombudsman. The heavy turnover and political turmoil associated with the 1964 and 1966 elections perhaps provided the opportunity and the incentive for such altered behavior.[5] More recently the Democratic "class of 74" or "Watergate babies" honed the practices of constituency service to a fine art, employing mobile offices, holding district teas, and otherwise devoting great effort and imagination to the care and feeding of their constituents.[6] Whereas formal position and the intangible stock of credit congressmen build up increase with seniority, less senior incumbents devote greater effort to constituency service and thereby develop more positive images than their less constituency-oriented seniors.

Recognizing the several partly conflicting effects of seniority on congressional reputations, additional analyses probed deeper into the subject. Still more comprehensive analyses included indicators of institutional leadership positions: subcommittee chairs and membership on the Democratic Steering and Policy Committee for Democrats, and membership on the Policy Committee and Committee on Committees for Republicans. And by devising a new measure that divides congressmen into the pre-1964, 1964–1973, 1974 (Watergate), and 1976 (freshmen) cohorts, the generational conception of seniority can be tested (Tables 6.6–6.8).

The addition of institutional position significantly ($p < .001$) improves the ability to predict whether the incumbent has a good reputation for district service. Democratic subcommittee chairs enjoy much enhanced recollections of district service among their constituents, but membership on important party committees also ap-

Table 6.6. Relationship of incumbent activities and allocations to district service recollections in United States

Variable	Seniority[a]	
	Continuous	Categorical
Weekly visits	.273**	.252**
Medium caseload	−.018	−.019
Heavy caseload	.255*	.212*
Medium staff	−.049	−.056
Large staff	.252	.269†
Seeks grants	.100	.102
Publicizes grants	.329*	.342*
Democratic incumbent	.117	.039
Subcommittee chair	.479**	.516**
Democratic leader	.316†	.329†
Republican leader	.257*	.196†
Year elected	.004	—
Before 1964	—	.035
1964–1973	—	.143
1974–1975	—	.282*
District offices	−.078	−.097
Constant	−1.753**	−1.532
Chi-square/df	57/13**	62/15**

a. $n = 1478$. **$p < .01$.
*$p < .05$. †$p < .10$.

pears to have an impact, somewhat more so for Democrats. Classifying congressmen by cohorts also improves the model. The Watergate class fares especially well with respect to constituent recollections of district service. The original significant seniority effect on district service was apparently spurious. The continuous seniority measure muddled the higher evaluations of the "class of '74" and the party and institutional leadership positions of more senior members.

Institutional position also matters to constituents' expectation of helpfulness, the second measure of congressmen's reputation (Table 6.7). *Ceteris paribus* subcommittee chairs are more likely to be highly evaluated, but this effect is offset by a negative effect for members of the Steering and Policy Committee, which includes all the sub-committee chairs in the sample. Being a Republican party leader has no effect one way or the other. In contrast to reputation for district service, there is a marginally significant tendency for younger representatives to enjoy more positive expectations, probably explained by the perception that pre-1964 members of Congress are less accessible than younger colleagues.

Finally, the introduction of formal position and seniority cohorts also changes some conclusions about the third measure of reputation, constituency attentiveness (Table 6.8). Although a member's reputation is significantly related to holding a subcommittee chair,

Table 6.7. Relationship of incumbent activities and allocations to expectations of access in United States

| Variable | Seniority[a] | |
	Continuous	Categorical
Weekly visits	.072	.103
Medium caseload	−.012	.001
Heavy caseload	.138	.109
Medium staff	.040	.006
Large staff	.383*	.383
Seeks grants	.244**	.227**
Publicizes grants	.229*	.166
Democratic incumbent	.002	.062
Subcommittee chair	.392**	.405**
Democratic leader	−.453*	−.485*
Republican leader	.147	.126
Year elected	.013†	—
Before 1964	—	−.360*
1964–1973	—	.041
1974–1975	—	−.020
District offices	−.226**	−.232**
Constant	−1.651**	−.670*
Chi-square/df	45/13**	49/15**

a. $n = 1465$.   **$p < .01$.
*$p < .05$.   †$p < .10$.

Table 6.8. Relationship of incumbent activities and
allocations to constituency attentiveness in
United States

Variable	Seniority[a]	
	Continuous	Categorical
Weekly visits	.189*	.177*
Medium caseload	.175†	.206*
Heavy caseload	.295*	.178†
Medium staff	.219†	.191†
Large staff	.296†	.336†
Seeks grants	.120	.164
Publicizes grants	.474**	.319*
Democratic incumbent	.060	−.100
Subcommittee chair	.253*	.347**
Democratic leader	−.189	−.144
Republican leader	.221	.078
Year elected	.000	—
Before 1964	—	.416†
1964–1973	—	.765**
1974–1975	—	.912**
District offices	−.340**	−.376**
Constant	−1.505**	−1.852**
Chi-square/df	44/13**	78/15**

a. $n = 1483$.   **$p < .01$.
*$p < .05$.   †$p < .10$.

formal position matters somewhat less than for the two other reputational measures, making only a marginally significant $(p < .10)$
improvement in the model. But when the cohort measure of seniority replaces the continuous measure, it dramatically improves
the model. The class of '74 stands out, with the 1964–1973 congressmen trailing narrowly, and the pre-1964 congressmen trailing
even more, though still significantly ahead of freshmen (the omitted
category). Thus, freshmen do not establish themselves immediately,
but given a few years, their efforts can produce more noticeable
results than those of their more experienced colleagues, as apparently happened in the case of the Watergate class.

Overall, there is little support for the notion that constituency reputation simply increases with every year in office. Rather, access to institutional power positions which accompanies increasing tenure appears to have some impact. On the other hand, younger congressmen are more motivated to try to build good constituency reputations, as demonstrated by the consistently high reputation of the class of '74.

The consideration of formal leadership and seniority generation does not weaken the associations between incumbent activities and constituent evaluations. In fact, they strengthen the relationships in the case of staff size. In other words, the activities and resource allocations of congressmen produce real effects on their reputations, which are not merely incidental by-products of institutional position or electoral generation.

There is little reason to conduct a similar examination of seniority effects in Britain, where seniority does not lead directly to leadership positions in the party or Parliament. The favor of party leaders largely determines an MP's journey up the ministerial ladder. Indeed, promising MPs usually begin their progression toward leadership at a fairly early stage in their parliamentary careers. MPs who do not attain early apprenticeship positions are likely to spend their careers as backbenchers.

Moreover, in Britain positions of government responsibility do not generally enhance their occupants' ability to do things for their constituencies. Given the lack of staff and other support services, an MP who assumes a leadership position probably has less time to allocate to constituency work. This trade-off between the two realms of activity in Britain contrasts with the situation in the United States where abundant support services enable congressmen to sustain high levels of effort in both realms. Generally held norms of fairness in Britain also deny the legitimacy of using one's ministerial position to benefit one's constituency. According to Roy Gregory, few members would risk the political "uproar" that a particularistic influence attempt could provoke, given that potential electoral benefits are small and that most of those on the ministerial ladder represent safe constituencies: "When the rules of acceptable conduct make it impossible publicly to claim or acknowledge the credit for success, thereby in effect excluding the prospect of reward, there is not much incentive to risk the penalties that would almost certainly be inflicted on anyone caught in the act of trying to bring home the bacon."[7]

Although constituency service activity has increased in recent years, and younger MPs have taken on the welfare role at a faster rate than their more senior colleagues, there is virtually no relationship between tenure in office and reputation among constituents.[8] Although more recently elected MPs have somewhat better reputations for casework access and general attentiveness, the relationship is rarely significant. Division of MPs into Labour members currently holding subcabinet, undersecretary, Parliamentary Private Secretary, and Whip positions, members with previous service in such positions but not currently serving, opposition spokesmen, and all remaining backbenchers produced only a few significant relationships. Ministerial position tends to lower the likelihood of having a good reputation for district service, though not for being helpful to people with a problem or being generally attentive to constituency problems.

Constituent Characteristics and Member Reputations

The activities and resource commitments of incumbents clearly affect constituent perceptions and evaluations. In a nutshell, members who visit the constituency most often, handle the largest number of cases, employ the largest staffs (U.S.), emphasize grantsmanship (U.S.), and hold the most frequent surgeries (UK) enjoy the most positive reputations as "good constituency men," to use a British term. So far little has been said about the characteristics of constituents. The activities and resource allocations of members must be perceived by constituents in order to have an impact. Thus, the level of information possessed by constituents and their personal experience with their representative could significantly shape their evaluations.

Consider first a member's reputation for district service (Table 6.9). Personal, impersonal, and second-hand contacts are all significantly associated with reputation for district service, but over and above these relationships, caseloads, grant publicity, and visits to the constituency continue to show significant effects in the United States, as does holding a subcommittee chairmanship. In Britain, caseloads, solicitation of cases, and frequent surgeries continue to show significant relationships with recollections of district service, as does being a backbencher or Liberal MP.

It is not clear just how member activities and resource allocations

Table 6.9. Relationship of district service recollections to member activities and constituent characteristics

Variable	United States[a]	Great Britain[b]
Contact		
Personal	.575**	.605**
Media	.944**	.633**
Second-hand	.485**	.560**
Party identification		
Independent/none	−.290*	.177
Minor	—	−.020
Same as member	.075	.162
Subcommittee chairman	.392**	—
Watergate class	.113	—
Seeks grants	.103	—
Publicizes grants	.267†	—
Solicits cases	—	.598**
Weekly visits	.287**	.025
Caseload		
Moderate	−.116	−.078
Heavy	.180†	.411**
Staff		
Medium	−.056	—
Large	−.059	—
Surgeries		
> Monthly	—	−.034
≥ Weekly	—	.294*
Backbench	—	.442**
Liberal incumbent	—	.533†
District offices	.023	—
Constant	−2.528**	−2.678**
Chi-square/df	270/15**	136/14**

a. $n = 1422$.   *$p < .05$.
b. $n = 857$.   **$p < .01$.
               †$p < .10$.

can affect constituent perceptions, if not through constituents meeting members or their staff, reading, hearing, or hearing about the representative, receiving mail, and seeing the incumbent on TV. The reports of individual contact should incorporate the effects of member activities and resources, but these contact reports apparently do not fully capture all of the effect of member efforts. An incumbent's reputation will increase among those not helped directly, among those who do not know someone else who has been helped directly, and even among those who have not read, heard, or seen the incumbent. Perhaps some subtler reputational benefit extends beyond contacts to general hearsay. Or possibly some significant fraction of the constituency forgets contact with the representative but nevertheless shows the effects of that contact.[9]

In contrast to the incumbent's reputation for district service, personal contacts seem to incorporate the influence of incumbent activities on expectations of helpfulness. Only seeking grants continues to exert a direct effect in the United States, and heavy caseloads do so only in Britain (Table 6.10). Previous satisfactory experience with a case is by far the strongest correlate of favorable expectations, with knowledge of someone else's experience also showing a very strong relationship, especially in Britain.[10] Party identification bears a stronger relationship to favorable expectations in Britain than in the United States, whereas reported contacts are more important in the United States.

Finally, in the case of reputation for constituency attentiveness the American pattern resembles that for recollections of district service (Table 6.11). A number of the district level factors, such as visits, caseloads, and staff continue to show direct effects on reputation even after the inclusion of personal contact measures. The impressive seniority (cohort) effects of Table 6.8 are largely unaffected by the addition of constituent variables, although differences between the Watergate class and the adjacent 1964–1973 group of congressmen become smaller.

In the British analyses district factors show little or no significant effect above that incorporated in the individual contact measures. The only exceptions are the familiar relationship for Liberal MPs and a rare, marginally significant relationship for year elected. Reported contacts show a major association with mentions of constituency attentiveness as a reason for liking the MP, and again, constituents who share the MP's party affiliation are more likely to mention his or her constituency attentiveness.

Table 6.10. Relationship of "very helpful" expectations to member activities and constituent characteristics

Variable	United States[a]	Great Britain[b]
Contacts		
Personal	—	—
Media	.682**	.223*
Hearsay	.421**	.194
Party identification		
Independent/none	−.118	.239†
Minor	—	−1.044*
Same as member	.212**	.501**
Satisfactory casework experience	1.370**	1.273**
Heard about satisfactory		
casework experience	.554**	1.507**
Moderate caseload	−.016	−.118
Heavy caseload	.147	.208†
Medium staff/surgeries	−.065	.052
Large staff/surgeries	.059	.200
Seeks grants	.187*	—
Publicizes grants	.049	—
Subcommittee chair	.065	—
District offices	.036	—
Visits	—	−.035
Backbench	—	−.083
Liberal MP	—	.155
Year elected	—	.011
Constant	−1.723**	−.061
Chi-square/df	298/14**	106/15**

a. $n = 1351$. *$p < .05$.
b. $n = 523$. **$p < .01$.
†$p < .10$.

In sum, the activities that representatives undertake and the resources they allocate find some reflection in the evaluations formed by their constituents. A dollar of federal spending in a congressional district may not produce a proportionate improvement in the congressman's electoral fortunes. But seeking out grants and publicizing the grants awarded do result in a greater proportion of constituents who recall something special the representative has done for the district, who believe he or she would be helpful if the occasion arose, and who like the representative's attentiveness to the constituency. The number of cases that a congressional office handles also has no direct relationship to the representative's vote. But heavy caseloads

Table 6.11. Relationship of constituency attentiveness to member activities and constituent characteristics

Variable	United States[a]	Great Britain[b]
Contacts		
Personal	.362**	.905**
Media	1.376**	.405**
Hearsay	.515**	.275†
Party identification		
Independent/none	−.235†	−.096
Minor	—	−.414
Same as Member	.088	.298*
Subcommittee chair	.165	—
Year elected		
Before 1964	.380	—
1964–1973	.781**	.024†
1974–1975	.857**	—
Moderate caseload	.173†	−.147
Heavy caseload	.130	−.108
Medium staff	.258†	−.104
Large staff	.127	−.113
Seeks grants	.108	—
Publicizes grants (cases)	.128	.219
District offices	−.272**	—
Liberal MP	—	.690*
Backbench	—	−.034
Weekly visits	.202*	.062
Constant	−3.425**	−3.464**
Chi-square/df	238/15**	89/15**

a. $n = 1472$.   *$p < .05$.
b. $n = 638$.   **$p < .01$.
                 †$p < .10$.

are associated with a greater proportion of satisfied constituents, a fact that would seem relevant to electoral margins. Committee position, too, has no direct impact on a congressman's electoral showing. But subcommittee chairs enjoy higher esteem among their constituents than those not so well positioned. With less consistency, other factors, such as frequent trips home and large staffs, also show some connection to favorable constituent evaluations. Representatives' activities produce political benefits by enhancing their reputation. Although the relationships are not always linear nor overwhelmingly strong, they are there.[11]

The Bases of General Reputations

District service is not the only means by which representatives earn personalized electoral support. If the party system and the legislative institutions permit the representative to serve as a tribune of the district and advocate policies favorable to it in the legislature, a policy-based personal vote becomes possible. Such a policy-based personal vote is a realizable goal for most congressmen but a largely unrealizable one for most MPs. In recent years, however, the iron facade of party discipline in the Commons has begun to show a small crack or two, and it is conceivable that voting for individual MPs on the basis of their policy stands might someday extend beyond unusual cases like Enoch Powell's visibility on immigration questions, as it did in earlier periods of British history.[12]

Yet another possible basis of a personal vote is personal attributes and characteristics of the representative that are largely divorced from either district service or policy positions. Constituents may simply like a representative, or feel pride that one of theirs has achieved high office, or feel flattered that the representative makes himself or herself accessible to them. Judgments about personal attributes probably are not entirely divorced from either district service or policy positions. Presumably constituents find more reason to like and admire a representative who serves their interests than to like and admire one who does not. Still, we all know and like people with whom we disagree, so the partial independence of personal affection and approval of behavior can be taken as a given.

A number of the member activities and resources measured in this study refer specifically to the realm of constituency service, such as caseloads, solicitation of casework, and project workers. Others, however, are multipurpose. Washington staff may serve many ends, such as policy formulation and advertising, perhaps even more so than constituency service. Similarly, frequent visits to the district undoubtedly reflect a representative's desire to establish a personal bond with constituents as much as to perform an activity directly instrumental to serving the district.[13] To a lesser extent the same may be true for surgeries in Britain. Even those activities explicitly connected to constituency service, such as publicizing cases and grants, may serve broader ends as well, increasing the representative's visibility and contributing to the general sense that he or she is on top of things.

Thus, a complete treatment must take up the question of reputation in a broader sense, one that includes policy and personal components as well as constituency service. To determine whether the allocations and activities of representatives affect the most general evaluations constituents form, over and above their evaluations of district service, two survey questions were used. The first is often called the "popularity" question. Many polling organizations regularly ask the public how well they think the president or prime minister is handling his or her job or, alternatively, whether they approve or disapprove of the executive's performance. The CPS/NES study included a version of this question directed at the performance of individual representatives. The question reads, "In general, how would you rate the job that (name of MP or congressman) has been doing—very good, good, fair, poor or very poor?" The second question is the open-ended one, "Is there anything you like (dislike) about (name of MP or congressman)?" For purposes of the statistical analysis we did not make use of the absolute number of comments but rather created a simple measure distinguishing those who reported liking something from those who did not.

Activities and Reputations

Both MPs and congressmen are popular with their constituents. Americans are four times as likely to mention something they like about their congressman as to mention something they dislike. And the British are twice as likely to mention a like as a dislike. Job ratings of representatives are even more positive, with congressmen again faring especially well. Americans offered positive ratings over negative ones by an 11:1 ratio in 1978 and by a 7:1 ratio in 1980.[14] Although Britons are somewhat less enthusiastic about their members, approval of MPs exceeds disapproval by more than 3:1. One baseline against which to judge such figures is that congressmen in both years were rated much more highly than President Carter, and MPs were rated about equally with Prime Minister Callaghan.

Like their reputations for constituency service, members' general reputations are affected by their activities and allocation of resources (Tables 6.12–6.14). Congressmen with large Washington staffs have higher job ratings and receive more favorable comments by con-

Table 6.12. Relationship of member evaluation to member resource allocations

Resource	Job rating very good	Like something about member
United States		
Washington staff		
0–7	40%	37%
8–11	46	46
12+	53	56
District staff		
0–4	46	43
5–8	50	50
9+	42	39
Project workers		
None	47	46
1 or more	46	43
District offices		
1	57	52
2	40	43
3	48	42
4	30	33
5	26	39
All	46	45
Great Britain		
Paid employees		
0–2	34	24
3–4	36	24
All	35	24

Table 6.13. Relationship of incumbent evaluations to incumbent activities in United States

Activities	Job rating very good	Like something about member
Visits		
< Monthly	48%	45%
> Monthly	43	42
≥ Weekly	50	49
Cases		
≤ 30/week	46	43
31–90	45	46
90+	52	46
Congressman time on casework		
0%	47	48
≤ 25%	40	40
26–50%	59	50
Solicits casework		
No	55	46
Yes	45	45
Publicizes casework		
No	46	44
Yes	45	50
Handles local casework		
No	49	47
Some	36	40
All	44	42
Seeks grants		
No	44	43
Yes	49	48
Publicizes grants		
No	44	38
Yes	46	45

stituents. Congressmen who do more casework, visit the district frequently, seek grants, and publicize grants have somewhat better reputations by either measure. Congressmen who publicize casework receive a slightly higher number of positive comments from constituents. A plausible explanation for these findings is that Washington staff have multiple uses, whereas the other activities and resource allocations refer more specifically to district service. Because congressional reputations have both a policy and a nonpolicy component, and because Washington staff have both policy and non-

Table 6.14. Relationship of member evaluations to member activities in Great Britain

Activities	Job rating positive[a]	Like something about member
Visits		
< Weekly	29%	18%
≥ Weekly	37	26
Surgeries		
≤ Monthly	26	20
> Monthly	36	23
≥ Weekly	46	38
Cases		
< 25/week	30	22
25–50	34	20
> 50	46	39
MP time on constituency affairs		
≤ 33%	31	20
34–50%	39	27
> 50%	34	23
Solicits casework		
No	33	22
Only at elections	22	20
Yes	35	24
Publicizes casework		
No	28	16
Yes	35	25
Handles local casework		
No	29	16
Reluctantly	36	25
Yes	34	24

a. Because fewer British constituents rate their MP's performance as "very good," this column combines "good" and "very good" responses.

policy functions, the two correspond more closely than do general reputation and resource and activity measures that refer specifically to constituency service.

The British data are consistent with this conjecture. Because the policy component of the MP's reputation is perforce quite small, given the constraints of party discipline, constituency service makes up a relatively larger part of the MP's image. Therefore, the relationships between constituency service and general reputation are stronger in Britain than in the United States.

When the joint relationship between member activities and general reputation is examined, the American patterns appear weak and inconsistent (Tables 6.15–6.16). Large Washington staffs and subcommittee chairmanships are the only resources positively associated with favorable evaluations of congressmen, however measured. Seeking grants leads to positive comments but not to higher job ratings. Frequent visits to the district leads to higher job ratings but not to positive comments. Most striking of all, though Democratic incumbents received significantly more positive job ratings, they have a significantly lower probability of receiving a positive com-

Table 6.15. Relationship of member allocations and activities to job ratings

Variable	United States[a]		Great Britain[b]
Weekly visits	.194**	.164*	.173*
Medium caseload	−.075	−.044	.226*
Heavy caseload	.007	.007	.104
Medium staff	.160†	.204*	—
Large staff	.656**	.732**	—
Surgeries			
> Monthly	—	—	.176†
≥ Weekly	—	—	.392*
Publicizes cases	—	—	.060
Seeks grants	.083	.080	—
Publicizes grants	−.021	.037	—
Democratic incumbent	.252**	.294**	—
Liberal incumbent	—	—	.352†
Subcommittee chair	—	.212*	—
Republican leader	—	.166†	—
Democratic leader	—	−.397*	—
Backbencher	—	—	−.142†
Year elected	−.007	−.001	.012
District offices	−.051	−.066	—
Constant	1.905**	1.301*	.006
Chi-square/df	28/10**	38/13**	29/9*

a. $n = 1043$.   *$p < .05$.
b. $n = 549$.   **$p < .01$.
$\qquad\qquad$ †$p < .10$.

Table 6.16. Relationship of member allocations and activities to positive comments about member

Variable	United States[a]		Great Britain[b]
Weekly visits	−.131	−.242	.254**
Medium caseload	.004	.022	−.066
Heavy caseload	.109	.010	.267*
Medium staff	.080	.086	—
Large staff	.269†	.451**	—
Surgeries			
> Monthly	—	—	.069
≥ Weekly	—	—	.604**
Publicizes cases	—	—	.123
Handles local cases	—	—	−.076
Seeks grants	.211**	.158*	—
Publicizes grants	.078	.084	—
Democratic incumbent	−.393**	−.506**	—
Liberal incumbent	—	—	.462*
Subcommittee chair	—	.570**	—
Backbencher	—	—	−.098
Year elected	−.001	—	.003
Before 1964	—	−.406*	—
1965–1973	—	.097	—
1974–1975	—	.188*	—
District offices	−.172*	−.258*	—
Constant	.267	.283	−.985
Chi-square/df	41/10**	70/13**	63/10**

a. $n = 1355$.   *$p < .05$.
b. $n = 857$.   **$p < .01$.
   †$p < .10$.

ment. This finding is not materially affected by the addition of education or the constituent's level of interest in politics. Job ratings also have no relationship with seniority, but the Watergate class has a significantly higher probability than freshmen of receiving a positive comment, whereas the pre-1964 group of congressmen has a significantly lower probability than freshmen.

In contrast to the cloudy American picture, the size of the MP's caseload, frequency of surgeries, and frequency of visits all contribute positively to both job ratings of MPs and the likelihood of positive comments about them. Liberals enjoy more favorable reputations, other things being equal. Tenure in office matters not at all.

Constituent variables such as reported contacts with the representative, party identification, and assessments of the congressman's voting record (U.S.) have a major impact on how constituents evaluate congressmen, but incumbents' activities and resources continue to affect their reputations over and above these constituent variables (Table 6.17). Staff sizes and subcommittee leadership in the United States and frequency of surgeries and Liberal incumbency in Britain are the prime examples of this pattern. Moreover, the oldest generation of congressmen are less positively evaluated by their constituents, other things being equal. This relative disadvantage may, of course, be offset by these congressmen's greater propensity to hold subcommittee chairs.

Of the constituent variables, personal contact with representatives or their agents is related to more favorable reputations in both countries, but the other forms of contact show different relationships in the United States and Britain. Contact through the mail and the media significantly increase constituent ratings of congressmen, but these less personal forms of contact have little bearing on the reputations of MPs. Conversely, hearsay or second-hand contact equals or even exceeds the effect of personal contact in Britain but appears to be the weakest avenue of contact between representatives and their constituents in the United States.

The most important single influence on general assessments of a congressman is the constituent's evaluation of the congressman's voting record. Only 40 percent of the constituents offer such a judgment, and only about 5 percent express disagreement with the congressman's voting, but among those with an opinion, that opinion bears a massive relationship to evaluations of the congressman.[15]

Finally, on the matter of party affiliation, constituents evaluate members of their own party more favorably, but the effect of party does not dominate the evaluations constituents form. Other constituent characteristics and some member activities show equally strong effects. Identifiers with the British minor parties (nationalists) are least likely to say something positive about their member, as are American independents. But the independents rate congressmen more highly than do members of the opposition party.

In sum, the correlates of general reputations are similar in both

Table 6.17. Relationship of member allocations and activities to generalized evaluations

Variable	United States		Great Britain	
	Job rating[a]	Like[b]	Job rating[c]	Like[d]
Weekly visits	.010†	—	.076	.174*
Medium caseload	—	—	.100	−.164
Heavy caseload	—	—	−.065	.152
Medium staff	.134†	.201*	—	—
Large staff	.413**	.322*	—	—
Surgeries				
> Monthly	—	—	.145†	.003
≥ Weekly	—	—	.453**	.588**
Publicizes cases	—	—	.159	.169
Handles local cases	—	—	—	−.061
Seeks grants	—	.136†	—	—
Democratic Congressman	—	−.450**	—	—
Liberal MP	—	—	.540*	.543*
Subcommittee chair	.180*	.341**	—	—
Backbench	—	—	−.140†	−.084
Year elected	—	—	.012	.005
Before 1964	—	−.272*	—	—
Voting record				
Agree	1.517**	1.486**	—	—
Somewhat agree	.456**	.939**	—	—
Pro/con	−.449**	.097	—	—
Disagree	−1.142**	−.169	—	—
Personal contact	.358**	.665**	.304**	.603**
Impersonal contact	.292**	.849**	.066	.133†
Second-hand contact	.109†	.431**	.524**	.652**
Party identification				
Independent/none	.191*	−.365**	.242*	.104
Minor	—	—	−.641*	−.635*
Same as member	.295**	.242**	.548**	.411*
Constant	1.175**	−1.428**	−.225	−1.088†
Chi-square/df	493/13**	717/15**	99/15**	173/16**

a. n = 1269. c. n = 549. *p < .05.
b. n = 1626. d. n = 857. **p < .01.
　　　　　　　　　　　　　†p < .10.

countries. Partisanship plays some role in determining evaluations, and selective attention to information about or from representatives may also underlie some of the relationships. But reality in the form of the representatives' activities and characteristics clearly has something to do with how constituents subjectively assess their representatives. The efforts put forth by the MPs are understandable in light of the accumulating evidence that those efforts shape the evaluations formed by their constituents.

Reputation and Reported Contacts

Contacts with, by, and from MPs and MCs have a strong association with the visibility of the representative, with the representative's reputation for constituency service, and with general evaluations of the representative. But what determines the levels of contact reported by constituents? Conceivably contacts are determined primarily by personal or random factors outside the representative's control. If this were so, contacts would continue to be important, but nothing representatives could do would increase contacts. They would be at the mercy of such things as their constituents' general level of interest in politics, or exogenous local or national circumstances that somehow cause their constituents to monitor information about them.

In fact, the things representatives do affect the likelihood that their constituents report contacts. Indeed, the things representatives do could not enhance their reputations except by constituents learning about their activities through the media, personal contacts, hearsay, and publicity efforts. The reported contacts which relate so strongly to evaluations of the representative are themselves affected by the representative's activities and resource allocation decisions.

The surveys provide data on eight forms of contact: met personally, heard speak, talked to staff, mail, newspaper or magazine, radio, TV, and hearsay. Analysis of constituent reports reveals several general patterns. First, the size of Washington staffs in the United States and the number of surgeries in Britain are the only measures of member activities or resource allocation that significantly increase every form of contact with the member, except talking to staff in the United States (Table 6.18). Number of cases and frequency of visits in Britain are associated with higher levels of contact for half the eight forms. The corresponding relationships in the United States

Table 6.18. Relationship of contact reports to Washington staff size (United States) and frequency of surgeries (Great Britain)

Contact in United States	Washington staff size		
	0–7	8–11	12+
Met	13%	13%	20%
Heard	11	11	25
Staff	8	8	9
Mail	48	52	57
Read	44	53	58
Radio	23	27	32
TV	43	42	51
Hearsay	25	27	43

Contact in Great Britain	Frequency of surgeries		
	≤ monthly	> monthly	≥ weekly
Met	10%	14%	18%
Heard	5	8	7
Staff	3	4	6
Mail	23	31	34
Read	27	33	49
Radio	6	6	12
TV	15	14	27
Hearsay	10	15	18

are weaker. Second, in both countries the more personal forms of contact—meeting, hearing, and talking to staff—are predicted less well by the level of the member's activities than the less personal forms. Third, with the exception of TV viewing, the statistical models predicting nonpersonal forms of contact are similar in both countries. Reports that the citizen has read something about the representative in a newspaper or magazine and reports of second-hand contact, as from a friend, relative, or co-worker, are the forms of contact that are most successfully explained by member activities.

Given these general patterns, it is sufficient to report analyses of four forms of reported contact in each country: met the representative personally, read something about the representative, heard about someone else's contact, and saw the representative on TV (Tables

6.19 and 6.20). As for the effects of representatives' activities on reported contacts, the size of staff and frequency of surgeries are still related to the probability of contact even when all other factors are considered. A large Washington staff for a congressman and frequent surgeries for an MP contribute to significantly higher contact reports among their constituents. In Britain, the MP's personal presence in the constituency also has consistently significant effects on reported contacts, but no such relationships emerge in the United States. Heavy caseloads contribute to higher reports of contact, other than TV, in Great Britain, but in the United States such effects are present only in TV contact. Finally, in the United States those offices which described special efforts to get grants get some response from their constituents. On the whole, representatives' activities and resource allocations show clear associations with constituent reports, and, if anything, those associations are stronger in Britain.

As for representatives' characteristics, seniority has a positive

Table 6.19. Correlates of contact reports in United States

Variable	Met[a]	Read[a]	Hearsay[b]	TV[c]
Medium staff	−.093	.134†	−.131	−.149
Large staff	.228†	.368**	.316*	.241†
Heavy caseload	—	—	—	.143*
Seeks grants	.132†	.009	.296**	.151*
Publicizes grants	—	—	.446**	—
Same party identification as incumbent	.234**	.046	.268**	.011
High school	.040	.393**	.074	.057
Some college	.212*	.548**	.408**	.044
College	.431**	.854**	.546**	.006
Subcommittee chair	.134	.026	.194*	.238**
Year elected	−.008	−.014*	−.039**	−.004
Campaign spending	.001†	.002**	.002**	.003**
Constant	−.938†	.383	1.070*	−.303
Chi-square/df	45/10**	112/10**	122/11**	81/11**

a. $n = 1697$.   *$p < .05$.
b. $n = 1542$.   **$p < .01$.
c. $n = 1539$.   †$p < .10$.

Table 6.20. Correlates of contact reports in Great Britain

Variable	Met[a]	Read[a]	Hearsay[b]	TV[a]
Weekly visits	.333	.177*	.409**	.052
Surgeries				
> Monthly	.035	.028	.129	−.251*
≥ Weekly	.265†	.564**	.251†	.604**
Medium caseload	.022	.233*	.217†	−.295*
Heavy caseload	.033	.395**	.555**	−.120
Same party identification				
as MP	.421**	.351**	.274**	.267**
Education				
9–10 yrs.	−.034	.020	.133	−.181
> 10 yrs.	−.166	.191†	.304*	−.252
Backbench	−.117	−.048	.115	−.178†
Liberal MP	.279	1.056**	.490*	2.474**
Year elected	.005	−.010	−.027*	−.023*
Constant	−1.848*	−.317	−.172	.844
Chi-square/df	31/11**	74/11**	50/11**	116/11**

a. $n = 902$. *$p < .05$.
b. $n = 857$. **$p < .01$.
†$p < .10$.

effect on reported contacts: the more recent the representative's election, the lower the contact level. The effect appears largest for hearsay, especially in the United States. Whereas seniority does not bear any consistent relationship to constituent evaluations of representatives, it frequently bears a significant relationship to constituents' reports of contact. People indeed are more likely to have heard something about a more senior representative than a less senior one. Institutional position is especially important with respect to the representative's TV coverage. In the United States, holding a subcommittee chair assumes greatest importance for TV exposure, and the only significant effect for backbenchers in Britain is the marginally negative relationship for TV exposure. Liberal MPs have the highest level of contacts, especially through the media. As for the effects of campaign spending, which is a highly relevant consideration in the United States, though not in Britain, money is of least importance in relation to meeting incumbents personally and is of most importance for TV exposure, a pattern exactly as common sense and familiarity with American campaign practices would predict.[16]

Among constituents' characteristics, party affiliations are consistently more important in Britain. Sharing the representative's party relates positively to all types of reported contacts, whereas some types of contacts show no relationship to party identification in the United States. Education of the constituents shows fairly similar effects across the two countries. Education typically relates positively to contacts, with the principal exception of TV, which shows no relationship whatsoever. The more highly educated read more and hear more but do not watch more.

Overall, statistical predictions of personal meetings are not so impressive as predictions of less personal forms of contact. The two forms of contact may differ in that the personal forms may reflect the constituent seeking out the representative, whereas the other forms presume that representatives seek out constituents. Still, those MPs who go home most often and hold the most frequent surgeries have the most constituents who report personal meetings. Why congressmen who have the largest Washington staffs should rate higher on personal meetings is not as clear, unless the staff makes it possible for the representative to spend more time in the district.[17]

Just as the activities representatives undertake and the resources they allocate find a positive reflection in constituents' evaluations of their district service, these activities also find a positive reflection in the more general evaluations of representatives by their constituents. How citizens rate the job performance of their representatives and what citizens like and dislike about their representatives depend significantly on the decisions those representatives make and the manner in which they behave. Politicians do not dance before the proverbial blind audience. The audience actually has a rather discerning eye. Whether or not there are any direct effects of representatives' activities on vote totals, there are direct effects of their activities on constituents' reports of contact, evaluations of district service, images of representatives, and overall performance evaluations. And such factors are hardly irrelevant to the vote representatives receive.

7

The Personal Vote

It is now an accepted part of the psephologist's
conventional wisdom that the personalities of the
local candidates and their campaign efforts are
worth only a derisory number of votes.

Congressional elections are local, not national
events: in deciding how to cast their ballots,
voters are primarily influenced not by the
President, the national parties, or the state of the
economy, but by the local candidates.

No candidate is worth 500 votes.

Incumbency is without question the most
important single factor in congressional elections.

The significance of the personal vote in contemporary
congressional elections is unquestioned. The claim that incumbency
is the single most important factor in House elections may well be
true if interpreted in the broadest sense of incumbency as a factor
in raising money and discouraging opposition as well as a criterion
of vote choice. Even if party identification continues to have primacy
in vote choice, the syndrome of factors encapsulated by "incumbency" follows a close second. Numerous studies have described
the effects of the personal characteristics, record, and activities of
House incumbents on voting behavior in recent House elections.[1]
Thus, the American analyses reported below should come as no great
surprise.

As the quotations which head this chapter indicate, however, the
conventional wisdom about modern British elections assigns the
personal vote for MPs to a category somewhere between the trifling

and the insignificant. In a classic study Philip Williams calculated that marginal MPs with eight years or more of service have swings from 2 percent (Conservatives) to 3.5 percent (Labour) better than marginal MPs with less service.[2] With such apparently small proportions of the vote contingent on MPs' personal characteristics and efforts, the personal vote appears to be inconsequential for all but the most electorally insecure MPs.

Yet MPs themselves, who have to stand for re-election, assign greater importance to their personal efforts. MPs queried in 1967 universally believed that their personal reputations and activities made some difference in their majorities. And as Dennis Kavanagh observed, "Candidates work hard enough to lead one to believe that they, at least, think their efforts can be decisive." Similarly, after conducting a survey of candidate selection in the Labour Party, John Bochel and David Denver commented: "Most political scientists would suggest that the 'candidate effect' in British politics is minimal ... This view is not, on the whole, shared by Labour selectors ... Although there are some interesting differences between selectors in different types of seat, the data leave no room for doubt that overall selectors place a good deal more weight upon the candidate than would electoral analysts."[3]

Like all else, conventional wisdom usually changes, albeit gradually, in recognition of current realities. Thus, the famous quotation "no candidate is worth 500 votes" contrasts with the conclusions contained in a more recent Nuffield election study. John Curtice and Michael Steed concluded from their study of vote shifts in the case of 18 marginals:

> It is clear that Labour kept down the swing in its marginal constituencies, particularly in those with less than a 2% two-party majority ... A major reason for the low swing, particularly the very low swing in the most marginal seats, is the effect of a change in incumbent MP since 1974. Because of the greater attention he can command in the media and the constituency services he can render, an incumbent MP is more likely to be able to establish a personal vote, consisting of those who support him as an individual rather than as a party representative. Where an MP does build such a personal vote in his favour, that vote will be lost if he is defeated. If he does lose, by the time of the next election the new incumbent MP may have acquired his own personal vote. The combined effect of these two personal votes would be a lower

swing against the second incumbent at the following election . . . These 18 clear cases amount to strong evidence of the
personal vote that an MP can build up . . . For the period from
1974 to 1979, it would appear that the double effect amounted to
around 1500 votes in an average sized constituency . . . It is, of
course, in marginal seats that MPs have the greatest incentive to
work for such personal votes.[4]

To an American, the difference between 500 and 1500 votes might
seem like a trifling matter, but in the average British constituency
60,000 or so individuals vote, so that relative to the electoral base,
the difference is larger than it first appears. More important, of course,
are suggestions that the revisions of the conventional wisdom reflect
not the oversights of earlier studies but the recognition of recent
trends.

This matter of temporal variation is one too quickly forgotten in
America. The academic consensus today stresses the significance of
incumbency, but only a decade ago the accepted portrait of congressional elections was entirely different. The consensus then described
House elections as low information, party line affairs, buffeted by
national effects produced by particular presidential candidates and
administrations—in short, much more like the British system. This
portrait, which was based on 1950s data, held sway until studies in
the early 1970s.[5] These later studies provided the impetus for another
extensive congressional elections survey in 1978, which in turn gave
rise to the present consensus. So despite widespread agreement on
the outlines of contemporary House elections, that agreement has
crystallized quite recently. In a later section of this chapter we will
do what we can to illuminate the question of temporal change,
though our efforts are unavoidably constrained. The main point of
the chapter, however, is to establish the present magnitudes of the
personal vote in the two countries, and then explore the apparent
bases of this vote.

The Impact of Incumbency

Analyses of individual voting decisions in the 1978 and 1980 U.S.
House elections and the 1979 British General Election appear in
Table 7.1. The estimated models treat the vote for or against the
congressional and parliamentary candidates of the incumbent Democratic and Labour parties as a function of long-term partisan affil-

Table 7.1. Summary vote equations

Variable	United States 1978[a]	1980[b]	Great Britain 1979[c]	
Party identification				
Strong Republican	−.08	−.86**	−1.86**	Strong Conservative
Weak Republican	.05	−.68**	−1.43**	Weak Conservative
Independent Republican	.08	−.44*	−.16	Other
Independent Democrat	.27†	.49*	−.46**	Liberal
Weak Democrat	.25†	.48*	1.33**	Weak Labour
Strong Democrat	.36*	.92**	2.09**	Strong Labour
Executive job rating				
Good	.05	.08	1.11**	Good
Fair/don't know	−.09	−.22	.77**	Fair/don't know
Incumbency status				
Democrat	.67**	.85**	.31*	Labour
Republican	−.85**	−.45*	−.28*	Other
Constant	.00	−.39	−1.51**	
Chi-square/df	258/10**	292/10**	1233/10**	
Correctly predicted	76%	76%	89%	

a. $n = 846$.   *$p < .05$.
b. $n = 707$.   **$p < .01$.
c. $n = 1527$.   †$p < .10$.

iations, reactions to the recent performance of the administration or government, and the incumbency status of the constituency (Democratic, Labour, Republican, Conservative, Liberal, and so forth). Thus, incumbency enters the picture as a black box—whatever effects adhere to the labels will require additional exploration and explanation. The American results provide no great surprises, but the British results are highly suggestive. They show that if party affiliations and ratings of Prime Minister Callaghan are held constant, Labour MPs ran significantly better than Labour candidates contesting open seats and Labour candidates challenging MPs of other parties ran significantly worse than Labour candidates contesting open seats. Although only three Liberal constituencies with 55 constituents and four Nationalist constituencies with 78 constituents appear in the sample, the effects of all the incumbency variables were at least marginally significant in a second analysis:

Labour MP	−.31	$(p < .05)$
Conservative MP	−.23	$(p < .10)$

Nationalist MP $-.39$ $(p < .10)$
Liberal MP $-.96$ $(p < .01)$

Liberal incumbency was a particularly strong factor in deflecting voters from the decisions they would make on the basis of party identification and Callahan ratings alone, but in general, if a candidate was not an incumbent MP in 1979, it was good not to have to run against one.

In the United States, the estimated effects of incumbency are much larger and more precise than in Britain. For Democratic incumbents the effect was nearly the same in 1978 and 1980, but the effect for Republicans was almost twice as large in 1978 as in 1980. This disparity is probably explained by the difference between the 1978 off-year election and the more partisan, ideologically charged 1980 Reagan landslide. With a general pro-Republican tide running in 1980, the difference between Republican incumbents, who on average already win by relatively high margins, and Republican candidates in open seats diminished. In contrast, the difference between Democratic incumbents and open seat candidates increased marginally for the same reason. Year-to-year variation aside, however, the electoral effect associated with incumbency status in the United States is of the same order as that associated with strong party identification, *ceteris paribus*.

In the United States the ratings of Carter's performance showed no effect in either year, whereas in Britain the ratings of Callaghan's performance showed extremely strong and significant effects.[6] The impact of party identification, while significant in both countries, shows a much stronger relationship to the vote in Britain. There is a temporal difference in the effects of party identification in the United States. In 1980 the party identification effects showed a fairly symmetrical pattern about the omitted reference category of Independent. On the Democratic side, weak identifiers and independent leaners differed little, if at all, and showed a voting pattern that was weaker than but opposed to Republicans leaners and weak identifiers; the strong identifiers of the two parties are polar opposites. In contrast, the effects of party identification in 1978 were weak and muddled. The three Republican categories were indistinguishable from the Independents, and the Democratic categories were not nearly so distinct from the Independents and Republicans as in 1980. Again, this temporal difference probably has its roots in the more partisan nature of the 1980 election.

Because the impact of a variable in a probit analysis depends on the values assumed by other included variables, additional perspective on the results is obtained by calculating illustrative probabilities of voting for the Democratic/Labour candidates as a function of the incumbency status of the district. These calculations appear in Table 7.2. To each category of party identification we assign the modal executive rating for that category then use the equations in Table 7.1 to calculate the probability of a Democratic or Labour vote as incumbency varies.[7] For the United States the 1980 equation is used, on the assumption that an American presidential election provides a more appropriate comparison to a British general election than would an off-year election.

The stronger effect of party identification and the weaker effect

Table 7.2. Estimated probabilities of vote for in-party by party identification, executive performance, and district incumbency status

Great Britain[a] Party identification/ executive performance	Non-Labour	Open	Labour
Strong Conservative/Fair	.00	.00	.01
Weak Conservative/Fair	.01	.02	.03
No party/Fair	.15	.23	.33
Liberal/Fair	.07	.12	.19
Weak Labour/Good	.74	.82	.89
Strong Labour/Very good	.92	.95	.98

United States[b] Party identification/ executive performance	Republican	Open	Democratic
Strong Republican/Very poor	.04	.11	.33
Weak Republican/Very poor	.06	.14	.41
Independent Republican/Very poor	.10	.20	.51
Independent/Poor	.20	.35	.68
Independent Democrat/Good	.39	.57	.85
Weak Democrat/Good	.39	.57	.85
Strong Democrat/Good	.56	.73	.93

a. From Equation 3, Table 7.1.
b. From Equation 2, Table 7.1.

of incumbency status in Britain interact to produce a much smaller impact of constituency incumbency status on individual votes. In particular, the impact of Conservative party identification was so strong in 1979 that candidate incumbency status made little or no difference among Conservative identifiers: all of the 81 strong Conservatives in Labour districts voted against the incumbent. This contrasts sharply with the American case, where a one-third minority of strong Republicans reported support of Democratic incumbents. For those not attached to the Conservative Party, however, the effects of incumbency status are more pronounced. Voters offering no party identification, for example, were twice as likely to vote for an incumbent Labour candidate as for a Labour candidate running against an incumbent of another party. The case is similar for Liberals, and even weak Labour identifiers show a nontrivial effect of incumbency status. In the United States, the general effects of incumbency (looking across the rows) are relatively much stronger, being perhaps two thirds or so as great as the effects of party identification (looking down the columns).

There is no good way of producing a single estimate of comparative incumbency effects, but an "ideal type" calculation is useful. Suppose a constituency has a distribution of party identification and executive ratings which exactly mirror the national distribution. Then the estimates suggest that such a constituency in Britain would vote 44 percent for a Labour MP, 39 percent for a Labour candidate opposing a nonincumbent candidate of another party, and 36 percent for a Labour candidate opposing a sitting MP. In the United States the comparable figures for Democratic support would be 66 percent, 41 percent, and 27 percent. Thus, the American incumbency effect in such an ideal comparison is five times that apparent in Britain, but no doubt British party managers, candidate selectors, and candidates themselves would be more than mildly curious about what underlies the 8 percent range in Britain.

While there is no denying its much smaller size in Britain, an incumbency effect indeed showed up in the 1979 election, an effect somewhat larger than is generally recognized in the literature. Did British incumbents do better than nonincumbents because of a personal vote built up by an MP's behavior in office? Consider several of the components of the personal vote identified in American research and how they do or do not apply to Britain. The most obvious explanation of the House incumbency advantage points to the sheer quantity of electorally productive resources provided free to all incumbents—staff, offices, long distance, the frank, and travel. Estimates of the value of these resources range beyond a million dollars per term. Such considerations are irrelevant for minimally supported MPs. Another partial explanation of the House incumbency advantage inheres in the differential campaign funding of incumbents and challengers. In Britain, however, campaigns are much cheaper, constituency spending is severely limited, candidates do not raise money individually, and spending decisions are more centralized. Thus, the financial muscle of MPs is not a plausible hypothesis.[8]

Other less tangible factors partially explain the House incumbency advantage. Strong incumbents deter strong challengers, and incumbent strength is at least to some extent a self-fulfilling prophecy which results when weak challengers are the only ones willing to make the race. Here again, the case is different in Britain. Unlike American candidates, who await the proper time to run, many aspiring MPs look for a suitable location, a winnable if not safe district. A reputation as a good candidate is an important qualification for the nomination in such a district, and a prime means of earning such a reputation is to wage a strong campaign in a hopeless district. In the Parliaments of the 1970s, one-half of all MPs had lost at least once before winning their seats, and one-fourth had lost twice or more. Thus, incumbent MPs are less likely to get an electoral free ride than are incumbent congressmen, given that ambitious challengers in Britain cannot hope to impress future selection committees by merely "going through the motions."[9]

These considerations suggest that the incumbency effect in Britain is very personal. Its existence must reflect the particular characteristics and activities of particular candidates. Such a vote is contingent; it depends on who MPs are, what they do, and how constituents perceive and evaluate their persons and activities. At least that is one plausible hypothesis about what lies inside the black box of British incumbency.

Components of the Personal Vote

In the United States the incumbency advantage is known to arise from a variety of considerations. As Gary C. Jacobson summarized, "*all* of the things members of the House are purported to do in pursuit of re-election pay off." Analyses reveal that incumbent job ratings, the things constituents like and dislike, expectations of access, and other more specific evaluations, alone or in combination, have a significant impact on the vote. Because there is so much overlap (technically, shared variance) in many of the constituent evaluations, simpler equations often perform as well statistically as more complicated ones and yield a clearer picture by reducing multicollinearity. Yet the omission of any variable anywhere found significant opens one to the charge of misspecification. Unfortunately, such statistical dilemmas have no mechanical resolution. Thus, we proceed by presenting a number of specifications which incorporate major considerations discussed in the literature. These specifications attempt to balance statistical power with substantive clarity.[10]

David Mayhew argued that congressmen engage in three general categories of activity. First, they advertise, defined "as any effort to disseminate one's name among constituents in such a fashion as to create a favorable image but in messages having little or no issue content." Second, they claim credit for government decisions, activities, and projects which are intimately connected to the flow of particularized benefits to constituents individually or to the district generally. Third, congressmen take positions, where the critical consideration is the stand taken rather than the outcome actually realized.[11] A comprehensive model of voting for House members should incorporate each of these factors as well as party identification and presidential approval.

Table 7.3 reports four equations for the 1978 and 1980 elections which typify the general pattern of results. Although the second equation for each year is slightly superior in a statistical sense, the substantive picture offered by the first is somewhat richer. Presumably the most basic effect of advertising is to enhance visibility. In turn, congressmen find visibility, measured here by name recall, desirable because it makes a significant contribution to the vote.[12] The effects of incumbent recall are invariably significant and fairly stable (bouncing around in the .47 to .57 range in 1978 and the .35 to .40 range in 1980) across a variety of specifications.

As for claiming credit for particularized benefits, such activities do indeed redound to the congressman's credit. Recollections of something special done for the district generally have at least a marginally significant effect on the vote, and mention of a constituency relevant "like" about the member has a somewhat weaker

Table 7.3. Vote for incumbent congressmen

Variable	1978		1980[c]	
	(1)[a]	(2)[b]	(1)	(2)
Recall incumbent	.52**	.49*	.37*	.38*
Recall challenger	−1.31**	−1.20*	−.75**	−.55**
Challenger contact	−.15†	−.18*	−.56**	−.51**
Party identification				
Independent	.79**	.80**	.59**	.81**
Same as Congressman	1.55**	1.47**	1.17**	1.09**
Voting record				
Satisfactory	.84**	.37	—	—
Somewhat satisfactory	.40*	.23	—	—
Neutral	−.24	−.39	—	—
Not satisfactory	−.30	−.24	—	—
Carter job rating:				
Rep incumbent				
Good	.21	.00	.44*	.32†
Fair/don't know	.52*	.41†	—	—
Poor	.78*	.52†	.51**	.40*
Dem incumbent				
Good	.26	.20	.24†	.15
Fair/don't know	.26	.08	—	—
Constituency				
attentiveness	.26†	.14	.19	.04
District service	.36*	.30†	.21	−.10
Expectation of helpfulness				
Very helpful	1.47**	—	1.56**	—
Somewhat helpful	1.12**	—	.70**	—
Don't know	1.16**	—	.39*	—
Member job rating				
Very good	—	2.00**	—	3.11**
Good	—	1.39*	—	2.37**
Fair	—	.55†	—	.96*
Don't know	—	.30†	—	1.54**
Constant	−1.45*	−1.09*	−.85**	−2.11**
Chi-square/df	315/19**	331/20**	241/13**	319/14**
Correctly predicted	87%	88%	80%	86%

a. $n = 749$.   *$p < .05$.
b. $n = 751$.   **$p < .01$.
c. $n = 656$.   †$p < .10$.

and less stable association with voting decisions. By far the strongest effect among the constituency service variables, however, is the constituent's expectation of helpfulness, which shows a highly significant, stable, and quite large impact on electoral support for the incumbent, though the pattern of the estimates differs across the two elections. In 1978 "not helpful" responses are associated with support levels lower than the other categories of responses, but the latter do not differ among themselves; in contrast, the 1980 pattern is virtually linear.

The third class of congressional activities, position taking, is represented in the 1978 election study by the constituent's evaluation of the member's voting record. About 40 percent of the sample and 55 percent of the voters have opinions on this subject. Although projection and other forms of rationalization may bias the responses to such items, the variables that represent positive evaluations of the voting record generally relate to electoral support in a statistically significant and substantively nontrivial manner. The one surprising outcome in 1978 appears in the significant negative associations between evaluations of Carter's performance as president and electoral support for Republican incumbents. In districts with Republican congressmen, the less favorably voters regard Carter, the more likely they are to support the Republican incumbent. Such effects do not appear in equations like those reported in Table 7.1. This pattern is much weaker in the 1980 election, though a change in question format creates a comparability problem.[13] Generally, the relationship between approval of Carter and support for Democratic incumbents is slightly positive but rarely significant. (The category "Democratic incumbent, Carter rating poor" was suppressed in these equations. The other coefficients measure differences relative to this baseline.)

Finally, what of the challenger? For the most part House incumbents in recent times have had it in their power to determine their own fate. By successfully building up their image and personal vote, they can do much to discourage strong challenges. The results show just how important it is to discourage such challenges: challenger name recall in 1978 and recall and contact in 1980 have an extremely large impact on the vote: their combined impact is in the same general range as party identification and the expectation of being very helpful. Thus, a well-financed, credible challenger who can penetrate constituents' political consciousness is bad news for an incumbent congressman.[14]

The second and fourth equations differ from the first and third only in substituting incumbent job ratings for expectations of helpfulness.[15] Incumbent job ratings bear the largest relationship of any variable examined to incumbent electoral support. Moreover, as the wording of the survey question would suggest, job ratings appear to function as a general, all-inclusive evaluation of the incumbent's personal qualities and activities. To explain, notice that reactions to the member's voting record in 1978 become insignificant in the presence of job ratings, as does mention of constituency attentiveness. The effect of recollecting something special done for the district also diminishes but retains marginal significance. Numerous additional estimations show that the many other considerations previously related to member reputations fade to insignificance when job ratings are included, strongly suggesting that their effects are indirect, occurring through their impact on job ratings. Thus, job ratings constitute the single best measure of an incumbent's personal standing with constituents, but performance ratings incorporate the effects of numerous other variables further removed in the causal chain.

The British situation differs from the American in that the effects of several of the constituency service variables are smaller and less stable than their American counterparts. Party and executive evaluation effects dominate the British vote; much less variance is associated with support for individual incumbents. Hence, the relationships are weaker to begin with, and intercorrelation among variables makes the effects correspondingly less stable. As a result, the choice of specification is more critical for evaluating the precise impact of constituency services. A series of reasonable specifications may approximate the truth (Table 7.4).

Partisan and executive rating effects are invariable and more or less noncontroversial. The estimated partisan effects are massive and incredibly stable; they offer a statistical picture seldom seen by survey analysts. On a lesser scale but still impressive are the estimated effects of Callahan ratings. These too are substantively large and fairly stable.[16] Undoubtedly Democratic congressmen would not have been quite so unconcerned about the political fortune of Jimmy Carter if the Labour effects had appeared in their equations. Perhaps more surprising but equally noncontroversial from a statistical standpoint are the effects of name recall of both incumbent and challenger. These are as stable as one could imagine. Given the

Table 7.4. Vote for incumbent MPs

Variable	Great Britain[a]			
	(1)	(2)	(3)	(4)
Recall incumbent	.45**	.44**	.43**	.43**
Recall challenger	−.35**	−.33**	−.34**	−.34**
Party identification				
None	1.01**	1.00**	1.03**	1.03**
Other	.93**	.99**	1.01**	1.03**
Same as MP	2.43**	2.43**	2.44**	2.45**
Callahan job rating:				
Lab incumbent				
Good	.65*	.61*	.48†	.48†
Fair/don't know	.41†	.40†	.29	.31
Other incumbent				
Good	.66*	.62*	.52*	.50*
Fair/don't know	.98**	.96**	.86**	.86*
Poor	1.12**	1.10**	1.03**	1.03**
Constituency attentiveness	.28*	—	—	.04
District service	.08	—	—	—
Expectation of helpfulness				
Very helpful	—	.36*	—	.10
Somewhat helpful	—	.05	—	−.09
Don't know	—	−.08	—	−.19
Member job rating				
Very good	—	—	1.03**	.90**
Good	—	—	.52**	.46*
Fair	—	—	.54**	.53**
Don't know	—	—	.43*	.46*
Constant	−2.25**	−2.27	−2.60**	−2.51**
Chi-square/df	737/12**	745/13**	755/14**	760/18**
Correctly predicted	86%	86%	86%	86%

a. $n = 1109$. **$p < .01$.
*$p < .05$. †$p < .10$.

dominance of partisanship and executive ratings, candidate visibility in Britain has an electoral effect much smaller than in the United States, but the effect is large enough to evoke some political interest.

The picture becomes less clear with constituency service variables. The first equation includes the constituency attentiveness and recollection of constituency service variables. The latter variable never shows significant effects and is consequently omitted from subsequent analyses. Constituency attentiveness does show a significant relationship to the vote, but one considerably smaller than simple name recall. The second equation substitutes the expectation of helpfulness variables for the two constituency service variables of the first equation. A very helpful expectation has a significant relationship to the vote, larger than that shown by the constituency attentiveness variable, and its impact applies to more voters, 30 percent versus 20 percent. If both variables are included simultaneously, the coefficient of each becomes smaller and attains a lower significance level (.14 and .31 respectively, both significant at the .10 level). Addition of the constituency attentiveness variable to the second equation does not make a significant addition to the overall goodness of fit, whereas addition of the helpfulness variables to the first equation does (as indicated by the standard likelihood ratio test). These results suggest that the constituency attentiveness and helpfulness variables overlap to a considerable extent and that helpfulness is somewhat the stronger indicator of the specific impact of constituency service.

The third equation substitutes MP job approval for the constituency service variables, and the fourth equation combines all the previous ones. The results in Britain are even clearer than in the United States. MP job rating is by far the strongest indicator of the MP's personal effect on the vote; the relationships are large in magnitude and highly significant, and they appear to appropriate the systematic effect of all the constituency service variables. Of course, job ratings would be expected to incorporate a greater proportion of the sum total of the MP's activities because of the general question wording.

Overall, the statistical results suggest that if one is interested specifically in the constituency service component of the personal vote, the expectation of helpfulness is probably the most appropriate measure.[17] But if one is interested in the personal vote per se and can tolerate some ambiguity about just what it represents, MP job ratings are the most suitable measure. To be sure, because job ratings have some partisan basis (Table 6.15), there is a likelihood that they include a partisan rationalization component which does not reflect an MP's personal efforts and activities. This would lead to overestimation of the magnitude of the personal vote using job ratings. Yet constituency service, while probably the largest single component of the personal vote, represents only one sphere of activity; hence it probably underestimates the magnitude of the personal vote. If both measures are employed, they provide a good chance of "bracketing" the true personal vote.

Based on the preceding analyses, what is the vote-getting potential of the individual MP or congressman? As explained earlier, a single numerical estimate is not possible. It is possible, however, to illustrate the probabilities of incumbent support across different configurations of voter attitudes as in Table 7.2. Again, each partisan category is assigned the modal executive rating for that category. For the British sample we assume the voter recalls the incumbent's name but not the challenger's; for the American sample we assume the voter recalls neither. Also in the American sample we assume that the voter has no evaluation of the congressman's voting record, does not remember anything special he or she has done for the district, and offers no constituency relevant "like" about the congressman. Again, these assumptions reflect modal patterns in the samples. The resulting tables report probabilities of voting for the MP and congressman within the major party identification and incumbency status configurations as variations occur in expectations of helpfulness (Table 7.5) and member job ratings (Table 7.6).

Cross-national differences in the personal vote show up clearly in the tables. In Britain the effects of party affiliations are much larger than the effects of incumbency status. Even those who evaluate the MP most positively are very unlikely to vote for him or her if they do not share the same party. In the United States, however, the effects of incumbency status are much larger relative to the effects of party identification. The contrast is particularly evident in the most positive category of evaluations: those who judge the congressman most positively are very likely to vote for him or her, even if they do not share the same party.

Despite the relatively smaller personal vote in Britain, it is more than a trivial matter. Labour identifiers do provide some support for

Table 7.5. Estimated probabilities of incumbent vote by expectation of helpfulness

Incumbent's party	Voter's identification	Not helpful	Somewhat helpful	Very helpful
	Great Britain[a]			
Labour	Labour	.89	.90	.94
	None/other	.33	.35	.47
	Conservative	.08	.08	.14
Conservative	Labour	.11	.12	.20
	None/other	.55	.57	.69
	Conservative	.94	.95	.97
	United States[b]			
Democrat	Democrat	.71	.89	.98
	Independent	.40	.67	.90
	Republican	.20	.44	.76
Republican	Democrat	.34	.61	.87
	Independent	.60	.83	.96
	Republican	.80	.94	.99

a. From Equation 2, Table 7.4.
b. From Equation 3, Table 7.3.

positively regarded Conservative MPs, and Conservative identifiers for positively regarded Labour MPs. Both groups of identifiers evidence some failure to support negatively regarded MPs of their party. And those not identified with the two largest parties show greater susceptibility to the efforts of a particular MP. Party and evaluations of national leaders count for far more, to be sure, but individual MPs can do nothing about party affiliations and next to nothing about evaluations of national leaders; they can do something about their personal reputations.

Partisan Differences

Are there partisan differences in the personal vote? Constituency service, for example, is said to be a tool more enthusiastically taken up by Democrats than Republicans. The mid-60s increase in the incumbency advantage is associated with the large Democratic class of 1964, and the Democratic class of 1974 is noted for its diligent and innovative district service practices. Indeed, in 1978 Democratic incumbents received a 60 percent higher proportion of district attentiveness responses to the open-ended likes/dislikes items than did Republican incumbents.[18] In Britain, Liberals have a penchant for "grass-rooting." Unfortunately, too few Liberal MPs are included in the study to permit any systematic analysis. The interviews, however, reveal numerous suggestions that Labour MPs more easily assume the welfare officer role than Conservatives. And the Williams study did find a larger personal vote for experienced Labour MPs than for Conservatives.

Table 7.7 contains some of the House vote equations from Table 7.3 estimated separately for Democratic and Republican incumbents. The 1978 results (Equation 1 of Table 7.3) give an ambiguous picture. On the one hand, constituency attentiveness and district

Table 7.6. Estimated probabilities of incumbent support by member job ratings

Great Britain[a] Member's party	Voter's identification	Job rating			
		Poor	Fair	Good	Very good
Labour	Labour	.77	.90	.90	.96
	None/other	.19	.37	.37	.57
	Conservative	.03	.09	.09	.20
Conservative	Labour	.05	.13	.13	.27
	None/other	.39	.60	.59	.77
	Conservative	.87	.95	.95	.98

United States[b] Member's party		Strongly disapprove	Disapprove	Approve	Strongly approve
Democrat	Democrat	.19	.54	.93	.99
	Independent	.10	.37	.86	.96
	Republican	.02	.13	.60	.84
Republican	Democrat	.04	.20	.72	.91
	Independent	.08	.52	.93	.99
	Republican	.27	.63	.96	.99

a. From Equation 3, Table 7.4.
b. From Equation 4, Table 7.3.

Table 7.7. Vote for incumbent congressmen, separately by party of incumbent

Variable	1978		1980	
	Dem.[a]	Rep.[b]	Dem.[c]	Rep.[d]
Recall incumbent	.34†	1.04**	.28†	.75*
Recall challenger	−1.34**	−1.39**	−.63*	−.63†
Challenger contact	−.22*	−.03	−.39*	−.75**
Party identification				
Independent	.63*	.87**	.84**	.70*
Same as Congressman	1.46**	1.76**	1.15**	1.04**
Voting record				
Satisfactory	.92*	.23	—	—
Somewhat satisfactory	.12	.73*	—	—
Neutral	−.31	−.37	—	—
Not satisfactory	−.41	−.12	—	—
Carter rating				
Good	.25	−.62†	.10	−.06
Fair/don't know	.19	−.20	—	—
Constituency attentiveness	.39*	.10	.19	−.37
District service	.48*	.33	−.22	.28
Expectation of helpfulness				
Very helpful	1.24**	2.08**	—	—
Somewhat helpful	1.13**	1.22**	—	—
Don't know	1.09**	1.46**	—	—
Congressman job rating				
Very good	—	—	3.26**	3.00**
Good	—	—	2.48**	2.28**
Fair	—	—	1.28*	.23
Don't know	—	—	1.82**	1.08*
Constant	−1.17	−1.27	−2.31**	−1.40*
Chi-square/df	178/16**	152/16**	190/12**	130/12**
Correctly predicted	88%	86%	84%	87%

a. $n = 424$. c. $n = 392$. *$p < .05$.
b. $n = 322$. d. $n = 264$. **$p < .01$.
†$p < .10$.

service are significant on the Democratic side but not the Republican. On the other hand, the expectation of helpfulness shows a considerably stronger effect for Republicans. For Democrats, the only difference is essentially between a constituent believing the incumbent would not be helpful (the omitted category) and any other response. For Republicans, the relationship between the different responses and the vote is much stronger. In 1980 equations the picture is similar but the differences are not so large: the Republican coefficients are much the same, but the Democratic ones show more spread, and that for a "very helpful" expectation goes to 1.55.

The second two columns of Table 7.7 examine the importance of job ratings separately for the parties. Here there is little, if any, important interparty difference. The Democrats show a larger spread between the "poor" response (the base category) and the "fair" and "don't know" responses, but the spread between the poor and the positive responses is very similar for both parties.

Table 7.8 reports equations estimated separately for Labour and Conservative MPs. As in the United States, the picture for Britain is somewhat unclear. The expectation of helpfulness shows a significant association with the vote for Labour MPs but not for Conservatives. Similarly, the constituency attentiveness variable, too, is significant for Labour but not for Conservatives (not shown). These findings suggest that constituency service does make a significant contribution to the vote for Labour MPs, but not for their Tory counterparts. But the other equations raise doubts about that inference. The job ratings measure suggests that there is no apparent difference between the personal support for Labour and Conservative MPs. Possibly, the personal votes for Labour and Tory MPs have different bases, being constituency service in the case of Labour and something else in the Tory case, but what would be that something else? At this time the data permit no firm conclusion as to which party's incumbents, if either, profit more from the personal vote.

The Personal Vote and Member Activities

Chapter 5 developed the argument that member activities affect their electoral fortunes through a multistep process: member activities and resource allocations create opportunities to contact constituents and induce favorable evaluations that lead to electoral support. Thus, member activities create electoral support indirectly.

Table 7.8. Vote for incumbent MPs, separately by party of incumbent

Variable	Labour[a]	Tory[b]	Labour[a]	Tory[b]
Recall incumbent	.62**	.41**	.62**	.40*
Recall challenger	−.31*	−.50**	−.36*	−.47**
Party identification				
None	1.18**	.87**	1.19**	.90**
Other	1.35**	.02	1.31**	.16
Same as MP	2.53**	2.49**	2.51**	2.50**
Callahan rating				
Good	.58*	−.70**	.45†	−.69**
Fair/don't know	.37	−.21	.27	−.21
Expectation of helpfulness				
Very helpful	.60†	.09	—	—
Somewhat	.41	−.03	—	—
Don't know	.31	−.29	—	—
MP job rating				
Very good	—	—	.95**	.93**
Good	—	—	.63*	.37
Fair	—	—	.65*	.45†
Don't know	—	—	.51†	.35
Constant	−2.79**	−.76**	−2.85**	−1.28**
Chi-square/df	271/10**	449/10**	276/11**	452/11**
Correctly predicted	85%	87%	84%	88%

a. $n = 412$. *$p < .05$.
b. $n = 607$. **$p < .01$.
          †$p < .10$.

Some researchers have searched without success for direct effects. Our efforts too were relatively unproductive, but there are some things of a positive nature to report.

Difficulties already encountered multiply at this point. First, the analysis is one step further down the causal chain, and competing factors such as partisanship and executive ratings exert more influence on votes than on evaluations. Second, given the low turnout in American elections, roughly half of the previous cases are lost. Third, because incumbents running without opposition must be dropped from the analysis, still more of the American cases are lost and, more importantly, more of the distinct configurations of district level variables are lost—the number of districts appearing in the American equations drops from about 70 to less than 60. Given the higher British turnout and the quaint British custom of providing each MP with an opponent, less of the British data is lost, especially on the elite side.

Despite these problems, some positive findings appear for both countries, though they are considerably stronger for Britain. Caseloads and grants had something to do with the vote for congressmen in 1978.[19] Most striking, however, is the large, robust, and highly significant effect of large Washington staffs (Table 7.9). This is the largest effect found of an incumbent asset or activity. When individual level variables are added to the analysis, the coefficient on large staff reaches 1.5 and remains significant at the .01 level.

A different sort of analysis applies to Britain. Discussions of British elections rely heavily on the concept of "swing," the average of one party's gain plus the other party's loss. Though the concept has little meaning when more than two parties compete, British politicians and commentators on British politics still thought and talked

Table 7.9. Vote for Congressman as function of member activities and allocations

Activity/allocation	1978[a]
Weekly visits	−.11
Caseload	
Medium	.28†
Heavy	.21
Staff	
Medium	.12
Large	1.06**
Seeks grants	−.20
Publicizes grants	.31†
Year elected	−.03*
Constant	2.36**
Chi-square/df	28/8**
Correctly predicted	77%

a. $n = 537$.   **$p < .01$.
*$p < .05$.   †$p < .10$.

in terms of swing and deviations therefrom in 1979. A noteworthy feature of the 1979 election was that the traditional uniform swing showed much less uniformity than usual: North Britain swung to the Conservatives by 4.2 percent, while South Britain swung by 7.7 percent. Thus, most analysts computed regional swing figures rather than a single national figure. We follow this practice in the analysis which follows.[20]

Many of the MPs and agents expressed the belief that diligent constituency work could amplify swings to their party and, more crucially, dampen swings against their party. It is a straightforward matter to test the accuracy of this belief. Information from the MP's or agent's interview was used to form a simple index of constituency involvement. In order to retain as many parliamentary districts as possible, we selected activities with little missing data. The MP received one point for each of four activities: encourages cases, publicizes successful cases, handles local cases, and holds surgery at least twice monthly. The 101 districts for which data are available range from zero to four on this index (the exact distribution is 16, 21, 28, 31, 5). After dropping retirees, seats won in by-elections after 1974, and seats held by Liberals and Nationalists, 85 constituencies remained. Do accounts of constituency work in these 85 constituencies bear any relation to objectively measured swings in the vote? They most certainly do.

The swing in the sample districts is significantly related to the relevant regional swing, to some demographic variables, and to their score on the index of constituency involvement (Table 7.10).[21] Variations in constituency work (0 to 4) apparently account for swings of something between 1.5 and 2 percent for Conservatives and between 3 and 3.5 percent for Labour. Thus, depending on party, variations in constituency attentiveness have an electoral effect potentially as large as one-quarter to one-half of the observed regional swings. The figure for Labour is almost twice that for Conservatives, being larger in magnitude but consistent in ratio with the earlier estimates of Williams. These figures are realistic bounds on the personal vote, since it is well within the capability of the average MP to determine where he or she scores on the index of constituency work. Also, the estimates are in the general ballpark, though again they are somewhat larger than those provided by Curtice and Steed.[22]

Table 7.10. Effect of constituency work on swing

Variable	Conservative seats[a]		Labour seats[b]	
	(1)	(2)[c]	(3)	(4)[c]
Regional swing[d]	.59**	.56**	.83**	.79**
Constituency work	.42*	.44*	−.74†	−.88*
Immigrant population	−4.24**	−4.03**	−1.17	—
Metropolitan cities	.19	—	2.23*	1.92*
Nonmetropolitan cities	−.89	—	.17	—
Constant	1.15	1.22	2.45	3.06
r-square	.41	.39	.55	.52

a. $n = 55$.

b. $n = 33$.

c. Equations (2) and (4) omit nonsignificant demographic variables included in equations (1) and (3).

d. Swing is defined as the average of gain in Conservative share of vote and loss in Labour share. Figures are drawn from the *Times Guide to the House of Commons*.

*$p < .05$.

**$p < .01$.

†$p < .10$.

Temporal Change in Magnitude of the Personal Vote

There is no doubt that the personal vote of American congressmen has increased over the course of the past two decades. Various factors have contributed to this development, including constituency service, but the lack of suitable time series data prevents any definitive assessment of the relative importance of the hypothesized influences. In Britain, there are suggestions that the personal vote is growing larger, but for the most part those suggestions are based on impression and anecdote rather than systematic analysis. While such analyses do show that the party vote is declining and that the geographic heterogeneity of the vote is increasing, they do not locate the source of these trends in variations in the personal vote for MPs.[23]

In Chapter 4 we exploited the existence of earlier surveys in Britain and the United States to provide at least one benchmark for identifying temporal change. Comparison of the 1958 and 1978 American election studies indicates that the proportion of citizens requesting information or help from their congressman tripled over the two decades. Moreover, the constituency attentiveness component of the congressman's image increased significantly. Similarly, comparison of the 1966 Butler-Stokes survey with the 1979 Gallup survey suggests that the proportion of British citizens requesting personal service from their MP increased somewhat between the mid-1960s and late 1970s, while the constituency attentiveness component of the MP's image grew dramatically. This evidence suggests that constituency service is more salient to constituents now than in earlier decades. The increasing salience of constituency service also turns out to exert an increasingly strong effect on constituent voting behavior.

Equivalence of variables once again is essential to this conclusion. Some of the individual survey questions, such as name recall and party identification, present little problem of equivalence, but others require more work. Matching coding categories of the open-ended items creates comparable measures of candidate evaluation, but because the questions themselves differ across surveys, a residue of ambiguity inevitably remains.[24]

In the United States, challenger variables are simple. So few people have anything at all to say about challengers that all comments must be reduced to the two categories, positive evaluation and negative evaluation. These become dummy variables that take on a value of one if the voter says anything positive and negative, respectively. The same consideration governed creation of a single incumbent negative evaluation variable. Positive evaluations of incumbents are sufficiently common, however, to form three categories. Constituency attentiveness takes on a value of one if the voter mentions anything about the incumbent in that category. Policy agreement is coded one for any positive response dealing with policy, ideology, or general philosophy. And candidate attributes have a value which is the total number (integers, 1–4) of positive comments about the incumbent's record and experience, leadership qualities, or personal qualities. Of course, responses in this large category may have their basis in policy, constituency service, partisan rationalization, or other considerations.

In both 1958 and 1978 Americans who make any negative comment about the incumbent or positive comment about the challenger demonstrate a significantly lessened probability of incumbent support (Table 7.11). A negative evaluation of the challenger is the largest single influence on the probability of support for the con-

Table 7.11. Voting behavior in races with incumbent congressmen

Variable	1958[a]	1978[b]
Recall incumbent	1.00**	.72**
Recall challenger	−.77**	−1.08**
Party identification		
Same as incumbent	1.18**	.92**
Opposite incumbent	−1.17**	−.73**
Democratic incumbent	.60**	−.09
Incumbent		
Candidate qualities	.61**	.52**
Constituency attentiveness	.48	.77**
Policy agreement	−.33	.75**
Negative evaluation	−1.69**	−1.36**
Challenger		
Positive evaluation	−1.29**	−1.25**
Negative evaluation	1.89**	.66**
Constant	−.17	.77**
Chi-square/df	571/11**	378/11**
Correctly predicted	90%	86%

a. $n = 721$.   b. $n = 755$. $**p < .01$.

gressman in 1958, but the effect of this evaluation falls by two-thirds in 1978. This may be a feature of the peculiar 1978 group of challengers, so it is hard to speculate about the decline. Name recall is significant in both years, though the relative magnitudes of its effect on the incumbent and challenger shifts around. The impact of party identification shows the expected decline between 1958 and 1978 but remains a major correlate of the vote. Moreover, 90 percent of the voters express a party identification, whereas far fewer express negative evaluations of the incumbent or any evaluation of the challenger.[25] Another party effect, the Democratic tide running in 1958, shows up in the extra bonus accruing to Democratic incumbents in that year; in 1978 no such national force is apparent.

The most interesting effects are those attached to the several types of positive evaluation of incumbents. The broad category of incumbent personal qualities has about the same association with the vote in 1958 and 1978, but real differences appear in the effects of the other two positive evaluations. The effect of constituency attentiveness increases in magnitude between 1958 and 1978 and goes from statistically insignificant to highly significant. Of course, the larger number of voters underlying the 1978 category may account for the enhanced statistical precision of the estimate, but on balance it appears that between 1958 and 1978 the impact of constituency attentiveness on the vote increased at the same time as constituency attentiveness became more salient to the electorate. Equally interesting is the effect of policy agreement. The effect is statistically insignificant and negative in 1958 but positive and highly significant in 1978. Again, an increase in the number of constituents in the category may enhance the 1978 statistical estimate, but some real change appears likely. For the still small proportion of the sample which mentions a policy or ideological matter, perceptions of how the congressman relates to it are quite as important as party identification, *ceteris paribus*.

In Britain, we carried out an analysis parallel to that reported for the United States. To construct the candidate evaluation measures for Britain, we relied on the open-ended probes following the MP job rating question in 1966 and the likes and dislikes questions in 1979. Only one response was coded in 1966, so in order to maintain as much comparability as possible, only the first response coded in 1979 was utilized (Table 7.12).

Party identification remains by far the most important correlate of support for MPs, though its impact has slipped a bit. The strong pro-Labour tide of 1966 was replaced by a weaker anti-Labour tide in 1979. Candidate visibility has roughly the same impact across the two elections. The candidate evaluation measures, however, show indications of change that are even more striking than in the United States. Whereas no measure of MP evaluation has a significant effect in 1966—and one, constituency attentiveness, has a negative effect—two of the four measures have significant effects in 1979. The MP's personal qualities show a highly significant association with the 1979 vote and an effect almost five times larger than in 1966. As in the United States, this is a large category, and responses may reflect the MP's activities in various realms. Of special interest is the effect of constituency attentiveness, which moves from a negative effect in 1966 to a positive and statistically significant one in 1978. Finally, while MP policy agreement remains in-

Table 7.12. Voting behavior in races with incumbent MP, 1966 v. 1979

Variable	1966[a]	1979[b]
Recall incumbent	.54*	.44**
Recall challenger	−.32*	−.36**
Party identification		
Same as incumbent	1.81**	1.46**
Opposite incumbent	−1.05**	−.99**
Labour incumbent	.54**	−.18*
Incumbent candidate qualities	.11	.51**
Incumbent constituency attentiveness	−.21	.23†
Incumbent policy agreement	.10	.41
Incumbent negative evaluation	.06	−.00
Constant	−.82**	−.49**
Correctly predicted	92%	86%

a. $n = 781$.   *$p < .05$.
b. $n = 1109$.   **$p < .01$.
                   †$p < .10$.

significant, its effect attains a reasonable magnitude. If the category contained more people, it would probably reach statistical significance.

The upshot is that in both the United States and Britain temporal change appears to have occurred. In both countries contemporary voters attach greater importance to the qualities of the individual candidates, the constituency services they provide, and the policies they espouse than did the voters of a few decades ago. To be sure, these results are not conclusive. With only two time points, unusual elections cannot be differentiated from trends. Moreover, questions of the comparability of survey questions make one hesitant to express as much confidence in the results as the statistical tests indicate. At the same time some systematic evidence presumably is preferable to no systematic evidence, and this evidence comports with the less systematic observations made in the literature and in our interviews. On balance, the case for temporal change is more positive than not. Contemporary congressmen and MPs have greater ability to control their fates than did their predecessors of a few years ago, though MPs still remain far behind congressmen in this matter.

This chapter has shown the existence of, estimated the magnitude of, and explored the nature of the personal vote for representatives in Great Britain and the United States. The electoral advantage which accrues to a hard-working congressman is far greater than that accruing to a similarly hard-working MP. But the efforts of the MP do have a discernible effect, an effect which may be growing in importance. The beliefs expressed by MPs about the electoral consequences of their activities (Chapter 3) appear to reflect reasonably accurate perceptions of reality.

In both countries constituency service is a major component of the personal vote and probably an increasingly important component of constituent support for members. In the United States, a congressman's policy views as embodied in his or her voting record also appear to be an increasingly important component of the personal vote. In Britain, MP policy stands appear to have an increased importance, but the results are too weak to draw any firm conclusion.

To show that constituency service contributes to a personal vote obviously does not prove that vote seeking is the basic motivation for constituency service. Possibly members do it simply because it is part of the job, as British observers traditionally conclude. But members themselves are aware of the electoral consequences of their actions, and those facing the greatest degree of electoral insecurity are the most diligent in serving their constituencies, other things being equal. Thus, MPs as well as congressmen engage in constituency service at least in part as a means of enhancing their prospects of re-election, and at least in part their efforts pay off.

Part III

THE LARGER
IMPLICATIONS

8

Particular Interests and General Benefits

The existence of a personal vote correlates with larger features of a political system. Representatives elected with a substantial personal vote are better situated to survive the ebbs and flows of electoral tides set in motion by reactions to national conditions and national party leaders. They are also better situated to resist the threats and blandishments of party leaders than those who owe election solely to the party labels attached to their names. Security and independence breed demands for personal influence which further reinforces security and independence. These propositions do not compose any simple, one-directional causal chain. Some representatives do constituency service in hopes of earning a nonprogrammatic personal vote which will offset the electoral costs of personal policy independence; others service their districts and demonstrate independence of party as complementary strategies calculated to help them survive adverse national tides. Constituency service, policy independence, and electoral outcomes are intertwined in a complex of mutual causation, which may differ somewhat from country to country.

Regardless of the specific causal links, the existence of a personal vote based on constituency service or policy independence exacerbates the tensions inherent in any polity between the whole and its parts. If representatives operate as free agents, coordinated action by the government becomes more difficult, and responsibility for government policy becomes more diffused. Whereas constituents gain from the increased services rendered by their representative and the faithful articulation of their views, they lose from their lessened ability to assign political responsibility and from the simple fact that what is good for individual legislative districts is not necessarily good for the nation as a whole.[1]

This chapter examines two specific aspects of the individual versus collective problem. First we consider an example of the disjunction between individual and collective responsibility for government policies and their effects. Second, we consider the suggestion that recent deteriorations in parliamentary party cohesion relate to MPs' efforts in their constituencies.

Legislators, Legislatures, and Executives

In 1975 Richard Fenno asked: "If our Congressmen are so good, how can our Congress be so bad? If it is the individuals who make up the institution, why should there be a disparity in our judgments?" While traveling with representatives in their districts, he had observed that individual congressmen regularly receive praise and honor, while the collective Congress just as regularly receives criticism and opprobrium. In fact, representatives "run for Congress by running against Congress."[2] Each representative champions his or her district's interests against those of other congressmen who are "the tools of big business," "the minions of labor bosses," "the big spenders," "the mean-spirited reactionaries," and other suitable menaces. Such a strategy is understandable enough for Republicans, who have been in the minority for two decades, but scarcely for Democrats.

The 1984 elections provided more than one example of the phenomenon. Many Democrats searched for ways to protect themselves from the impending Reagan landslide. A common pattern was for Democratic incumbents to paint themselves as independent-minded legislators who used their committee assignments and staff resources to promote the district's best interests. The Democratic chairman of the House Budget Committee, Jim Jones of Oklahoma, went so far as to send a mailer to his constituents detailing the points of disagreement between himself and Tip O'Neill, Democratic Speaker of the House.[3]

Particular examples find a more universal reflection in national surveys that assess the relative performance or trustworthiness of Congress and its members. In recent years such surveys typically show that only a quarter to a third of the population approves or trusts the Congress, while one-half to two-thirds of these same citizens approve or trust their individual representative. For example, citizens' job ratings of congressmen in 1978 contrast sharply with the same citizens' ratings of Congress (Table 8.1). Whereas incumbent congressmen enjoy an 11:1 ratio of positive to negative judgments, the collective Congress is on the short end of a 16:22 ratio. The most extreme examples of this behavior occur in the 225 cases where citizens simultaneously rate the incumbent as good or very good and the Congress as poor or very poor. These citizens are not nearly balanced out by the 11 citizens who offer the opposite rating pattern.

Comparable data for Great Britain provides a contrast to the United States, though the qualitative pattern is similar. Ratings of individ-

Table 8.1. Member ratings by institution ratings

Member	Very good	Good	Fair	Poor	Very poor	Don't know	
			Congress				
Very good	1%	4%	6%	2%	1%	2%	15%
Good	0ª	5	15	6	1	4	31
Fair	0ª	3	11	4	1	4	22
Poor	0	0ª	1	1	1	0ª	3
Very poor	0	0ª	0ª	0ª	0ª	0ª	1
Don't know	0ª	3	10	4	1	10	28
	1	15	42	17	5	20	
			Parliament				
Excellent	1	3	5	1	1	1	12
Good	1	5	9	3	1	3	23
Fair	1	3	12	3	1	2	22
Poor	1	1	3	1	1	0ª	7
Very poor	0ª	0ª	1	0ª	1	1	3
Don't know	2	7	14	5	2	6	34
	6	19	43	14	7	12	

a. Less than 0.5 percent of the samples fall into this cell.

ual MPs show a 3:1 ratio of favorable to unfavorable, which though impressive in an absolute sense, is not impressive relative to congressmen. Parliament as a whole, moreover, fares better than the Congress with a favorable to unfavorable ratio of 25:21. As compared to Americans, British electors do not adore their MP or scorn their Parliament. Nevertheless, a weak version of Fenno's puzzle is evident in Britain, where the MP ratio is nearly three times more favorable than the Parliament ratio, as compared to 15 times more favorable for the corresponding ratios in the United States.

There are a number of reasons for citizens to evaluate their legislators and their legislature so differently. In some cases differentiating the member from the institution is only natural. A Republican voter, for example, would have no reason to hold a Republican representative responsible for the perceived outrages of a heavily Democratic Congress. There are at least three reasons why a systematic discrepancy between member and institutional evaluations is normal in single-member, plurality systems. The first arises from members' ability to take policy positions different from the overall position of the institution. The second arises from the simple fact that all members do not share the partisan label of the majority. The third arises from constituents' tendency to apply different standards of evaluation to the representative and the institution.

Policy independence leads directly to higher support for individual members than for the collective institution. Assume that constituents evaluate both the legislature and their legislator on a common set of policy dimensions and that the geographically defined single-member districts are not perfect microcosms of the nation. A legislator with any personal freedom whatsoever can then take positions that will be evaluated at least as positively by constituents as will be the output of the legislature as a whole. Such an argument underlies Randall Calvert and Mark Isaac's model of the incumbent party's vote loss in midterm elections.[4] So long as individual candidates have some freedom to tailor their positions to their particular districts, they will naturally be perceived more favorably than an institution, such as Congress, or an officeholder, such as the chief executive, that in effect is constrained to adopt a single national position.

Given the important effects of voting record on the job rating of congressmen (Table 6.17), discrepant policy evaluations probably explain some part of Fenno's puzzle in the United States. The difficulties of governing in the United States include problems of cohesion in the political parties, which are attributed in large part to the differing constituencies to which party members consider themselves accountable. *A priori*, it seems likely that the discrepancy between views of Congress and its members stems in part from the ability of individual congressmen to achieve a closer policy "fit" with their district than can the collective Congress.

In Britain, the policy explanation conflicts with the prevailing image of the MP as mere cannon fodder for centralized, highly disciplined parties. Yet such an image is overdrawn, and it ignores noteworthy contrasting facts. For one thing, there have been increasing defections from the party whip in recent years. For another thing, there has been an increase in the number of "free," or unwhipped, votes. These provide an opportunity for an MP to vote his or her constituency, as in the United States. Finally, despite the MPs' strong ties to party, they do personalize their positions by placing differential emphasis on some party stands relative to others in speeches, literature, and personal communications with constituents.[5] Even though the policy explanation still seems implausible in the case of Britain, MPs may have some slight and even increasing ability to separate themselves from party and achieve a better fit with their constituencies.

A pure party evaluation model yields the discrepancy in approval of legislators and legislature as a natural feature. Consider the illustrative table:

| | Legislature evaluation | |
Member evaluation	Approve	Disapprove
Approve	a	b
Disapprove	c	d

The puzzle of discrepant judgment occurs when $(a + b) > (a + c)$, or more simply, when $b > c$.

Assume that all voters and all legislators belong to one or the other of the parties, that party cohesion is perfect, and that voters form evaluations on purely partisan grounds. Then the electorate would divide into four classes:

	Voter	Representative
a	Majority	Majority
c	Majority	Minority
d	Minority	Majority
b	Minority	Minority

In group *a*, majority party identifiers represented by majority party legislators approve both their legislator and the legislature. The opposite case is group *d*, the minority party identifiers in districts that elect majority party legislators. These voters are unhappy with both their representative and the institution. Principal interest centers on group *b*, minority party identifiers in districts that elect minority party legislators (who like their legislator but not the legislature), versus group *c*, majority party identifiers in districts that elect minority party legislators (who like the legislature but not their legislator). If districts are of approximately equal size and district majorities are similarly equal, then *b* will be greater than *c*. That is, those districts that do elect minority party legislators perforce contain more minority than majority identifiers. Assume, for example, that two-thirds of the districts return a majority party member and that every member receives 65 percent of the vote in his or her district, as was roughly the situation in the United States in 1978. Then:

$$a = .65 \times .67 = .44$$
$$b = .65 \times .33 = .21$$
$$c = .35 \times .33 = .12$$
$$d = .35 \times .67 = .23$$

As a result, member approval equals 65 percent, while institutional approval equals 56 percent.

Thus, the paradox is a logical consequence of a situation in which legislators and the legislature are not differentiated at all: it is a pure artifact of partisanship. In the United States, ratings of congressmen are so little related to partisanship that the party explanation lacks plausibility. In Britain, ratings of MPs are somewhat more strongly related to partisanship, so the party explanation may be of greater applicability. Still, even in Britain MP ratings are much more than reflections of party identification, prompting doubts that party is the entire story.

A third explanation of the disparity between individual and collective judgments emphasizes the differing standards by which the individuals and the collectivity are judged. The institution is held up against programmatic standards more so than its members, who instead are judged according to their personal characteristics, accessibility, and solicitude for the concerns of constituents. Using

Harris surveys conducted for the Obey Commission, Glenn R. Parker and Roger Davidson showed the following:

> 1. Well over half the citizens evaluate Congress either on the basis of policy (overwhelmingly *domestic* policy) or on the basis of the congressional manner of doing business, its lack of coordination, conflict, and slowness. These evaluations have a pronounced negative cast.
>
> 2. More than one-third of the citizens evaluate individual congressmen on the basis of their constituency service. The next most common standard is their personal attributes. Such evaluations are overwhelmingly positive.
>
> 3. Only a tiny minority evaluates congressmen in terms of policy.[6]

Thus, the third explanation of the disparity in judgments involves a disparity in popular expectations. If representatives are applauded for their admirable personal qualities and their constituency activities, while the legislature is condemned for its inability to deal with major national problems in an efficient, mature manner, then the members have every incentive to emphasize personal qualities and constituency service and to avoid responsibility for national problems. The puzzle becomes potentially self-perpetuating.

The 1978 NES/CPS study shows that more than three-quarters of the positive comments that constituents make about congressmen pertain to constituency attentiveness and personal attributes, whereas only one-sixth make reference to policy, ideology, or party considerations (Table 1.9). Similarly, in Britain more than three-quarters of all positive comments refer to the MP's personal qualities and constituency attentiveness (Table 1.5).

Evaluations of the Congress and the Parliament present a notable contrast. In each survey the institutional performance rating question was followed by one that sought to elicit the citizen's reason for the rating. The findings for the United States are fully in accord with those in the Parker and Davidson study. The three largest categories contain negative references to issues, to the performance of Congress relative to important problems, and to the nature of the congressional process and relations with the executive branch. In Britain the views are less negative but otherwise similar to those in the United States. Rather general and vague views about the good that Parliament has done compose the largest category, but after that are unions and strikes, inflation, other issues, and the problems of the larger Labour government. The disparity between individual and collective standards is present in Britain as well as in the United States.

That national legislatures are judged on their performance should surprise no one. What is more interesting is how little the individual members, in either country, appear to be judged on their contributions to the resolution of national problems. Perhaps that too should come as no surprise in Britain where incumbent behavior is sufficiently constrained that it would not be reasonable to hold MPs personally accountable for merely doing what their position requires them to do.[7] In the United States, however, the near absence of national standards underlying judgments of legislator performance is genuinely surprising and more than a little disturbing. To interject a caveat, however, national performance and policy considerations are not always so irrelevant to incumbent job ratings when data other than likes and dislikes comments are examined. For example, judgments about the national government's inflation performance have significant effects on the job rating of Democratic congressmen.[8] Similarly, judgments about government performance on the national problem that citizens identify as most important show a statistically significant effect. Such effects are not terribly robust, being quite sensitive to which other variables are included in the analysis, but some effect of national performance judgments usually appears. Surprisingly, however, in 1980 when national conditions presumably were more salient and when the Republicans ran a more party-oriented campaign, judgments about national conditions were not related to ratings of Democratic congressmen. Whether this reflects a counterintuitive temporal difference between 1978 and 1980 or stems from the change in question format cannot be determined.

Differences between popular evaluations of legislators and legislatures are mirrored by differences between evaluations of legislators and executives. As with ratings of the national legislature, ratings of executives, both U.S. presidents and British prime ministers, are significantly related to evaluations of government performance and the partisanship of the citizen. As a result, the relationship between ratings of the executive and ratings of incumbent legislators are not terribly strong, especially in the United States.

Another interesting feature of the executive ratings is that they are more positive than the institutional ratings in both countries.

That is, President Carter fared better among the citizenry than did the Congress, despite his troubles and the decade of congressional resurgence. To be sure, his perceived inability to lead Congress was held against him by many people, but perceived congressional unwillingness to work with Carter was held against the Congress by even more people. In Britain, Prime Minister Callaghan not only was more favorably rated than the Parliament but also was fully as favorably rated as the individual members, taking account of the six times larger category of no opinion about MPs. The implication seems clear: the legislative institutions share the blame with the executive for national problems and government performance, but they lack the human quality which may lead at least some voters to temper their performance ratings with sympathy or other human emotions.[9] The representatives, in contrast, have it both ways, especially in the United States. They take advantage of the human quality and escape much of the blame for national problems as well.

In sum, both American and British citizens hold their representatives in high regard. This constituent approval has relatively little partisan basis in the United States and no more than a moderately partisan basis in Britain. Moreover, national problems and the performance of the larger government in dealing with them have relatively little impact on incumbent ratings, though in the United States, at least, approval of a representative's voting record bears a strong relationship to judgments about his or her overall performance. In great part, approval of congressmen and MPs stems from their personal efforts to enhance their visibility and provide services to their constituents. This basis of constituents' evaluations contrasts sharply with the basis for judgments of the legislative institution and the executive. In this realm reactions to national problems, government performance, and, in Britain, partisanship underlie popular judgments.

For the United States, the significance of this disparity in standards of evaluation seems clear. In discussing the widespread tendency of congressmen to run for Congress by running against Congress, Fenno remarked, "In the short run, everybody plays and nearly everybody wins. Yet the institution bleeds from nearly 435 separate cuts." To Fenno's observation we would add that not only have congressmen managed to separate themselves from Congress, but they have largely managed to separate themselves from the successes and failures of the president as well. The 1984 election is a case in point.

As a result, electoral incentives for party cohesion ("We may either all hang together, or most assuredly . . .") have diminished, and the task of presidential leadership has become all the more difficult.[10] In turn, the ability of the citizenry to assess responsibility for government performance has declined.

In Great Britain, things have not gone nearly so far as in the United States. Although the basis for evaluating individual MPs differs from that for evaluating Parliament and the prime minister, the connection between the electoral fates of the MPs and the prime minister remains far tighter than in the United States. Individual MPs continue to bear collective responsibility for government performance. To the extent that trends described in Chapter 4 persist, however, shared responsibility may diminish, though the parliamentary form of government makes it difficult to imagine that Britain will ever approach the United States in this regard.[11]

Constituency Service and Cross-Voting in Britain

American political commentary stresses the close association between electoral independence and policy independence.[12] When representatives owe their elections to their own efforts, party leaders and the executive have fewer rewards to offer and fewer sanctions to threaten. In turn, less party unity and more policy independence reinforce electoral independence. Though one cannot say which comes first, independence in the two realms tends to go together. The covariance is an empirical one, however, not a logical one. A representative might construct a large personal following via nonprogrammatic activities such as constituency service, then use the "cushion" provided to support a party platform or presidential program not in accord with policy positions popular in the district. But in such cases the legislator is freely choosing to follow party or president, and no doubt the party or president must tread more lightly when dependent on such followers rather than on followers whose freedom of choice largely ended when they accepted the party nomination.

In Congress the parties have weakened so much that members are relatively free to tailor their voting records to their individual districts and states. So long as they support the party on organizational votes and do not actively work against the party's presidential candidate, they remain party members in more or less good standing. In Britain, the modern MPs' options are more limited. They can occasionally introduce private member's bills and file Early Day Motions, they can vote their constituencies on free votes, and they can adjust their campaign emphasis. In the 1970s, however, the iron facade of party discipline in the Commons began to show fissures. Attuned observers already have speculated that various embryonic trends in Britain are related, such as more constituency work, increased dissension, and escalating demands for backbench participation.[13] But while the temporal trends suggest a correlation between electoral and policy independence, a cross-sectional correlation provides more compelling evidence. That is, do MPs who provide high levels of constituency service also vote more independently in Parliament? Excluding ministers, whips, opposition spokesmen, and those elected in by-elections, the MP study included 68 backbench MPs who served during the 1974-1979 Parliament. Because pressures on the governing party backbenchers (Labour) are likely to be more intense than pressures on the opposition backbenchers, these backbenchers were divided by party.

To measure dissent, one can combine abstention, a weak form of dissent, with cross-voting, a stronger form, but something may be gained by examining them separately as well.[14] Another important question involves the number of times an MP dissents, the number of distinct bills dissented on, and the number of distinct policy areas encompassed by an MP's dissents. For any given number of dissents, the MP who disagrees vehemently about a single bill or issue is less independent than one who scatters his or her dissents across different bills in different policy areas. Thus, seven different behavioral measures are examined (Table 8.2). The measure of constituency involvement is the additive index, which gives one point each for soliciting cases, publicizing cases, handling local cases, and holding surgeries more than twice monthly.[15] Positive relationships mean that dissent increases as constituency work increases.

Labour backbenchers dissented more frequently by all measures than their Conservative counterparts. In part, this reflected Labour's position as the governing party responsible for initiating action during a troubled period in British politics. Additionally, the Conservative front bench chose to abstain or allow a free vote on several of

Table 8.2. Correlations between constituency service and dissent in Parliament[a]

	Index	
	Labor MPs	Conservative MPs
Times MP cross-voted	.50**	−.08
Bills on which MP cross-voted	.32*	−.13
Policy areas on which MP cross-voted	.35*	−.12
Times MP abstained on whipped vote	.06	.01
Bills MP abstained on whipped vote	.15	−.06
Areas MP abstained on whipped vote	.15	−.10
Total times MP cross-voted and abstained (Norton-Schwartz-Crowe measure)	.49**	

a. Entries are Pearson correlations.
*$p < .05$.
**$p < .01$.
Source: For the data on dissent, see Philip Norton, *Dissension in the House of Commons, 1974–1979* (New York: Oxford University Press, 1980).

the most divisive issues, in particular Devolution, when the whips would have met with resistance in their ranks.

There is a relationship between dissent and constituency service for Labour MPs, but not for Conservative MPs. Every correlation is positive for Labour, and those for actual votes as opposed to abstention are significant at conventional levels. The strongest relationships are for total number of dissents and total number of cross-votes. The results leave little doubt that Labour MPs who were the most active in their constituencies were also the most likely to dissent.[16]

Thus, preliminary evidence points to a relationship between constituency service and the propensity to exercise a degree of policy independence in the Parliament, at least for the period 1974–1979. Again, this does not imply any simple causal link. On the one hand, local support based on constituency service may embolden MPs to dissent. On the other hand, MPs who dissent on the basis of conscience may feel compelled to compensate for the disapproval of activists with heightened levels of constituency service. Or both service and dissent may reflect a common third factor, such as the expectations of local activists or the desire to dissociate oneself and insulate oneself from an unpopular Labour government. Whether these or other possibilities underlie the relationships is not known. The point is simply that electoral independence and policy independence tend to occur together.

In sum, every polity experiences conflicts between the demands of its component parts and the welfare of the polity as a whole. Such conflicts are most evident in the economic realm. For example, corporations and unions in the United States demand restrictions on imports, at a tangible cost to consumers of hundreds of thousands of dollars per job and a potentially much larger cost to export industries and the national economy.[17] Only the difficulty of measuring the best national course of action hides the existence of such conflicts in other spheres of government activity. Government policies affect their citizens in differential fashion, and those adversely affected understandably resist, even if their costs contribute to a more general good.

Although the problem is universal, single-member district electoral systems institutionalize it by making elected representatives formally responsible only to small portions of the polity. Texas representatives espouse the sentiment that Massachusetts citizens can freeze in the dark, not out of maliciousness, but because they represent Texas oil producers, not Massachusetts consumers. Appalachian representatives draft and oversee clean air laws that waste money and contribute to acid rain not out of stupidity, but out of a calculated effort to protect the eastern coal industry from the inroads of cleaner Western coal. In the abstract, single-member district systems do not provide elected representatives with compelling personal incentives to pursue common interests.[18]

Some of our colleagues downplay the significance of the preceding arguments.[19] After all, representatives defend parochial interests because voters apparently want them to, and are voter preferences not paramount? Does it make good sense to accept the principles of populist democracy and simultaneously criticize the product of those principles? Clearly, constituency service does cater to real demands, and just as clearly policy independence enables representatives to articulate the strongly held views of their constituents. But such arguments should not make one overlook the coordination problem institutionalized in single-member district systems. A representative highly sensitive to local concerns can be locally responsible and nationally irresponsible.

Pork barrel projects are the classic example. In the pure case where the benefits are concentrated in a single district and the costs spread across all districts, a representative will favor a project for his or her district so long as the benefits are 1/435 as great as the costs. If a coalition of legislators forms to pass each of their projects, the result will be a great waste of societal resources. While all policy areas do not provide such extreme examples, the logic of the argument is general. Coherent policy, defined weakly as policy which is more than the summation of particularized interests, is a characteristic collective action problem of single-member district systems.[20] Polities having such electoral systems can develop cooperative solutions to such problems, as in the British system of party government, but the parochial pressures institutionalized in single-member districts must be offset or overridden by some formal or informal mechanisms. Examples of formal mechanisms include cabinet government and restrictions on private member bills. An example of an informal mechanism is a strong party system.

Other factors exacerbate the collective action problem. Among them are:

1. Independently elected executive. Citizens can split their tickets between parochially minded congressmen and more generally minded presidents, as in the United States, rather than being forced to make a unified choice, as in Britain.

2. High professionalism in the legislature. As politics becomes an attractive career, the stakes of losing increase. Incumbents grow more averse to risks and place a higher premium on relatively noncontroversial parochial activities.

3. Party decomposition. As the party ties of citizens weaken, the value of the personal relationships between them and their representatives grow more important. The decline in automatic partisan support necessitates continual work to maintain the needed level of contingent support.

4. New campaign technology. The capacity to target messages to selected audiences allows candidates to unravel their bundles of policy proposals even further and appeal to increasingly particularized interests.

The list could go on but the preceding examples suggest the range of possibilities. One problem with the view that there is no such thing as excessive constituency service, because voters are getting the kind of representation they value most, is that service can exacerbate the coordination problems inherent in the electoral system.

If voters fully understood the larger consequences of getting what they want in the small, they might find it less attractive. Moreover, constituents' demands for district service are to some degree endogeneous rather than spontaneous. The value that constituents place on service may reflect the behavior of other political actors, including the representative. Voter expectations about constituency service are molded by what the representative does. A representative who emphasizes service establishes strong expectations about service among his or her constituents. The behavior of a new representative can be constrained by the expectations established by the previous incumbent. And even the behavior of neighboring representatives can spill over into the expectations of constituents. Part of the reason that constituents rate constituency service highly is that contemporary representatives do so much of it and advertise it so heavily. In short, there is no way to know what constituents really want when what they want is partly manufactured by what they have been getting.[21]

The constituency service component of representation can gain a momentum of its own without voters or representatives consciously controlling the process. MPs complained about the growth of the welfare officer role but felt that they had to respond to the pressures even though they did not feel that it was the proper function of the MP. In the United States, the increased retirement rates of congressmen in the 1970s reflected a decline in job satisfaction coincident with the rising importance of the constituency service role.[22] The importance of service can grow without anyone especially wanting it to do so. Representatives can get trapped by the escalating expectations of voters and the competitive spur of their colleagues. Those in marginal seats or those who otherwise feel insecure attempt to distinguish themselves by extraordinary constituency work. This creates expectations that spill over to other districts, raising the overall level of activity. The trend rises a notch when challengers promise to outperform the incumbents. Whether this process has inherent limits is not known, but the process is the uncontrolled result of the separate choices of numerous political actors, many of whom neither know nor appreciate the consequences.

9
Implications for Political Institutions

Students of elections sometimes are asked why they do not concentrate their efforts on "real politics," defined as the beliefs, calculations, and behavior of interest group leaders, high-level bureaucrats, substantive experts, and key elected officials. This query implies that public policy is determined by elites, not by voters. The citizenry at large supposedly pays little attention to political affairs, has no clear ideas about most issues, and votes largely on the basis of long-standing class, partisan, and other allegiances. Why study mere followers when there are more important and exciting actors to study?

As unrepentant students of elections we disagree profoundly with such viewpoints. To understand legislative policy making, one must understand the electoral relationship between representatives and their constituents. Candidates devise methods to convince voters to put them in office, and voters respond to these efforts positively or negatively. If voters respond only to party appeals, legislative policy making will take a different form than if voters base their choices on the personal voting records or constituency service of their representatives. The nature of voter response is a critical variable, and voter response *is* a variable, not something etched in stone at the inception of a political system. Voter response changes at times, and the behavior of representatives is one of the stimuli for change.

This final chapter reviews the central findings of our study and discusses them with reference to pertinent institutional features of the British and American systems. Then we throw scholarly caution to the winds and proceed to a wide-ranging discussion of the relevance of our arguments to behavior observed in electoral systems other than single-member district.

Review of the Findings

In both the United States and Britain, citizens expect their representatives to protect constituency interests and to provide ombudsman services to individual constituents (Chapter 1). Members of Parliament devote much of their time and members of Congress much of their resources to constituency service (Chapter 2). A noteworthy feature of constituency service is that it is a relatively noncontroversial activity. Few voters consider it unimportant, and most are satisfied by the services they receive (Chapters 2 and 6). Consequently, legislative members who engage in extensive service activity are better known (Chapters 1 and 6), more favorably evaluated (Chapters 2 and 6), and more successful electorally (Chapter 7) than those who are less solicitous of their constituencies. MPs with records of extensive constituency service enjoy more favorable swings (Chapter 7). In 1979 this phenomenon enabled some Labour members in marginal seats to retain office despite the large national swing to the Conservatives.[1]

Representatives undertake constituency work with a variety of motives, but by their own testimony the electoral incentive is significant, especially for those in marginal seats, who are the largest providers of constituency service (Chapter 3). Representatives believe that casework has both a positive and a negative electoral component: they can gain votes by extra efforts and lose votes by not living up to expectations. Analyses corroborate these beliefs: the activities representatives undertake affect their reputations (Chapter 6).

Most of the evidence presented in this study involves comparisons across individuals at a single point in time. Chapter 4, however, reported fragmentary evidence of changes in member behavior and constituent expectations over a fifteen- to twenty-year period. Constituency service figures more prominently in evaluations of members now than in earlier periods, and the electoral payoff of constituency service has grown over the past two decades (Chapter 7). The representatives themselves undertake more service activity today than previously and allocate a larger proportion of their personal time and other resources to their geographic constituencies.

Although there are numerous similarities between the two countries, the differences are clear. Congressmen adopt a less personal, staff-oriented style of constituency service, while MPs adopt a more personal, time-intensive style (Chapter 2). Congressional offices are small bureaucracies, whereas MPs are "mom and pop" operations.[2] The American party and electoral systems lead to greater payoffs for constituency service for congressmen than the corresponding British systems allow for MPs (Chapter 7). Not surprisingly, party affiliations affect representatives' reputations more in Britain than in the United States (Chapter 6), and evaluations of national leaders affect British voting behavior much more than American (Chapter 7).

Interaction between Rules and Behavior

Every political system is defined by a set of rules that encourage some types of behavior and discourage others, thereby giving rise to sentiments for and against change in the rules. The rules that govern entry into the legislature in Britain and the United States are broadly similar. In both countries legislative members represent single-member districts, they are elected by plurality rule, and their individual names appear on the ballot. Superimposed on this general similarity is a crucial difference. The ballot in the United States consists of many simultaneous contests for formally independent offices. In particular, voters can separate their presidential and congressional choices. In Britain, no such option exists. The voter who wishes Margaret Thatcher to lead the country has no option but to vote for the Conservative candidate for MP.

Some electoral rules encourage electoral independence; others discourage it. Other things being equal, if voters choose among individual candidates, the candidates have incentives to establish personal bases of support. Alternatively, if voters choose among undifferentiated party lists, such incentives are far weaker or nonexistent. Formally separating the choice of legislative and executive candidates fosters an "every man for himself" mentality. Formally linking the choice of executive and legislative candidates fosters a team mentality: candidates for the legislature and executive have personal incentives to cooperate in the pursuit of mutual success.

Another set of rules governs the legislature, determining how its members' behavior is channeled and constrained. Again, some rules encourage the independence of members while others discourage it. Rules that facilitate the provision of constituency services encourage independence, as do rules which facilitate credit claiming by individual members. From the perspective of these rules the contrast between Parliament and the Congress is striking. The resources available to congressmen exceed those available to MPs by several orders of magnitude. Congressmen have more than sufficient resources to engage in extensive constituency service and continue to meet their legislative responsibilities. As for credit claiming, the formal independence of Congress from the president and the decentralized structure of congressional committees combine to produce a vastly more influential rank and file than in Britain. Congressmen can alter the agenda, introduce and amend legislation, and influence bureaucrats to an extent only dreamed of by MPs. MPs lack the power to amend or delay legislation. They cannot control when a bill will be read. The number of days allocated to private member bills is severely limited, and the government easily obstructs bills to which it objects. With such limited capacity to protect and advance their local interests, MPs have difficulty in claiming credit for legislative activity and oversight on behalf of the constituency.

David Mayhew remarked about the Congress that, "if a group of planners sat down and tried to design a pair of American national assemblies with the goal of serving members' electoral needs . . . they would be hard pressed to improve on what exists." In contrast, if a group of planners sat down and tried to design an institution that magnified the dependence of legislative members on their national parties, they would be hard pressed to improve on what exists in Britain.[3] In the United States both the electoral and legislative rules encourage credit-claiming activities; in Britain, some of the electoral rules do, but the legislative institutions do not. Thus, incentives in Britain create a tension that is manifested in disputes with party leaders over such matters as backbench staff resources and committee powers. More than in the United States, the British legislative practices and electoral rules are out of equilibrium. Thus, there should be continued pressures for parliamentary change in Britain until the tension is resolved.

The temporal changes identified in Chapters 4 and 7 become relevant at this point. One explanation for the increased importance of constituency service in the United States connects it to changes in legislative rules which facilitate the performance of constituency service activities. The growth in congressional staff allowances and other congressional resources (Chapter 4) is the most obvious example. As congressmen gained the resources to do more, they did more, constituents came to expect more, and the constituency service function expanded in size and importance. In Britain, increased attention by MPs to constituency service is associated with demands for expansion of resources, but those demands remain largely unmet.

In the policy realm, however, changes in the unwritten rules of the game in Britain have attracted notice. In particular, the widely shared belief that a government defeat on a three line whip is tantamount to a vote of no confidence has deteriorated.[4] MPs now dissent more frequently than in the past, and that dissent is associated with constituency service and the personal vote it produces (Chapter 8). Similarly, pressures for an enhanced backbench role in the policy-making process, expanding and strengthening the select committee system, is associated with increased MP independence and increased attention to constituencies.

Once again we reiterate that our argument presupposes no linear series of causes and effects. To say that decentralizing or fragmenting institutional changes contributes to representatives' independence says neither that the institutional changes always precede the independence nor the reverse. Changes in the magnitudes of representatives' personal votes can stimulate demands for institutional change, just as such changes can alter the magnitudes of personal votes. As congressional job security increased in the late nineteenth century, rank and file congressmen fought to gain increased control over the appropriations process. Somewhat later they strengthened their hold over the committee system and restrained the coordinating power of the party leadership. Similarly, the 1960s increase in the House incumbency advantage was intertwined with the ongoing decentralization of the House into what has been termed "subcommittee government."[5] Neither the personal vote nor legislative rules are invariably the prime mover; rather, both are endogeneous, as are legislative institutions, the nature of the policy process, and the party system itself. Change one, and the others tend to adjust accordingly.

In sum, one source of institutional change lies in the degree of consistency between legislative and electoral rules. When electoral rules create incentives for a personal vote and legislative rules deny representatives the opportunity to establish it, stress arises in the system, or to put it in other terms, the rules are in disequilibrium. Indeed, we suggest an even stronger hypothesis: there is an inherent tendency for single-member district, plurality rule systems to move in the direction of greater decentralization and independent electoral standing. Generally speaking, electoral institutions are more difficult to change than legislative ones, because electoral institutions are enshrined in the constitution of a political system. Moreover, because single-member district systems produce two-party competition,[6] the established parties resist electoral rules changes, such as proportional representation, as witnessed by the contemporary Labour and Conservative response to Alliance demands for proportional representation. Thus, resolution of the tension between electoral and legislative rules will more than likely occur in the legislative rules, consistent with the trend in both Great Britain and the United States toward a weakening of centralized control. British party leaders have been far more successful than their American counterparts in resisting backbench pressures, but backbench demands for a greater piece of the action continue unabated.

Although the independence of representatives, the coherence of the policy process, and the structure of legislative institutions follow an internal logic, the nature of the larger environment can force large adjustments in their interrelationships. For example, the development of the welfare state has contributed to the growth of the MPs' constituency role. People must have a need for ombudsman services before they will value them. The postwar governments of both the United States and Great Britain have established a diverse array of domestic programs. This increased impact of government decisions on citizens' welfare naturally produces an increase in the demand for representatives' intervention. To some extent, then, the increased importance of constituency service and the concomitant growth in the personal vote reflect the growth in the welfare, administrative, and regulatory functions of the modern state.

Less tangible factors also affect this system of relationships. So long as the electoral and legislative rules create the incentive, representatives will attempt to fashion a personal vote. But the motive force of the incentive will be stronger when the parties are unpopular and national conditions are unfavorable. In Britain, backbench demands intensified during a period in which the national parties lost much support, when the British economy experienced considerable difficulty, and when the Liberals and Nationalists made strong showings.[7] Much the same can be said of the United States. Incumbents always will see value in a buffer against electoral adversity, but the value of that buffer rises as expected adversity rises.

Finally, legislators are not the only relevant actors in a political system. They share policy-making power with executives, high-level bureaucrats, interest group leaders, experts, and others who are prepared to invest considerable resources in pursuit of their own goals. These other actors can alter the system of relationships. Consider the transformation of the decentralized and fragmented early nineteenth century British Parliament into the centralized body of the post World War II years, explained by such factors as the rise of constituency party organizations allied with parliamentary party leaders and the gradual assumption of procedural control of the Commons by the cabinet. Using ballot records for elections in double-member districts, Gary Cox shows that party discipline in the Commons followed the rise of party voting in the electorate; he argues that the rise of party voting in the electorate reflected the decreasing importance of the individual MP.[8] Not only did the assumption of procedural control of the Commons by the cabinet drastically diminish the MPs' impact on public legislation, but MPs gradually lost the ability to deliver particularized benefits to their constituents. Their earlier capacity to enact private bills eroded when committees were staffed with disinterested members, as Civil Service patronage steadily declined and as the victory of free trade removed tariff policy, a prime source of legislative particularism, from the political agenda. One still wonders why MPs allowed the cabinet to assume their prerogatives, but the victory of free trade and the near abolition of patronage probably reflected the wishes of other important interests in the society. So, the loss of individual policy influence and of the ability to deliver benefits, though not the prime mover, led to a decline in the personal vote and to the domination of the policy process by the executive.

In sum, backbench MPs are deferential because they have so little personal support in their districts. Increase the level of the personal vote, and the shape of parliamentary institutions will change to accommodate it, party cohesion will decline, and policy making will decentralize.[9] Rank-and-file congressmen are obstreperous because they have so much personal support in their districts. Decrease the level of the personal vote, and congressional institutions will change to accommodate the decrease, party cohesion will increase, and policy making will become more centralized. The argument works equally well in reverse: Centralize policy making, and ultimately the personal vote will decline. Or follow the argument from either of the intermediate points: alter the institutions, and the personal vote will adjust; or change the level of party cohesion, and the personal vote will adjust. In each case, large personal votes go with fragmentation and decentralization, small personal votes accompany coordination and centralization.

Legislator Independence in Multimember District Systems

Looking beyond the United States and Great Britain, one should not be surprised to find that other single-member simple plurality systems, too, have high levels of constituency service, as in New Zealand, Canada, and India.[10] The logic of our argument suggests, however, that proportional representation systems, especially those with large districts, have low levels of constituency service. Lacking personal electoral ties to specific geographic areas, representatives from proportional systems should have less incentive to provide for the needs of individual constituents. Indeed, constituency service constitutes a collective action problem for parties in proportional representation systems: although service is of value to constituents and for that reason is potentially of electoral value to the party, individual MPs may wish to "free ride" on the efforts of fellow party members since they do not personally capture all the benefits of service.[11]

West Germany presents a naturally controlled experiment in the impact of different electoral systems on constituency service, since approximately half of its MPs are elected from single-member districts, with the remaining half selected from party lists in proportions designed to approximate a proportional representation result in the Bundestag. German candidates prefer to stand in districts, apparently because district-elected members on average have greater electoral security. Party leaders typically stand in districts. For their part, marginal constituencies prefer to nominate candidates with high personal visibility. Gerhard Loewenberg reported that "national or land leaders prominent within the party, especially Mayors, are regarded as particularly attractive candidates."[12]

Comparing the behavior of German candidates elected from party lists with those elected from districts is no simple matter. Many candidates run both ways simultaneously, and their behavior may reflect a mix of incentives. Moreover, MPs elected from the party lists typically associate with some district as an "alternate" or "shadow" representative. Despite these confounding factors, MPs elected from districts engage in more constituency service than those elected from lists. Expectations of service among German voters are high, Loewenberg reported, and dissatisfaction with "a member's attention to constituency errands is a major reason for failing to be renominated for a constituency seat." Such expectations are manifest in the vote as well: "2 to 3 percent of the electorate split their vote because of a preference for a constituency candidate of a party other than the one whose land list they endorsed."[13]

Despite theoretical arguments and the West German case, representatives in some proportional representation systems devote considerable time and effort to servicing their constituencies.[14] Therefore, unless we are prepared to accept different theories of legislative behavior for representatives in different electoral systems, we must show that there is some component of electoral self-interest in proportional representation system constituency service. The extent to which members in such systems actually face "free rider" incentives with respect to constituency service depends on the specific implementation of the electoral rules. Some proportional representation systems provide legislative members with substantial incentives to undertake constituency service activities, while others do not. Systems that provide such incentives exhibit tendencies similar to those found in single-member simple plurality systems, namely high constituency attentiveness and decentralized policy-making institutions within the legislative.

The Personal Vote in Proportional Representation Systems

A great variety of electoral systems are designed to achieve results more proportional than the Anglo-American single-member simple plurality or "first past the post" system. The existing possibilities range from the single-transferable vote in small districts, as in Ireland, to proportional representation using party symbol ballots in a single nationwide district, as in Israel. The incentive effects of a proportional representation list system, where the choice is primarily between parties, differ greatly from those of a single-transferable vote system, where electors rank order the individual candidates. Moreover, even within list systems incentive effects may vary considerably as a function of such matters as the number of representatives elected from each district, the availability of personal or preference votes, and the possibility of combining choices from different lists.[15]

If candidates in a transferable vote system are constrained to support the same policies, incumbents will be attentive to their constituencies as a means of distinguishing themselves from other candidates of their party. Candidates of the same party in Ireland frequently try to distinguish themselves from their colleagues by offering easier access and better services. Indeed, they sometimes create a single-member district system de facto by observing informal agreements not to campaign in or service geographical areas of the constituency claimed by other candidates.[16] Moreover, as most constituent problems in Ireland are local, many members of the Irish Dail find it advantageous to serve on their local councils.

Systems with large districts and party list voting lie at the other end of the proportional representation spectrum. In these systems, such as Israel and the Netherlands, the personal benefits of constituency service to the MP are generally small, so the constituency service activities are explained by party pressures.[17] Because service activity can improve party fortunes as a whole, the parties devise means of counteracting individual incentive problems. One party strategy is to recruit prominent local figures for the party list. Where mayors or other local officeholders are powerful figures with substantial local followings, parties induce such figures to join the list as a means of adding to their electoral luster. Once elected, local officeholders often remain sensitive to local demands, especially if they continue to hold their local offices. These local notables feel somewhat independent of party leaders, realizing that they bring as much to the list as the list brings to them.

The value of the local notable strategy is illustrated by elections in the French Fourth Republic. According to Philip Williams, "a strong candidate was vital, for in spite of the list system, the voter still chose among men . . . The familiar candidate was an asset far more than liability." Constituency demands were taken seriously: "the Deputy, who neglected his Department was not lightly forgiven." After it became possible for voters to cross off those names on the list that they did not wish to support, a practice called panachage, the pressures for constituency work expanded. The electoral politics of the period depended so much on candidate appeal that the parties often were unable to discipline their deputies: "When a party was doing well in the country, it had little need to worry about discipline; once it began to do badly it could ill afford to apply it."[18] Indeed, on a number of occasions local notables took their supporters out of one party into another.

Like the French Fourth Republic, the Italian electoral system permits citizens to cast "preference votes" for candidates on the list. The importance of preference voting in Italy has increased since World War II, especially in the patronage-based politics of the South. In a vein far removed from clashes of great societal interests, an Italian deputy remarked, "I only know that when one of their cows has a bellyache, they come to me . . . maybe they look upon all the mayors they ever had like this."[19]

Whereas single-transferrable vote and "preference vote" systems permit and even encourage the development of personal voting, nothing of the sort can be expected in the pure party list systems with large electoral districts. The local notable strategy is not so effective in Scandinavia as in France and Italy. Apart from ballot considerations, there is no tradition of independently powerful mayors, and local councils tend to be large and composed mostly of amateurs who receive little compensation. While the councils elect an executive committee, administrative authority is lodged with civil servants. In such circumstances local officials do not develop strong personal followings, and though party leaders may include council members on the lists, they cannot expect much electoral advantage from doing so. For their part, local officeholders, lacking individual districts, are not strongly motivated to engage in constituency work; indeed, after election to the parliament MPs may give up their local office. On the whole, Scandinavian parliaments exhibit a somewhat lower level of professionalization than in other European countries. Re-election rates are relatively lower, and serving as an MP appears to be a less attractive occupation.[20]

Unable to rely on the individual incentives of their members, Scandinavian parties find it necessary to make more explicit use of the carrot and stick to ensure member attention to constituent needs. Parliamentarians inattentive to constituent requests may be moved lower on party lists or removed altogether, though there is no solid evidence on the use of such negative incentives. Danish lists provide positive incentives for constituency service. Most of the Danish parties use lists that allow members to receive whatever personal votes they get as well as a fraction of the party vote. Thus, the magnitude of the personal vote determines who is elected to the Folketing. But while members of the Folketing engage in service activities, the relationship of such activities to their own electoral support is far from clear, since a majority of service requests come from outside the district.[21] Denmark lacks the patronage structure of Italian local politics as well as the decentralized legislative institutions which might enable the deputies to construct a service-based personal vote. Like Britain, elements of the Danish system appear somewhat out of equilibrium.

One reason that list placement may not be an effective means for party leaders to induce constituency attentiveness on the part of the rank and file is that list composition requires attention to other more important considerations, such as the accommodation of functional and geographic interests. Some members may feel assured of high list placement regardless of how little attention they pay to individual constituents. Other members may expect low placement regardless of how much attention they show.

Perhaps it is no coincidence that the Scandinavian systems rely more heavily on the formal institution of ombudsman than do other systems. The presence of an active ombudsman steers individual requests for services away from MPs and out of the political arena altogether. Whatever its principal motivation, the ombudsman institution removes constituency service from the set of considerations over which the parties might compete. In fact, the existence of the ombudsman functions as a cooperative agreement among the parties which alleviates their collective action problem: constituents are provided with valued services, but no party or its candidates profit electorally. Competition is limited to other realms. From the standpoint of the parties, such an agreement has the advantage of buttressing central control by eliminating a primary basis of member independence.[22]

The Personal Vote and Legislative Policy Making

In proportional representation systems characterized by small electoral districts, multiple officeholding, and write-in or panachage provisions, members can be expected to develop personal followings in their constituencies. As in single-member simple plurality systems, these personal followings tend to insulate backbenchers from the demands of party leaders. Mayors and other local notables cannot be pushed about as easily as faceless designees of the party. Party leaders are forced to augment mobilization and direction with negotiation and persuasion. Moreover, a greater extent of legislative electoral independence and a lesser degree of party control should be accompanied by a greater decentralization of legislative institutions. The principal example of such decentralization is a committee system in which meaningful policy responsibilities devolve to component committees and in which neither committee memberships nor jurisdictions can be changed at the whim of party leaders. Is there any indication of such decentralization in proportional representation systems that encourage personal voting, such as the French Fourth Republic and Italy?

During the French Fourth Republic all legislation, government sponsored or not, was referred to committee for initial consideration. As in the United States Congress, Fourth Republic committees tended to attract members with constituency interests in the committees' jurisdictions. As Philip Williams observed, "Agriculture drew all but six of its forty-four members from the land, no urban deputy ever stayed on it . . . two-thirds of the labour committee came from industrial areas; merchant marine attracted only seaboard members; of eighteen representatives of the Midi wine-growers, thirteen were on Beverages." These constituency-oriented committees were relatively homogeneous and frequently rewrote government proposals in their subject areas; they also were favorably disposed toward private member legislation.[23] Even in the prestigious Finance Committee, government proposals fared little better. Although constituted as the principal legislative bulwark against distributive spending, the Finance Committee was forced to compromise with substantive committees. Legislative committee members often sat as substitutes for finance members during consideration of spending legislation, and floor amendments were common. On various occasions attempts to enforce party discipline on government budget and revenue proposals caused the government to fall.

Italy also reveals the connection between personal voting and decentralized policy making. Italian party leaders find it necessary to share control with parliamentary committees. In fact, committees can actually enact some legislation without final approval by the Chamber of Deputies.[24] Backbenchers have established rights to introduce private member legislation, and a significant fraction of enactments originate in this way, up to 30 percent in the 1963–1968 parliament. This legislation is usually distributive, favoring "either a restricted number of individuals" or "occupational categories, interest groups, and localities." Generally the government can get its preferred legislation through committee, but proposals may be stalled or heavily amended, and on occasion they die in committee.

The Italian Parliament has become an important arena for decision making since 1971, and this development stems primarily from the increased importance of committees. Italian party leaders have made substantial concessions to member preferences and seniority in staffing committees, defining their jurisdictions, and selecting their leadership. Today, many committees are heavily populated with program supporters. Consequently, recent parliaments have shown a penchant for distributive policies on the one hand and a difficulty in enacting corporatist "solutions" to public problems on the other. Comparing allocational politics in France and Italy, Tarrow observed: "The substitute for overall planning in Italy has been an increase in the amount of resources distributed through existing bureaucratic and parastate agencies . . . it enables politicians to deliver concrete benefits to constituents."[25]

At the other end of the spectrum, the dependence of Scandinavian MPs on the parties renders them relatively compliant to leader requests. Moreover, Scandinavian parliaments do not exhibit significant signs of decentralization. Rather, they conduct their business in the plenary fashion typical of the British House of Commons. There is greater reliance on institutions of government control, such as "questions" and "interpellations," and less reliance on mechanisms of parliamentary independence, such as the development of legislation in committee and committee review of government activity.[26]

Scandinavian party leaders exercise substantial control over parliamentary committees. They control the internal organization and conduct of committees and allow rank and file parliamentarians little independent influence on policy making. The Norwegian Storting provides a good example of a dependent committee system. Between 1950 and 1969, only 42 percent of returning committee members retained their previous assignment. Committee chairs frequently were appointed from outside the committee. Between 1945 and 1980 only 44 percent of the committee chairs had previously served on their committee. The committees have limited staff. Until 1977 they did not even have permanent secretarial assistance. Committee work is important to the operation of the Storting, but it has little independence from external structures of authority.[27]

In Denmark, according to John Fitzmaurice, neither committees nor individual MPs have much in the way of staffs: "the position of members is more like that of the British Parliament than like many other continental assemblies which often provide considerable backup for members." The Folketing is more occupied by bill reviewing than lawmaking. The Danish committee system has become somewhat stronger since the establishment of a permanent standing committee system in 1972. Some committees, notably agriculture are dominated by members with special links to related constituencies. But committee membership generally is determined more by the preferences of organized interest associations than by the preferences of individual members.[28]

Finally, the centralized legislative policy-making structures found in Scandinavia and the Netherlands contribute to the hierarchical control of administration. Article 90 of the Swedish Instrument of Government states: "During deliberations of the Riksdag or its committees no questions may be considered . . . concerning the appointment or dismissal of civil servants, decisions of the government or courts, relations between individuals and corporations, or the execution of any law, statute or enactment." In contrast, Italian and French deputies frequently interact directly with their bureaucratic counterparts, though they do not approach the actual influence of American congressmen.[29]

In summary, proportional representation systems display a good deal of variability in the relationship between party leaders and backbenchers. Unlike single-member simple plurality systems, proportional systems do not generally tend toward decentralization or centralization. Rather, those systems that encourage intraparty electoral competition, like the Irish, foster the personal vote, as do those systems that employ lists with small constituencies and write-in vote provisions, like the Italian and the Fourth French Republic. In all these cases, the existence of personal support for members results in relatively independent backbenchers whose expectations must be accommodated by party leaders. These accommodations in turn tend to produce decentralized policy-making institutions within the legislature and frequent legislative intervention in bureaucratic domains. Conversely, systems that have adopted a form of proportional representation which discourages close ties between members and constituencies generally exhibit much more centralized structures of policy making in which backbench involvement in policy development occurs at the sufferance of party leaders.

Thus, the consideration of multimember district systems reinforces the contention of this book that a key to understanding the structure of policy-making authority in a legislature, or indeed to understanding the place of the legislature in governmental decision making, lies in understanding the incentives of members to develop ties to geographical constituents. Pressures toward decentralization vary directly with the strength of those incentives. The adoption of a single-member simple plurality system tends to provide incentives in this direction, though the British experience suggests that sturdy party institutions may work to counter the tendency. With proportional representation systems, much depends on the particular rules of the electoral system.

Both major categories of electoral system face a characteristic collective action problem. For single-member simple plurality systems the problem is to achieve coherent national policy when individual members have little incentive to subordinate their personal activities to a larger end. These systems can fall prey to legislative parochialism. Single-member simple plurality systems can achieve the collective good of coherent policy only by reining in the natural inclinations of members through party control of legislative careers, minimal levels of member resources, and party domination of the policy agenda. These are important components of the modern British solution to the collective action problem. The United States has yet to evolve a solution, and American citizens, not to mention congressmen, would no doubt find the British solution singularly unattractive. Moreover, because electoral rules are harder to change than legislative ones, British-type solutions are precarious; they hold strong pressures in check.

For multimember proportional representation systems the collective action problem is to provide for the needs, wants, and problems of constituents as individuals when MPs have little personal incentive to do so. Parties in such systems have an inherent problem in the realm of service responsiveness.[30] They must develop alternative mechanisms to induce members to serve individual constituents. Taking account of service activity in composing a party list is one such mechanism, but it interferes with stronger considerations. Cooptation of locally important politicians by the legislative parties works somewhat better, but at the price of party cohesion and control. The Scandinavian systems have evolved a more radical solution, the total elimination of service responsiveness from the legislature's purview though creation of an ombudsman.

These different cases show that the same representational trade-offs exist in every representative democracy. If representation of individuals waxes, representation of the collectivity wanes. If individual representatives play an important policy-making role, the ability of the larger system to act coherently lessens. All good things cannot be maximized by the same set of institutions and the same kind of individual behavior. By accident or intention, democracies have chosen different representational mixes, but all show indications of the inherent tension in varieties of representation.

The representation of particularistic, relatively nonprogrammatic constituency interests has ramifications for the structure of policy-making institutions, the conduct of the policy-making process, and ultimately the shape of public policy itself. Faithful representation of particularistic constituency interests goes with decentralized policy-making institutions. Such institutions tend to produce distributive policies rather than regulatory and redistributive policies. Decentralized systems insulate their domestic policies from both national and international forces, and they are prone to crises of immobilism.[31] The need to form and maintain winning coalitions dictates policies that are compatible with the system's politics, and at times such policies are insufficient to deal with problems facing the society.

On the face of it, a government responsive to the individual needs of ordinary citizens is a good thing. There is much to be said for tempering cold bureaucratic rationality and anonymous universalistic policy making with the warm, humane interventions of elected representatives.[32] To some extent representatives must be encouraged to undertake this necessary task and be rewarded for their efforts. Without contraints, however, such behavior can corrode the conduct of democratic government by undermining the ability of that government to act in ways that improve the lot of its citizens.

In the end, some tension is inescapable. Individual representatives may be admirably faithful to the wishes of their constituents, but those same constituents may widely believe that their wishes are not reflected in public policy and effective government. One need neither condemn the citizenry for having too short-term or selfish a perspective nor condemn the representatives for pandering to the baser desires of their constituents. Constituents express a variety of legitimate wants, and representatives legitimately try to meet them. That all does not work to perfection reflects fundamental tensions of political life, and fundamental contradictions in political institutions, not just human failing. We can't always have everything we want.

Coding Categories Equated in Comparisons of Open-ended Responses, 1958 and 1978

Category	1958	1978
General, good man, bad man	0	201
Record and experience	1–2	211–297
Personal abilities and attributes	3,5,13	301–320
relevant to leadership		397,505
Personal qualities	4,6–9	401–497
Party	10–12	500–504
		506–508
Constituency attentiveness		
Helps with problems	—	321–322
Understands district	15	323–324
Keeps constituents informed	—	325–326
Listens, accessible	14	327–328
Local issues, projects	30–31	329–331
National domestic issues	20–29	900–1009
Foreign policy	40–49	1101–1197
Philosophy, ideology, general	32–39	601–697
approach to government		531–536
		800–897
Group references	50–69	1201–1297
Personal considerations	70–79	—
Other	80–90	701–723

Problems of Comparability in Open-ended Questions about the Congressional Candidates, 1958 and 1978

The 1978 NES/CPS study included the standard battery of "anything you like/anything you dislike" items. Up to four positive and four negative responses were recorded. The 1958 study contained two sets of open-ended items. The first reads: "Now how about Mr. (Name of Candidate). Forgetting about his party for a moment, do you think of him as being the right sort of person to be a congressman, or don't you have any opinion on this?" Those offering opinions were then asked the reason for their opinion, with up to two responses recorded. The format of the "right sort" item allows for up to two positive or up to two negative responses, rather than both, in contrast to the "like and dislike items." Following the "right sort" question, the interviewee was asked a number of questions dealing with the candidate's social class, religion, nationality, group affiliations, issue positions, and understanding of the problems of people like the interviewee. That portion of the interview ended with the question, "Is there anything else about Mr. (name of candidate) that made you want to vote for him?" and analagously, "against him?" Up to two responses were recorded for each of these questions. The "for and against" items are symmetrical, as are the "likes and dislikes" questions, giving equal attention to both the positive and the negative. In contrast, the "right sort" items are asymmetrical in two senses. First, they request positive or negative opinions, not both. Second, the wording of the question is itself asymmetrical in that a negative response is extremely negative, tantamount to an assertion that the candidate is not fit to serve in Congress. In contrast, the "likes and dislikes" items casually inquire into "anything in particular" that the interviewee likes or dislikes. Notice, too, that the "right sort" item explicitly asks for nonpartisan judgments.

Reservations about asymmetrical question wording are probably justified (Table B.1). The 575 respondents who passed through the "heard or read" filter in 1958 show a 7:1 ratio of positive to negative responses on the "right sort" question, but only a 3:1 ratio on the

Table B.1. Evaluations of House incumbents

Item	Responses
1958[a]	
Is he right sort?	
Yes	75%
No	10
Don't know	15
Anything else?	
For	47
Against	15
1978[b]	
Anything in particular?	
Like	54
Dislike	14

a. $n = 575$.
b. $n = 1545$.

"for and against" questions. In 1978, the 1545 respondents who passed through the contact battery filter gave a ratio of positive to negative responses of 4:1 in answering the "likes and dislikes" questions.

Thus, to compare the overall "positivity" of candidate images between 1958 and 1978 would be ill advised. If all the open-ended responses in 1958 were added together, the data would suggest that the positivity of candidate images had actually declined, a proposition that seems dubious on other grounds. If the more reasonable strategy of comparing responses to the 1958 "for and against" questions with the 1978 "likes and dislikes" questions were adopted, the data would show that incumbent images were more positive in 1978. But this would amount to throwing away the bulk of the 1958 data. In view of the other problems of comparability, it is simply not possible to determine with confidence whether candidate images are any more or less positive today than in 1958.

NOTES

Introduction

1. See Duncan MacRae, *Dimensions of Congressional Voting* (Berkeley: University of California Press, 1958); Warren Miller and Donald Stokes, "Constituency Influence in Congress," *American Political Science Review* 57 (1963): 45–56; Donald Stokes and Warren Miller, "Party Government and the Saliency of Congress," *Public Opinion Quarterly* 26 (1962): 531–546.

2. John C. Wahlke, Heinz Eulau, William Buchanan, and LeRoy Ferguson, *The Legislative System* (New York: John Wiley, 1962); Roger Davidson, *The Role of the Congressman* (New York: Pegasus, 1969).

3. Morris Fiorina, *Congress: Keystone of the Washington Establishment* (New Haven: Yale University Press, 1977); Richard F. Fenno, *Home Style: House Members and Their Districts* (Boston: Little, Brown, 1978).

4. Heinz Eulau and Walter Karp, "The Puzzle of Representation: Specifying Components of Responsiveness," in Heinz Eulau and John Wahlke, ed., *The Politics of Representation* (Beverly Hills: Sage, 1978), pp. 55–71.

5. Donald Stokes, "Parties and the Nationalization of Electoral Forces," in William N. Chambers and Walter Dean Burnham, *The American Party Systems: Stages of Political Development* (New York: Oxford University Press, 1967). Katz argues that Stokes's methodology understated the size of the national component during the 1960s. Though Katz does not reanalyze the entire time series, it is likely that his alternative methodology would yield consistently higher estimates of the national component. Richard S. Katz, "The Attribution of Variance in Electoral Returns: An Alternative Measurement Technique," *American Political Science Review* 67 (Sept. 1973): 817–828.

6. See Robert S. Erikson, "The Advantage of Incumbency in Congressional Elections," *Polity* 3 (Spring 1971): 395–405; Robert S. Erikson, "Malapportionment, Gerrymandering, and Party Fortunes in Congressional Elections," *American Political Science Review* 66 (Dec. 1972): 1234–1245; David R. Mayhew, "Congressional Elections: The Case of the Vanishing Marginals," *Polity* 6 (Spring 1974): 295–317.

7. Edward R. Tufte, "The Relationship between Seats and Votes in a Two-Party System," *American Political Science Review* 67 (June 1973): 540–554.

8. Walter Dean Burnham, "Insulation and Responsiveness in Congressional Elections" *Political Science Quarterly* 90 (Fall 1975): 411–435; Randall L. Calvert and John A. Ferejohn, "Coattail Voting in Recent Presidential

Elections," *American Political Science Review* 77 (June 1983): 407–419; John A. Ferejohn and Randall Calvert, "Presidential Coattails in Historical Perspective," *American Journal of Political Science* 28 (Feb. 1984): 127–146; George C. Edwards, III, *Presidential Influence in Congress* (San Francisco: W. H. Freeman, 1980), pp. 70–78; Thomas E. Mann, *Unsafe at Any Margin: Interpreting Congressional Elections* (Washington, D.C.: American Enterprise Institute for Public Policy Research, 1978), p. 1; Gary C. Jacobson, "Incumbents' Advantages in the 1978 Congressional Elections," *Legislative Studies Quarterly* 6 (May 1981): 183; Morris Fiorina, "The Decline of Collective Responsibility in American Politics," *Daedalus* 109 (Summer 1980): 25–45; Morris Fiorina, "The Presidency and the Contemporary Electoral System," in Michael C. Nelson, ed., *The Presidency and the Political System* (Washington, D.C.: Congressional Quarterly, 1984), pp. 204–226. It is true that patterns in House and Senate elections diverged during the 1970s, with policy considerations playing a more prominent role in the Senate, but the outcomes of Senate elections were equally idiosyncratic. Individual policy stands and performance evaluations, not national issues and executive performance, most affected the results. See Barbara Hinckley, "The American Voter in Congressional Elections," *American Political Science Review* 74 (Sept. 1980): 423–439.

9. Ivor Crewe, "Do Butler and Stokes Really Explain Political Change in Britain?" *European Journal of Political Research* 2 (March 1974): 47–92; Dennis Kavanagh, *Constituency Electioneering in Britain* (London: Longmans, 1970), pp. 49–50; Anthony King, *British Members of Parliament: A Self-Portrait* (London: Macmillan, 1974).

10. John Curtice and Michael Steed, "Appendix 2: An Analysis of the Voting," in David Butler and Dennis Kavanagh, *The British General Election of 1979* (London: Macmillan, 1980), p. 394, 408–409, 428–429; John Curtice and Michael Steed, "Electoral Choice and the Production of Government: The Changing Operation of the Electoral System in the United Kingdom since 1955," *British Journal of Political Science* 12 (July 1982): 269.

11. On the lengthening of congressional careers, see Nelson Polsby, "The Institutionalization of the U.S. House of Representatives," *American Political Science Review* 62 (March 1968): 144–168. On the greater ease of reelection, see Charles O. Jones, *Every Second Year: Congressional Behavior and the Two-Year Term* (Washington, D.C.: Brookings Institution, 1967), p. 68; Samuel Kernell, "Toward Understanding 19th-Century Congressional Careers: Ambition, Competition, and Rotation," *American Journal of Political Science* 21 (Nov. 1977): 669–694. On careers generally, see H. Douglas Price, "The Congressional Career—Then and Now," in Nelson W. Polsby, ed., *Congressional Behavior* (New York: Random House, 1971). On the pattern of the contemporary congressional career, see Richard F. Fenno, *Home Style: House Members in Their Districts*, (Boston: Little, Brown 1978). The claim that members work harder at their responsibilities is our judgment. It is based on the lengthening of congressional sessions, the increase in the number of committee and subcommittee meetings, the expansion of district activities, and so forth, all of which are documented in the literature.

12. See Anthony King, "The Rise of the Career Politician and Its Consequences," *British Journal of Political Science* (July 1981): 263, 265; Donald D. Searing, "New Roles for Post-War British Politics: Policy Advocates and Professionalization in the House of Commons," Paper prepared for Annual Meeting of American Political Science Association, New Orleans, August 1985. On increased tenure of MPs, see Colin Mellors, *The British MP: A Socio-economic Study of the House of Commons* (Farnborough: Saxon House, 1978), chs. 2, 6. For several reasons King explicitly eschews the term "professional" in favor of the term "career." While King's reasons for drawing the distinction have some merit, they are not critical for our purposes. The terms are used interchangeably to refer to an individual committed to a primary career as a representative, at least until an opportunity to move to higher office becomes available.

13. For an illustration of the burdens willingly borne by practicing congressmen but happily set down upon retirement, see the swan song of Otis Pike (Democrat, N.Y., 1960–1978), *Congressional Quarterly Weekly Report*, Feb. 25, 1978, pp. 528–529.

14. "House members see electoral uncertainty where outsiders would fail to unearth a single objective indicator of it." Fenno, *Home Style*, pp. 10–11.

15. For the classic discussion of the influence of party identification, see Angus Campbell, Philip E. Converse, Warren E. Miller, and Donald Stokes, *The American Voter* (New York: John Wiley, 1960). Cf. John A. Ferejohn, "On the Decline of Competition in Congressional Elections," *American Political Science Review* 71 (March 1977): 166–176. On the effects of economic conditions on the congressional vote, see Donald R. Kinder and D. Roderick Kiewiet, "Economic Discontent and Political Behavior: The Role of Personal Grievances and Collective Economic Judgments in Congressional Voting," *American Journal of Political Science* 23 (Aug. 1979): 495–527; Gary C. Jacobson and Samuel Kernell, *Strategy and Choice in Congressional Elections* (New Haven: Yale University Press, 1981); Gerald H. Kramer, "The Ecological Fallacy Revisited: Aggregate versus Individual-Level Findings on Economics and Elections, and Sociotropic Voting," *American Political Science Review* 77 (March 1983): 92–111.

16. For the most recent discussion of the advantages of incumbency, see Gary C. Jacobson, *The Politics of Congressional Elections* (Boston: Little, Brown, 1983), ch. 3. On communications to constituents, see Glenn R. Parker, "The Advantage of Incumbency in House Elections," *American Politics Quarterly* 8 (Oct. 1980): 449–464; Albert D. Cover and Bruce S. Brumberg, "Baby Books and Ballots: The Impact of Congressional Mail on Constituent Opinion," *American Political Science Review* 76 (June 1982): 347–359. On district operations, see Morris Fiorina, *Congress: Keystone of the Washington Establishment* (New Haven: Yale University Press, 1977), ch. 7. On the growing use of technology by members, see Stephen E. Frantzich, "Technological Innovation among Members of the U.S. House of Representatives," *Polity* 12 (Winter 1979): 333–348; Stephen E. Frantzich, *Computers in Congress: The Politics of Information* (Beverly Hills: Sage, 1982). On electoral spending, see Gary C. Jacobson, *Money in Congressional Elections* (New Haven: Yale University Press, 1980).

17. Ivor Crewe, Bo Sarlvik, and James Alt, "Partisan Dealignment in Britain, 1964–1974," *British Journal of Political Science* 7 (April 1977): 129–190; James Alt, *The Politics of Economic Decline* (New York: Cambridge University Press, 1979); James E. Alt, Bo Sarlvik, and Ivor Crewe, "Partisanship and Policy Choices: Issue Preference in the British Electorate, February 1974," *British Journal of Political Science* 6 (July 1976): 203–290; Philip Norton, *Dissension in the House of Commons, 1974–1979* (New York: Oxford University Press, 1980); Peter Paterson, *The Selectorate: The Case for Primary Elections on Britain* (London: MacGibbon and Kee, 1967). On recent readoption fights, see David Butler and Dennis Kavanagh, *The British General Election of 1983* (London: Macmillan, 1984).

18. David Butler, *The British General Election of 1955* (London: Macmillan, 1955) p. 3; Kavanagh, *Constituency Electioneering in Britain*, p. 10. Cf. Philip Williams, "The M.P.'s Personal Vote," *Parliamentary Affairs* 20 (1966–1967): 23–30.

19. For the *locus classicus*, see Woodrow Wilson, *Congressional Government* (Baltimore: Johns Hopkins University Press, 1885). For a contemporary treatment, see Steven Smith and Christopher Deering, *Committees in Congress* (Washington, D.C.: Congressional Quarterly Press, 1984). See also George Goodwin Jr., *The Little Legislatures: Committees of Congress* (Amherst: University of Massachusetts Press, 1970).

20. Richard Fenno, *Congressman in Committees* (Boston: Little, Brown, 1973).

21. A. Lawrence Lowell, "The Influence of Party upon Legislation in England and America," *Annual Report of the American Historical Association for the Year 1901*, vol. I (Washington: Government Printing Office, 1902); Robert T. McKenzie, *British Political Parties: The Distribution of Power within the Conservative and Labour Parties*, 2d ed. (New York: Praeger, 1964).

22. See Lewis Namier, *The Structure of Politics at the Accession of George III* (London: St. Martins, 1957). On the French experience during the Third Republic, see Nathan Leites, *On the Game of Politics in France* (Stanford: Stanford University Press, 1959). On the problems posed by the American separation of powers, see James MacGregor Burns, *The Deadlock of Democracy* (Englewood Cliffs, N.J.: Prentice-Hall, 1963).

23. On the revolt against the Speaker, see Nelson W. Polsby, Miriam Gallagher, and Barry Spencer Rundquist, "The Growth of the Seniority System in the U.S. House of Representatives," *American Political Science Review* 63 (Sept. 1969): 787–807. On the expansion of committee rosters, see Louis P. Westefield, "Majority Party Leadership and the Committee System in the House of Representatives," *American Political Science Review* 68 (Dec. 1974): 1593–1604. On recent British developments, see Malcolm Ian Marsh, *Policymaking in the Post-Collectivist State: Party Government, Parliament, and Interest Groups* (Ph.D. diss., Harvard University, 1984; Methuen, forthcoming). Dodd makes a similar argument concerning the fragmentation of power in Congress but embeds it in a recurring cyclical pattern of decentralization-centralization. While the logic of the disintegrative phase is convincing, his theory of the integrative phase is not. Lawrence C. Dodd, *A Theory of Congressional Cycles: Solving the*

Puzzle of Change, Working Papers in Political Science no. P-85-3 (Stanford: Hoover Institution, June 1985).

24. Barbara Sinclair, *Majority Leadership in the U.S. House* (Baltimore: Johns Hopkins University Press, 1983).

25. On committee assignment, see Kenneth Shepsle, *The Giant Jigsaw Puzzle: Democratic Committee Assignments in the Modern House* (Chicago: University of Chicago Press, 1978). On subcommittee leadership selection, see Jack A. Goldstone, "Subcommittee Chairmanships in the House of Representatives," *American Political Science Review* 69 (Sept. 1975): 970–971.

26. Bernard Crick, *The Reform of Parliament,* 2d ed. (London: Weidenfeld and Nicolson, 1968); A. H. Hanson and Bernard Crick, *The Commons in Transition* (London: Fontana, 1970); S. A. Walkland and M. Ryle, *The Commons in the 70s* (London: Fontana, 1977); Norton, *Dissension;* Leon D. Epstein, "What Happened to the British Party Model?" *American Political Science Review* 74 (March 1980): 9–22.

27. King, "Rise of the Career Politician," pp. 280–281.

28. For a similar description of the current state of House policy making, see Steven S. Smith, "New Patterns of Decisionmaking in Congress," in John E. Chubb and Paul E. Peterson, ed., *The New Direction in American Politics* (Washington, D.C.: Brookings, 1985).

29. See Randall Ripley, *The Politics of Economic and Human Resources Development* (Indianapolis: Bobbs-Merrill, 1972), ch. 5; R. Douglas Arnold, *Congress and the Bureaucracy: A Theory of Influence* (New Haven: Yale University Press, 1979).

30. Calvert and Ferejohn, "Presidential Coattails."

31. Eric Uslaner, *Everyman out of His Humor: Energy Politics and Congressional Leadership,* unpub. ms., The University of Maryland, College Park, 1985.

32. P. C. Schmitter, *Corporatism and Public Policy in Authoritarian Portugal* (Beverly Hills: Sage, 1975), p. 9.

33. Even the strongest party system may be susceptible to such particularistic influences. Pennock argues that marginal agricultural constituencies critical for government majorities received special attention in early postwar British elections. J. Roland Pennock, "Responsible Government, Separated Powers, and Special Interests: Agricultural Subsidies in Britain and America," *American Political Science Review* 56 (Sept. 1962): 621–633.

34. John A. Ferejohn, *Pork Barrel Politics: Rivers and Harbors Legislation, 1947–1968* (Stanford: Stanford University Press, 1974); Arnold, *Congress and the Bureaucracy.* On the threat of backbench rebellion, see Robert Jackson, *Rebels and Whips* (London: Macmillan, 1968); Norton, *Dissension.*

35. "Under corporatism, the presence of institutionalized access to the decision-making process for all recognized groups diminishes the importance of personal ties between interest group representatives and government officials. Parliamentary lobbying is also of lesser importance because the consensus agreed upon by the government and group elites is regularly sustained by parliament. [In contrast] the more common forms of group

action under pluralism are personal contacts between interest representatives and government officials . . . Since parliament exerts an influence over policy content either directly through its legislative acts or indirectly through its members' contacts with government officials, interest groups usually devote considerable attention to lobbying parliament." Frank L. Wilson, "French Interest Group Politics: Pluralist or Neocorporatist?" *American Political Science Review* 77 (Dec. 1983): 896–897.

36. See e.g. Fiorina, "The Decline of Collective Responsibility"; Fiorina, "The Presidency." See also James L. Sundquist, *The Decline and Resurgence of Congress* (Washington, D.C.: Brookings, 1981).

37. J. J. Richardson and A. G. Jordan, *Governing under Pressure* (Oxford: Morton Robertson, 1979), pp. 84–87.

38. Miller and Stokes, "Constituency Influence in Congress"; David Butler and Donald Stokes, *Political Change in Britain* (London: Macmillan, 1974).

39. Since 1978 the biennial American election studies have been carried out by the University of Michigan Center for Political Studies (CPS), under the supervision of the Board of Overseers of the National Election Studies (NES) with the financial support of the National Science Foundation. The Inter-university Consortium for Political and Social Research distributes the data. We are grateful to all of these organizations for the contribution they have made to this study, though none have any responsibility for the conclusions and interpretations advanced.

40. Actually, over the course of the research we interviewed a total of 106 MPs or former MPs and 40 agents. Ten of the additional MPs were interviewed in connection with a 1978 pilot study; the rest were from constituencies outside our sample or were newly elected members. The figure 69 referred to in the text comprises interviews with MPs who stood for reelection from constituencies in the sampling frame.

1. Member Visibility and Member Images

1. Miller and Stokes provide the initial research on the 1958 SRC study. Donald Stokes and Warren Miller, "Party Government and the Saliency of Congress," *Public Opinion Quarterly* 26 (1962): 531–546; Warren Miller and Donald Stokes, "Constituency Influence in Congress," *American Political Science Review* 57 (March 1963): 45–56. On the 1978 study, see Thomas E. Mann and Raymond E. Wolfinger, "Candidates and Parties in Congressional Elections," *American Political Science Review* 74 (Sept. 1980): 617–632; Barbara Hinckley, "The American Voter in Congressional Elections," *American Political Science Review* 74 (Sept. 1980): 423–439. On MP visibility, see Ivor Crewe, "Electoral Reform and the Local MP," in Samuel E. Finer, *Adversary Politics and Electoral Reform* (London: Anthony Wigram, 1975).

2. Spontaneous name recall, used in the 1958 SRC study, is an overly demanding measure of candidate visibility compared to the actual requirement of recognizing the name on the ballot; an analogy is fill-in-the-blank tests versus matching tests. See Alan I. Abramowitz, "Name Familiarity,

Reputation, and the Incumbency Effect in a Congressional Election," *Western Political Quarterly* 28 (Dec. 1975): 668–684; Thomas E. Mann, *Unsafe at Any Margin: Interpreting Congressional Elections* (Washington, D.C.: American Enterprise Institute for Public Policy Research, 1978). See also Kent L. Tedin and Richard W. Murray, "Public Awareness of Congressional Representatives: Recall versus Recognition," *American Politics Quarterly* 7 (Oct. 1979): 509; Mann and Wolfinger, "Candidates and Parties"; Hinckley, "The American Voter"; Glenn R. Parker, "Interpreting Candidate Awareness in U.S. Congressional Elections," *Legislative Studies Quarterly* 6 (May 1981): 219–234. On the idiosyncratic nature of the 1978 survey, see Gary C. Jacobson, "Congressional Elections, 1978: The Case of the Vanishing Challengers," in Louis Sandy Maisel and Joseph Cooper, *Congressional Elections* (Beverly Hills: Sage, 1981); Robert B. Eubank and David John Gow, "The Pro-Incumbent Bias in the 1978 and 1980 National Election Studies," *American Journal of Political Science* 27 (Feb. 1983): 122–139; David John Gow and Robert B. Eubank, "The Pro-Incumbent Bias of the 1982 National Election Study," *American Journal of Political Science* 28 (Feb. 1984): 224.

3. Dennis Kavanagh, *Constituency Electioneering in Britain* (London: Longmans, 1970), pp. 49–50; Anthony King, *British Members of Parliament: A Self-Portrait* (London: Macmillan, 1974).

4. The U.S. measure of attentiveness comes from the survey item: "Some people seem to follow what's going on in government and public affairs most of the time, whether there's an election going on or not. Others aren't that interested. Would you say you follow what's going on in government and public affairs most of the time, some of the time, now and then, or hardly at all?" The response distribution is 24 percent, 35 percent, 26 percent, and 16 percent, respectively. The British measure is an additive index which assigns one point each to: watched the televised Conservative address, the televised Labour address, the televised Liberal address, listened to an election address on the radio, and read an address received in the mail. From low to high the response distribution is 16 percent, 7 percent, 6 percent, 28 percent, 30 percent, and 13 percent. On its face the British measure emphasizes campaign interest more than general interest. For the United States we broke education into the common categories: less than high school graduate, high school graduate, some college, college graduate. For Britain we broke education by year of leaving school: 14 or under, 15–18, 19 or older. Note that the equation in Table 1.3 could not be estimated when education and attentiveness were included simultaneously.

5. In the United States the tenure categories are: elected before 1964 (the Johnson landslide, Great Society, Vietnam), elected between 1964 and 1973, elected in 1974 (Watergate class), and elected after 1974. In Britain the categories are based in part on findings reported by Barker and Rush: elected before 1964, elected 1964 to 1973, and elected 1974 and later (resurgence of Liberals, growth of nationalist sentiment). Barker and Rush report greater constituency attentiveness by the 1964 and 1966 cohorts. Anthony Barker and Michael Rush, *The Member of Parliament and His Information* (London: Allen and Unwin, 1970), pp. 183, 191. A member of Congress is considered part of the Democratic leadership if he or she is a

member of the Steering and Policy Committee, and part of the Republican leadership if a member of the Committee on Committees or the Policy Committee. The 1978 NES/CPS survey included the districts of only two committee chairs with too few respondents (33 in the full sample, fewer after allowing for missing data) to permit separate estimates for committee and subcommittee chairs. Committee chairs were recoded as subcommittee chairs in the 1978 analyses. On the relationship between campaign spending and name recall, see Gary C. Jacobson, *Money in Congressional Elections* (New Haven: Yale University Press, 1980), p. 157.

6. The average population of a parliamentary constituency is about 90,000, of a congressional district about 525,000. In addition, most congressional districts are larger in area than parliamentary districts. The "second-hand" category (in Table 1.4) was not part of the list. It is constructed from responses to a question asking whether any of the constituent's friends, relatives, or co-workers had had contact in any of the other seven ways. The importance of such political hearsay is a well-known belief of practical politicians. For example, "whereas the Member does not look for extra constituency correspondence, he does what he is asked as best he can, in the knowledge that his letters to constituents may pass from hand to hand and the news of his helpfulness may spread through family, neighbours, local pub, and factory canteen, until dozens of other people know something of it." Barker and Rush, *The Member of Parliament,* p. 178.

Somewhat different contact levels were elicited by a 1972 survey sponsored by Granada TV. For example, 13 percent of the 1972 sample claimed they had seen their MP at a meeting, whereas in 1979 only 7 percent of the British sample made such a claim. Conversely, 16 percent of the 1979 sample reported seeing the MP on TV, as compared to 8 percent of the Granada sample. In general, however, the figures are in reasonable agreement: overall, 49 percent of the 1972 respondents had not heard or read about their MP in the past year, whereas a marginally smaller 44 percent of the 1979 sample reported no contact whatsoever. Given the seven-year difference, the between-elections timing of the Granada survey, and the small proportions responding to some of the specific contact possibilities, the figures seem in reasonable accord. See Crewe, "Electoral Reform," p. 531.

7. Richard F. Fenno, *Home Style: House Members and Their Districts* (Boston: Little, Brown, 1978).

8. For a general review, see Hannah Pitkin, *The Concept of Representation* (Berkeley: University of California Press, 1967); Jeremy Bentham, *The Constitutional Code,* in *The Works of Jeremy Bentham,* 11 vols., ed. John Bowring (London: Simpkin, Marshall, 1863) p. 160; John Locke, *The Second Treatise on Government* (New York: Bobbs-Merrill, 1952), pp. 84–91; Georg Hegel, *The Philosophy of Right,* ed. C. M. Knox (Oxford: Clarendon Press, 1952), pp. 193–208.

9. Ronald Butt, *The Power of Parliament,* 2d. ed. (London: Constable, 1969); Max Beloff and Gillian Peele, *The Government of the United Kingdom: Political Authority in a Changing Society* (London: Norton, 1980). On the national ombudsman, see R. Gregory and P. G. Hutchesson, *The Parliamentary Ombudsmen* (London: Allen and Unwin, 1975). On MP ac-

tivities, see D. N. Chester and N. Bowring, *Questions in Parliament* (Oxford: Oxford University Press, 1962); Bruce Cain and D. Ritchie, "Assessing Constituency Involvement: The Hemel Hempstead Experience," *Parliamentary Affairs* 35 (Winter 1982): 73–83; Philip Norton, " 'Dear Minister'—The Importance of MP to Minister Correspondence," *Parliamentary Affairs* 35 (Winter 1982): 59–72.

10. The 1972 Granada TV survey reported that the three aspects of the job considered most important—expressing voters' concern about the national issues, dealing with constituents' personal problems, and attending meetings in the constituency—all emphasized the members' local rather than national role. The three items mentioned least of all referred to official parliamentary duties. See Crewe, "Electoral Reform."

11. Morris Fiorina, *Congress: Keystone of the Washington Establishment* (New Haven: Yale University Press, 1977). On the life of backbench MPs, see A. H. Hanson and Bernard Crick, *The Commons in Transition* (London: Fontana, 1970); Barker and Rush, *The Member of Parliament*; Peter G. Richards, *The Backbenchers* (London: Faber and Faber, 1972); S. A. Walkland and M. Ryle, *The Commons in the 70s* (London: Fontana, 1977). On the effects of party discipline, see Robert Jackson, *Rebels and Whips* (London: Macmillan, 1968); Philip Norton, *Dissension in the House of Commons, 1945–1974* (London: Macmillan, 1975); Philip Norton, *Dissension in the House of Commons, 1974–1979* (New York: Oxford University Press, 1980); Richard Rose, *British MPs: A Bite as Well as a Bark?* Studies in Public Policy no. 98 (Glasgow: Centre for the Study of Public Policy, 1982).

12. Austin Ranney, *Pathways to Parliament* (London: Macmillan, 1965), pp. 114–117.

13. For the most recent review, see Richard S. Beth, "Recent Research on 'Incumbency Advantage' in House Elections: Part II," *Congress and the Presidency* 11 (Autumn 1984): 219–221.

14. Edmund Burke, "Speech to the Electors of Bristol," in *The Works of The Right Honorable Edmund Burke*, 16 vol. (London: F. C. & J. Rivington, 1827); John C. Wahlke, Heinz Eulau, William Buchanan, and LeRoy C. Ferguson, *The Legislative System: Explorations in Legislative Behavior* (New York: John Wiley, 1962).

15. Sidney Verba and Norman H. Nie, *Participation in America: Political Democracy and Social Equality* (New York: Harper & Row, 1972).

16. Fenno, *Home Style*, chs. 3–4.

17. On presidential support, see Morris Fiorina, "The Decline of Collective Responsibility in American Politics," *Daedalus* 109 (Summer 1980): 38. For British comparisons, see Norton, *Dissension*, p. 428. On more recent changes in Parliament, see Philip Norton, "The Changing Face of the British House of Commons in the 1970s," *Legislative Studies Quarterly* 5 (Aug. 1980): 333–358; John Schwarz, "Exploring a New Role in Policy Making: The British House of Commons in the 1970s," *American Political Science Review* 74 (March 1980): 23–37.

18. There were no comparable survey items in earlier studies to indicate whether British opinion has been shifting over time in the direction of independent voting by MPs. In the United States the proportion favoring

independent voting increased somewhat between 1958 and 1978, from 58 percent to 69 percent—an expected shift given the many other indications of a lessened American commitment to political parties. See Morris Fiorina, "Congressmen and Their Constituents: 1958 and 1978," in Dennis Hale, ed., *Proceedings of the Thomas P. O'Neill, Jr., Symposium on the U.S. Congress* (Boston: Pusey Press, 1982), pp. 33–64.

19. H. M. Drucker, *Doctrine and Ethos in the Labour Party* (London: Allen and Unwin, 1979).

20. Glenn R. Parker and Roger Davidson, "Why Do Americans Love Their Congressman So Much More Than Their Congress?" *Legislative Studies Quarterly* 4 (Feb. 1979): 53–62.

2. The Nature of Constituency Service

1. Heinz Eulau and Paul D. Karps, "The Puzzle of Representation: Specifying Components of Responsiveness," in Heinz Eulau and John Wahlke, ed. *The Politics of Representation* (Beverly Hills: Sage, 1978), p. 63; Richard F. Fenno, *Home Style: House Members and Their Districts* (Boston: Little, Brown, 1978), p. 241.

2. Fenno, *Home Style*, p. 101.

3. In the British sample only the fact of such second-hand experience was obtained. Satisfaction levels are not available.

4. Johannes contends that the estimated electoral effects of casework are lessened when turnout rates are taken into account. His argument is difficult to understand, but it seems directly contradicted by the finding noted in the text. John R. Johannes, *To Serve the People: Congress and Constituency Service* (Lincoln: University of Nebraska Press, 1984), p. 200.

5. The contact variables are created by collapsing the contact battery. Based on Parker's analysis, the responses were used to create two dummy variables: personal contact (met the incumbent; heard him or her at a meeting; talked to staff, agent, secretary or other employee), and media contact (newspaper or magazine, mail, radio, TV). See Glenn R. Parker, "Interpreting Candidate Awareness in U.S. Congressional Elections," *Legislative Studies Quarterly* 6 (May 1981): 219–234. The collapsing is necessary in order to reduce collinearity and to keep the number of variables in the analysis manageable.

6. Since there is not a clean measure of satisfaction with second-hand casework experience in Britain, the dummy variable takes on a value of one for all who report knowledge of friend, relative, or co-worker experience. The large and highly significant coefficient suggests that the effects of satisfactory second-hand experience are strong, given that the estimate is watered down by inclusion of a presumed minority who recall unsatisfactory experiences. Johannes does not distinguish between satisfied and dissatisfied responses when constructing his casework variable. Although the dissatisfied are a relatively small group, combining their highly negative reaction to the incumbent with the positive reaction of the satisfied can hardly fail to lessen the estimated effect of casework. Johannes, *To Serve*, p. 267n25.

7. John D. Macartney, "Political Staffing: A View from the District," Ph.D. diss., University of California, Los Angeles, 1975, pp. 113–114.

8. Bruce George, *Bruce George Report* 1979, p. 1.

9. Austin Ranney, "The Working Conditions of Members of Parliament and Congress: Changing the Tools Changes the Job," in Norman J. Ornstein, ed., *The Role of the Legislature in Western Democracies* (Washington, D.C.: American Enterprise Institute for Public Policy Research, 1979).

10. Johannes reports precisely the same figure for U.S. representatives during this time period. Johannes, *To Serve*, p. 42.

11. Bruce Cain, John Ferejohn, and Morris Fiorina, "The House Is Not a Home: British MPs in Their Constituencies," *Legislative Studies Quarterly* 4 (Nov. 1979): 509–510.

12. R. E. Dowse, "The MP and His Surgery," *Political Studies* 11 (Oct. 1963): 333–341.

13. Cain, Ferejohn, and Fiorina, "The House Is Not a Home," p. 506.

14. Similarly, "approximately 40% of all cases in 1977–78—using the rather narrow definition of this study—resulted in action favorable to constituents . . . The estimates double when the definition of success is broadened to include speeding up decisions and/or getting clear explanations of denials." Johannes, *To Serve*, p. 128. An intensive case study of the surgeries and "postbag" of one MP found that the MP's intervention was successful in 57 percent of 223 cases. Ronald Munroe, "The Member of Parliament as Representative: The View from the Constituency," *Political Studies* 25 (Dec. 1977): 585.

15. Macartney, "Political Staffing," p. 114.

16. Bruce E. Cain and David B. Ritchie, "Assessing Constituency Involvement: The Hemel Hempstead Experience," *Parliamentary Affairs* 35 (Winter 1982): 75–76.

17. Cain and Ritchie, "Assessing Constituency Involvement."

18. This congressional estimate is lower than those reported in previous studies owing to the narrow definition of "case" imposed on the respondents, distinguishing cases from projects. Cf. Johannes, *To Serve*, p. 35, Table 3.1.

19. R. Douglas Arnold, *Congress and the Bureaucracy: A Theory of Influence* (New Haven: Yale University Press, 1979), p. 29; J. Theodore Anagnoson, "Federal Grant Agencies and Congressional Election Campaigns," *American Journal of Political Science* 26 (Aug. 1982): 547–561.

20. Not only do minister's constituencies receive no special consideration in program or expenditure decisions, but in the context of the British system even the attempt to gain local advantage would impose serious political costs on a minister. Roy Gregory, "Executive Power and Constituency Representation in United Kingdom Politics," *Political Studies* 28 (March 1980): 63–83.

21. John A. Ferejohn, *Pork Barrel Politics: Rivers and Harbors Legislation, 1947–1968* (Stanford: Stanford University Press, 1974); Arnold, *Congress and the Bureaucracy*; Anagnoson, "Federal Grant Agencies"; Bruce A. Ray, "Congressional Promotion of District Interests: Does Power on the Hill Really Make a Difference?" in Barry S. Rundquist, ed., *Political Benefits* (Lexington: D. C. Heath, 1980).

22. On the shape of the federal grant system, see John Chubb, "Federalism and the Bias for Centralization," in John E. Chubb and Paul E. Peterson, ed., *The New Direction in American Politics* (Washington, D.C.: Brookings, 1985), pp. 273–306; Michael Reagan and John Sanzone, *The New Federalism* (New York: Oxford University Press, 1981).

3. Incentives for Serving the Constituency

1. Robert E. Dowse, "The MP and His Surgery," *Political Studies* 2 (Oct. 1963): 336; Anthony Barker and Michael Rush, *The Member of Parliament and His Information* (London: Allen and Unwin, 1970), p. 177.

2. Anthony King and Anne Sloman, *Westminster and Beyond* (London: Macmillan, 1973), pp. 13–14, 26–27.

3. Donald D. Searing, "The Role of the Good Constituency Member and the Practice of Representation in Great Britain," *Journal of Politics* 47 (May 1985): 348–381.

4. Austin Ranney, *Pathways to Parliament* (London: Macmillan, 1965); Michael Rush, *The Selection of Parliamentary Candidates* (London: Nelson, 1969); Max Beloff and Gillian Peele, *The Government of the United Kingdom: Political Authority in a Changing Society* (London: Norton, 1980), p. 91.

5. Leon Epstein, "British M.P.s and Their Local Parties: The Suez Case," *American Political Science Review* 54 (June 1960): 374–390; Ranney, *Pathways to Parliament*; P. McCormick, "Prentice and the Newham North East Constituency: The Making of Historical Myths," *Political Studies* 29 (March 1981): 73–90.

6. Byron Criddle, "Candidates," in David Butler and Dennis Kavanagh, *The British General Election of 1983* (London: Macmillan, 1984), ch. 10.

7. On administrative tribunals, see K. C. Wheare, *Maladministration and Its Remedies* (London: Stevens, 1973); R. E. Wraith and P. G. Hutchesson, *Administrative Tribunals* (London: Allen and Unwin, 1973); J. Farmer, *Tribunals and Government* (London: Weidenfeld and Nicolson, 1974).

8. R. Gregory and P. G. Hutchesson, *The Parliamentary Ombudsmen* (London: Allen and Unwin, 1975).

9. Beloff and Peele, *The Government of the United Kingdom*, p. 107.

10. On the frequency of surgeries, "those Members with less than nine years' service reported a notably greater frequency than their longer-serving colleagues . . . Among those with less than nine years' service the Members who had won their seats as 'gains' from another party held surgeries even more frequently than others." Barker and Rush, *The Member of Parliament*, p. 184.

11. "Some Conservatives to whom we spoke in our interviews feel that this constituency case-work aspect of Parliament has been developed deliberately by Labour candidates and Members for partisan reasons, and that this process began during and just after the Second World War." Barker and Rush, *The Member of Parliament*, p. 200. No further elaboration was given, so we are uncertain about the precise meaning of "partisan" here.

12. Various demographic characteristics of constituents, such as retire-

ment age and minority status, have little or no relationship to constituency effort. John R. Johannes, *To Serve the People* (Lincoln: University of Nebraska Press, 1984), pp. 52–53, 251n27.

13. The eigenvalue of the second dimension in both Britain and the United States fell well below 1.

14. The coefficients of scalability for the casework items in both countries were far below the conventional standard of .6. Across a variety of questions the coefficient of scalability was always in the .1–.2 range in the United States and the .3–.4 range in the United Kingdom. Stratification of the sample by party did not improve the scalability of the data for either country.

15. The relationships between each individual indicator of casework effort and the three predictor variables are summarized here. In the United States, previous electoral margin is the best predictor in the sense that it is significant in three out of the four equations and properly signed in all instances. The coefficients for the party and year elected variables are less stable. The party variable is significant only in the "number of caseworkers" equation and is improperly signed in the "solicits casework" and "publicizes casework" equations. The year elected variable is significant in the "solicits casework" equation but wrongly signed in the "number of caseworkers" and "handles local cases" equations. The model predicts best the "number of caseworkers" and "solicits cases"; it predicts less well "handles local cases" and "publicizes successful cases."

Interestingly, the model fits the British data somewhat better than the American: significant party differences appear in two instances, and the sign of the year elected variable is always positive and also significant in two instances. The chi-squares for the entire equations do not fail in any case. Of greatest relevance, previous electoral margin is equally as important in Great Britain as in the United States: the coefficient is statistically significant in three out of four instances and is correctly signed in all. The model best predicts whether the member "handles local government cases," the variable predicted worst in the United States analyses. But this should not distract from the similarities. In both countries those whose positions in the district are less secure are more likely than other representatives to undertake certain activities: soliciting cases and allocating caseworkers in the United States and handling local cases and the frequency of surgeries in the United Kingdom. Constituency orientation thus may vary in two ways: what kinds as well as how many casework activities representatives undertake. For a detailed report, see Bruce E. Cain, John A. Ferejohn, and Morris P. Fiorina, "The Constituency Component: A Comparison of Service in Great Britain and the United States," *Comparative Political Studies* 16 (April 1983): 67–91.

16. Seniority and marginality also have significant effects on congressional mass mailings. See Albert D. Cover, "Contacting Congressional Constituents: Some Patterns of Perquisite Use," *American Journal of Political Science* 24 (Feb. 1980): 125–135.

4. Temporal Change in Constituency Service

1. Morris Fiorina, *Congress: Keystone of the Washington Establishment* (New Haven: Yale University Press, 1977).

2. Ivor Crewe, "Do Butler and Stokes Really Explain Political Change in Britain?" *European Journal of Political Research* 2 (1974): 47–92; Ivor Crewe, Bo Sarlvik, and James Alt, "Partisan Dealignment in Britain, 1964–1974," *British Journal of Political Science* 7(2): 129–190; Philip Norton, *Dissension in the House of Commons, 1974–1979* (New York: Oxford University Press, 1980); John Schwarz, "Exploring a New Role in Policy Making: The British House of Commons in the 1970s," *American Political Science Review* 74 (March 1980): 23–37.

3. Norman Nie, Sidney Verba, and John R. Petrocik, *The Changing American Voter*, enl. ed. (Cambridge: Harvard University Press, 1979), pp. 11–12, 125–128.

4. Robert S. Erikson, "Malapportionment, Gerrymandering, and Party Fortunes in Congressional Elections," *American Political Science Review* 66 (Dec. 1972): 1234–1245; Walter Dean Burnham, "Insulation and Responsiveness in Congressional Elections," *Political Science Quarterly* 90 (Fall 1975): 411–435; John A Ferejohn, "On the Decline of Competitive Congressional Elections," *American Political Science Review* 71 (March 1977): 166–176.

5. Richard Born, "Generational Replacement and the Growth of Incumbent Reelection Margins in the U.S. House," *American Political Science Review* 73 (Sept. 1979): 811–817.

6. Steven H. Schiff and Steven S. Smith, "Generational Change and the Allocation of Staff in the U.S. Congress," *Legislative Studies Quarterly* 8 (Aug. 1983): 457–467.

7. David R. Mayhew, "Congressional Elections: The Case of the Vanishing Marginals," *Polity* 6 (Spring 1974): 295–317; Fiorina, *Congress*; Glenn R. Parker, *Homeward Bound: Explaining Change in Congressional Behavior* (Pittsburgh: University of Pittsburgh Press, 1986); Gary C. Jacobson, *Money in Congressional Elections* (New Haven: Yale University Press, 1980).

8. David Mayhew, *Congress: The Electoral Connection* (New Haven: Yale University Press, 1974).

9. Seniority differences do not account for all of the difference between the 1958 and 1978 figures for incumbents, however. The senior third of congressmen in 1978 had a recall figure of only 37 percent, still noticeably below the 1958 average for all incumbents.

As for challengers, in the 1978 NES/CPS study the sample voters reported casting only 21 percent of their vote for challengers, who actually garnered about 32 percent. In addition, the challengers in the study spent only four-fifths as much as all challengers, and the politically experienced challengers in the study, those with previous elective office, spent only half as much as all experienced challengers. In sum, information levels and positive-negative evaluation ratios are biased downward for 1978 challengers. See Gary C. Jacobson, "Congressional Elections, 1978: The Case of the Vanishing Challengers," in Louis Sandy Maisel and Joseph Cooper, eds., *Congressional Elections* (Beverly Hills: Sage, 1981).

10. Have information levels actually doubled in the past twenty years, the decline in name recall notwithstanding, or does the contact battery elicit a higher proportion of positive responses than the "heard or read" question? On first consideration the second possibility seems the more likely: today's incumbents possess greatly increased resources by which to communicate with their constituents, whereas their challengers, particularly the weak ones in the 1978 sample, have no obviously greater resource base. Yet doubling the information level for challengers required only a 20 percent absolute increase, whereas doubling the incumbents' information level required a 40 percent absolute increase, so perhaps the data are consistent with the increased resource advantage of incumbents over challengers.

11. Here too a caveat is in order. In 1958 constituents were asked to identify the incumbent immediately after receiving the names of the candidates. In 1978, however, a battery of like and dislike questions intervened. Possibly in racking one's brain for up to four each of things one likes and dislikes about a candidate, one might think of something that would create an association between a name and incumbency status.

12. Fiorina, *Congress*, p. 51.

13. As it turns out, in 1978 only 2 percent ($n = 15$) of those who could not identify the incumbent later reported casework experiences. The figure was 4 percent for district service. If the 1958 situation was comparable, failure to ask the questions of all the constituents probably led to little loss of information.

There are two dangers in the procedure used to generate the subsamples. The first is that the filters fail to correspond and thus do not produce comparable subsamples. The second danger is that the eliminated groups are simply ignored: if there are systematic differences between them, they would be overlooked in the adopted mode of analysis. But given that the omitted portion of the 1958 sample has no relevant data whatsoever, there is no obviously better way to proceed.

14. See John C. Wahlke, Heinz Eulau, William Buchanan, and LeRoy C. Ferguson, *The Legislative System: Explorations in Legislative Behavior* (New York: John Wiley, 1962).

15. In the 1958 SRC study responses were placed into a 70-category "Congressional Candidate Code." In the 1978 NES/CPS study the standard party/presidential candidate master code was augmented by a number of categories dealing specifically with congressional matters, yielding a classification with upward of five hundred categories. For the commonly offered responses, it is easy to identify the comparable categories in the two studies.

16. Twice as high a proportion of the sample, however, passes through that filter as passes though the "heard or read" filter in 1958.

17. Though there is some change in the personal attributes categories, when all the various personal characteristics and qualities are taken together, the proportion in this category is identical between the two years.

18. John Curtice and Michael Steed, "Appendix 2: An Analysis of the

Voting," in David Butler and Dennis Kavanagh, *The British General Election of 1979* (London: Macmillan, 1980), pp. 390–431; Bruce E. Cain, "Blessed Be the Tie That Unbinds: Constituency Work and the Vote Swing in Great Britain," *Political Studies* 31 (1983): 103–111; John Curtice and Michael Steed, "Electoral Choice and the Production of Government: The Changing Operation of the Electoral System in the United Kingdom since 1955," *British Journal of Political Science* 12 (1982): 249–298.

19. On the dominance of the party system in the 1950s and 1960s, see David E. Butler and Donald Stokes, *Political Change in Britain* (London: Macmillan, 1969), p. 425; Peter Pulzer, *Political Representation and Elections* (New York: Praeger, 1967), p. 98. For a discussion of its decline and accompanying changes, see Crewe, Sarlvik and Alt, "Partisan Dealignment"; Crewe, "Do Butler and Stokes"; Samuel Finer, *The Changing British Party System, 1945–1979* (Washington: American Enterprise Institute for Public Policy Research, 1980); Curtice and Steed, "Electoral Choice"; John Curtice and Michael Steed, "Appendix 2: An Analysis of the Voting," in David Butler and Dennis Kavanagh, *The British General Election of 1983* (London: Macmillan, 1984), pp. 333–373.

20. James Alt, *The Politics of Economic Decline* (New York: Cambridge University Press, 1979); William D. Nordhaus, "The Political Business Cycle," *Review of Economic Studies* (1975): 169–190; Samuel Brittan, "The Economic Contradictions of Democracy," *British Journal of Political Science* 5 (April 1975): 129–160.

21. John Bochel and David Denver, "Candidate Selection in the Labour Party: What the Selectors Seek," *British Journal of Political Science* 13 (Jan. 1983): 45–69; Philip Williams, "The Labour Party: The Rise of the Left," *West European Politics* 6 (Oct. 1983): 26–55.

22. T. W. Jackson, *Local Government* (London: Butterworth, 1976), pp. 112–121.

23. Beloff and Peele, *Government of the United Kingdom*, p. 251.

24. Anthony Barker and Michael Rush, *The Member of Parliament and His Information* (London: Allen and Unwin, 1970).

25. Barker and Rush, *The Member of Parliament*, p. 179.

26. Robert E. Dowse, "The MP and His Surgery," *Political Studies* 11 (Oct. 1963): 333–341; Barker and Rush, *The Member of Parliament*.

27. Ivor Crewe, "Electoral Reform and the Local M.P.," in S. E. Finer, ed., *Adversary Politics and Electoral Reform* (London: Anthony Wigram, 1975).

5. Unraveling a Paradox

1. Timothy E. Cook, "Review Essay," *American Political Science Review* 77 (Dec. 1983): 1018.

2. Gary C. Jacobson, *Money in Congressional Elections* (New Haven: Yale University Press, 1980).

3. Richard F. Fenno, *Home Style: House Members and Their Districts* (Boston: Little, Brown, 1978), Tables 2.1, 2.6; Lyn Ragsdale and Timothy Cook, "Representatives' Actions and Challengers' Reactions: Limits to Can-

didate Connections in the House," Paper delivered at Annual Meeting of Midwest Political Science Association, Palmer House Hotel, Chicago, April 12–15, 1984, Table 7, p. 21.

4. Fenno, *Home Style*, Table 2.6; Ragsdale and Cook, "Representatives' Actions," Table 7.

5. John R. Johannes and John C. McAdams, "The Congressional Incumbency Effect: Is It Casework, Policy Compatibility, or Something Else?" *American Journal of Political Science* 25 (Aug. 1981): 512, 538.

6. Paul Feldman and James Jondrow, "Congressional Elections and Local Federal Spending," *American Journal of Political Science* 28 (May 1984): 155.

7. See Ragsdale and Cook, "Representatives' Actions," Table 7; Linda Fowler, Scott Douglass, and Wesley Clark, "The Electoral Effects of Committee Assignments," *Journal of Politics* 42 (Feb. 1980): 307–322.

8. Paul Raymond, "When Politicians Talk, Nobody Listens: The Effect of House Candidates' Campaign Communications on Voting Behavior," Paper delivered at Annual Meeting of Midwest Political Science Association, Chicago, April 21–23, 1983.

9. Ragsdale and Cook, "Representatives' Actions," p. 21.

10. Johannes and McAdams, "Congressional Incumbency Effect," p. 538.

11. Feldman and Jondrow, "Congressional Elections," p. 159.

12. Jon R. Bond, Cary Covington, and Richard Fleisher, "Explaining Challenger Quality in Congressional Elections," *Journal of Politics* 47 (May 1985): 510–529.

13. Morris Fiorina, "Some Problems in Studying the Effects of Resource Allocation in Congressional Elections," *American Journal of Political Science* 25 (Aug. 1981): 543–567.

14. Imre Lakatos, "Falsification and the Methodology of Scientific Research Programs," in Imre Lakatos and Alan Musgrave, ed., *Criticism and the Growth of Knowledge* (Cambridge: Cambridge University Press, 1970); cf. Karl R. Popper, *The Logic of Scientific Discovery* (New York: Basic Books, 1959).

15. Washington staff is used because district staff, number of caseworkers, and number of project workers do not relate to any dependent variables of interest. These estimates of staff are drawn from the interviews with administrative assistants, not from the *Congressional District Data Book*.

16. Though in this case they are superior more often than not. Visits to the district only show a relationship when weekly or more frequent visits are differentiated from other frequencies. Caseload sometimes shows an effect when entered as a continuous variable, but it does so more dependably when the dummy representation is used. Washington staff generally shows effects either way but usually appears stronger and more robust as a dummy variable formulation. A number of variables, such as the percentage of incumbent's personal time spent on casework, show no statistical effects for any alternative specification.

17. For the various stages of the congressional career, see Fenno, *Home Style*, pp. 176–189.

18. Gary C. Jacobson, "Money and Votes Reconsidered: Congressional Elections, 1972–1982," *Public Choice* 47 (1985): 7–62.

19. Even with panel data the problem is not easily overcome. If the anticipation of future conditions affects present behavior, then simultaneity is present in the data if anticipations are relatively accurate.

20. Johannes and McAdams, "Congressional Incumbency Effect"; Feldman and Jondrow, "Congressional Elections"; Fiorina, "Some Problems."

21. Ten per cent seems a reasonable figure. The error in so straightforward a matter as vote report is at least that great in recent surveys. See e.g. Robert B. Eubank and David John Gow, "The Pro-Incumbent Bias of the 1978 and 1980 National Election Studies," *American Journal of Political Science* 27 (Feb. 1983): 122–139; David John Gow and Robert B. Eubank, "The Pro-Incumbent Bias of the 1982 National Election Study," *American Journal of Political Science* 28 (Feb. 1984): 224.

22. G. S. Maddala, *Econometrics* (New York: McGraw-Hill, 1977), pp. 292–294; J. Johnston, *Econometric Methods*, 2d ed., (New York: McGraw-Hill, 1972), pp. 281–291.

23. The standard error of a regression coefficient decreases as the dispersion of the variable around its mean increases.

24. For an experimental study of the effects of one form of member communications, see Alber D. Cover and Bruce S. Blumberg, "Baby Books and Ballots: The Impact of Congressional Mail on Constituent Opinion," *American Political Science Review* 76 (June 1982): 347–359. A study of local campaign resource allocation actually approached the fanciful experimental design described in the text. Candidates for the Monroe County Legislature in Rochester, New York, consented to conduct their campaigns according to this kind of experimental design (Republicans were regarded as sure winners by all concerned). Analysis of the data found that campaign contacting had a significant effect on voter preference, contrary to the earlier findings of nonexperimental studies. John C. Blydengurgh, "A Controlled Experiment to Measure the Effects of Personal Contact Campaigning," *Midwest Journal of Political Science* 15 (May 1971): 365–381.

6. Member Behavior and Constituent Response

1. Responses to the open-ended likes and dislikes questions were coded into about a dozen general categories in the 1978 NES/CPS election study. The constituency attentiveness category includes five subcategories: helps with problems (codes 321–322), understands district (323–324), keeps constituents informed (324–326), listens and is accessible (327–328), and local issues and projects (329–331). British Gallup coded the responses to the 1979 study using the American coding scheme as a model.

2. The estimates in Tables 6.4 and 6.5 are only a sampling of those carried out, but they provide an accurate picture of the patterns that emerged. Some variables, such as caseloads and grant activity, typically show substantively important and statistically significant relationships with member reputations. Others, such as types of staff, never do, so they were omitted from the final specifications. A few variables, such as the number of district

offices, show negative effects, when they show any, in violation of common-sense expectations. And some variables, such as seniority, manifest inconsistent sign and significance patterns but have some effect some of the time. As discussed in the preceding chapter, models that relate district level variables to individual level ones generally do not predict very well; the chisquare measures of goodness of fit are significant, but low. When individual level variables enter the analysis later in the chapter, the predictive power of the models improves greatly. The problem, incidentally, is more severe in Britain.

Because it was impossible to complete interviews for as many constituencies in Britain, each equation estimated with elite variables represents only 45–50 distinct configurations of elite variables (constituencies of MPs who stood for re-election and who provided—or their agent provided—a quantitative estimate of caseloads, number of visits, and so forth). The U.S. equations usually have approximately 70 distinct configurations of elite variables. Thus, a greater proportion of the British mass survey is unusable in these analyses, and fewer observations on the elite variables are available. In general, the statistical results for Britain are weaker, but whether this reflects the preceding considerations, reality, or both, is impossible to say.

3. In the preceding chapter the district offices variable was identified as a prime suspect for simultaneity bias. As was explained, the standard corrective for such a problem involves construction of an instrument for the suspect variable. In principle, this two-stage procedure yields a consistent estimate of the effects of district offices on constituent evaluations, purged of the reverse causal influence. In practice, however, instruments are seldom statistically adequate, so the actual results tend to be ambiguous. The original district offices variable typically shows a significant negative relationship in our analyses. The instrument is sometimes insignificant, as in the district service equation, but sometimes continues to show a significant negative relationship, as in the constituency attentiveness equation.

4. Chairmen of the standing committees and of the Appropriations subcommittees are subject to confirmation by a majority vote of the Democratic caucus. Over the past 25 years only about 5 percent of all subcommittee chair selections involved uncompensated violations of seniority. Randall B. Ripley, *Congress: Process and Policy*, 3d ed. (New York: W. W. Norton, 1983). The Democratic Steering and Policy Committee includes nine party leaders, including the chairs of Budget, Rules, Appropriations, and Ways and Means, eight other members appointed by the Speaker, and twelve members elected by regional caucuses. The members naturally tend to be experienced representatives.

5. Morris Fiorina, *Congress: Keystone of the Washington Establishment* (New Haven: Yale University Press, 1977), pp. 54–55. For the positive evidence, see Richard Born, "Generational Replacement and the Growth of Incumbent Reelection Margins in the U.S. House," *American Political Science Review* 73 (Sept. 1979): 811–817; Glenn R. Parker, *Stylistic Changes in Congress* (Pittsburgh: University of Pittsburgh Press, forthcoming), ch. 3. For the negative evidence, see John R. Alford and John R. Hibbing, "Increased Incumbency Advantage in the House," *Journal of Politics* 43 (Nov. 1981): 1042–1061.

6. Possibly because many of them were elected from districts previously considered safely Republican. In the 1974 elections the Republicans lost 43 seats and a total of 78 new Democrats were elected. A commitment to political reform was the hallmark of the new group, which soon made its mark by helping overthrow three standing committee chairmen. Charles M. Tidmarch, "The Second Time Around: Freshman Democratic House Members' 1976 Reelection Experiences," Paper delivered at Annual meeting of American Political Science Association, Washington, D.C., Sept. 1–4, 1977.

7. Roy Gregory, "Executive Power and Constituency Representation in United Kingdom Politics," *Political Studies* 28 (March 1980): 83.

8. Anthony Barker and Michael Rush, *The Member of Parliament and His Information* (London: Allen and Unwin, 1970).

9. In a British field experiment approximately half of those canvassed prior to the election did not recall being canvassed when interviewed a month after the election. John Bochel and David Denver, "Candidate Selection in the Labour Party: What the Selectors Seek," *British Journal of Political Science* 13 (1983): 45–69.

10. The expectation of access equations can be estimated in two ways. First, one can treat responses as observations on an ordinal scale (not helpful, somewhat helpful, very helpful). Second, one can treat responses as a dichotomy and attempt to differentiate very helpful responses from all others. Whereas the first method arguably makes fuller use of the information in the data, it has the disadvantage of eliminating numerous respondents (30 percent of the American sample, 35 percent of the British) who fall in the "don't know" and "depends" categories. Moreover, the small proportion of "not helpful" responses results in frequent statistical blow-ups. It would have been nice if one or the other method gave consistently superior results, but in the American sample the dichotomous estimation was far superior, and in the British sample the ordinal scale estimation was superior. In each case the alternative yielded no significant coefficients and overall equations (chi-squares) which were not significant.

11. Paul Feldman and James Jondrow, "Congressional Elections and Local Federal Spending," *American Journal of Political Science* 28 (May 1984): 147–163; John R. Johannes and John C. McAdams, "The Congressional Incumbency Effect: Is It Casework, Policy Compatibility, or Something Else?" *American Journal of Political Science* 25 (Aug. 1981): 512–542; John C. McAdams and John R. Johannes, "The Voter in the 1982 House Elections," *American Journal of Political Science* 28 (Nov. 1984): 778–781; John C. McAdams and John R. Johannes, "The 1980 House Elections: Re-examining Some Theories in a Republican Year," *Journal of Politics* 45 (Feb. 1983): 143–162. On committee positions, see Lyn Ragsdale and Timothy Cook, "Representatives' Actions and Challengers' Reactions: Limits to Candidate Connections in the House," Paper delivered at Annual Meeting of Midwest Political Science Association, Palmer House Hotel, Chicago, April 12–15, 1984; Linda Fowler, Scott Douglass, and Wesley Clark, "The Electoral Effects of House Committee Assignments," *Journal of Politics* 42 (Feb. 1980): 307–322.

12. Philip Norton, *Dissension in the House of Commons, 1974–1979*

(New York: Oxford University Press, 1980); John Schwarz, "Exploring a New Role in Policy Making: The British House of Commons in the 1970s," *American Political Science Review* 74 (March 1980): 23–37; Richard Rose, *British MPs: A Bite as Well as a Bark?* Studies in Public Policy no. 98 (Glasgow: Centre for the Study of Public Policy, 1982). On nineteenth-century voting for Parliament, see Gary W. Cox, "The Development of a Party-Oriented Electorate in England, 1832–1918," University of Texas at Austin, April 1984, mimeo.

13. Richard F. Fenno, *Home Style: House Members and Their Districts* (Boston: Little, Brown, 1978).

14. In the 1980 NES/CPS survey the response format of the question was changed to an approve-disapprove forced choice followed by a strength of feeling probe. With the "fair" option unavailable, the "don't knows" increased to 36 percent, and the ratio of positives and negatives declined to 7:1. Under the forced choice format the ratio of positive to negative ratings for Carter also declined. Unfortunately, the effects of question format cannot be separated from temporal change in this matter. Carter's performance evaluations did decline in commercial polls with unchanging items administered over time. There are no such temporally constant measures of incumbent performance.

15. The omitted reference category in the set of dummy variables contains those respondents with no opinion of the congressman's voting record. Thus, the coefficients in the table signify deviations from this "no knowledge" baseline. Survey questions which call for evaluations of matters about which constituents are not particularly well-informed, such as roll-call voting records, are of course prime candidates for rationalization. Whether or not a constituent shares the congressman's party affiliation, however, is barely related (gamma = .15) to his or her evaluation of the voting record. Although other bases for rationalization exist, this finding undercuts the most obvious one.

16. British campaign financing contrasts greatly with contemporary American practice. Expenses on behalf of specific parliamentary candidates are strictly limited by law. In 1979 the average candidate expenditure was in the neighborhood of 2000 pounds. Most of this amount goes for the printing of an election address which is then delivered free of charge by the Post Office. Candidates also have the right to use public halls for campaign meetings. Thus, the notion of "buying" an election is unknown at the parliamentary district level in the modern era. In addition, the differentials between candidates are too small to account for significant differences in electoral support. Michael Pinto-Duschinsky, "Financing the British General Election of 1979," in Howard Penniman, ed., *Britain at the Polls* (Washington, D.C.: American Enterprise Institute for Public Policy Research, 1979); Michael Pinto-Duschinsky, *British Political Finance, 1830–1980* (Washington, D.C.: American Enterprise Institute for Public Policy Research, 1981).

17. Congressmen with the largest staffs, however, do not visit the district as frequently as do members with medium-sized staffs. This is not just a function of experienced members with legislative responsibilities having

larger staffs and going home less often. Subcommittee chairs do go home less often, but they do not have larger personal staffs than other members.

7. The Personal Vote

Epigraph. Dennis Kavanagh, *Constituency Electioneering in Britain* (London: Longmans, 1970); Thomas Mann, *Unsafe at any Margin* (Washington, D.C.: American Enterprise Institute, 1978), p. 1; David Butler, *The British General Election of 1955* (London: Macmillan, 1955), p. 3; Gary Jacobson, "Incumbents' Advantages in the 1978 U.S. Congressional Elections," *Legislative Studies Quarterly* 6 (1981): 183.

1. Alan I. Abramowitz, "A Comparison of Voting for U.S. Senator and Representative," *American Political Science Review* 74 (Sept. 1980): 633–640; Albert D. Cover, "One Good Term Deserves Another: The Advantage of Incumbency in Congressional Elections," *American Journal of Political Science* 21 (Aug. 1977): 523–542; Morris Fiorina, "Some Problems in Studying the Effects of Resource Allocation in Congessional Elections," *American Journal of Political Science* 25 (Aug. 1981): 543–567; Barbara Hinckley, "The American Voter in Congressional Elections," *American Political Science Review* 74 (Sept. 1980): 423–439; Gary C. Jacobson, "Incumbents' Advantages in the 1978 Congressional Elections," *Legislative Studies Quarterly* 6 (May 1981): 183–200; John C. McAdams and John R. Johannes, "The 1980 House Elections: Re-examining some Theories in a Republican Year," *Journal of Politics* 45 (Feb. 1983): 143–162; Thomas E. Mann and Raymond E. Wolfinger, "Candidates and Parties in Congressional Elections," *American Political Science Review* 74 (Sept. 1980): 617–632.

2. P. M. Williams, "The M.P.'s Personal Vote," *Parliamentary Affairs* (1966–1967): 25–26.

3. For the results of the 1967 interview, see Anthony Barker and Michael Rush, *The Member of Parliament and His Information* (London: Allen and Unwin, 1970), p. 177; Dennis Kavanagh, *Constituency Electioneering in Britain* (London: Longmans, 1970), pp. 49–50; John Bochel and David Denver, "Candidate Selection in the Labour Party: What the Selectors Seek," *British Journal of Political Science* 13 (Jan. 1983): 48–49.

4. John Curtice and Michael Steed, "Appendix 2: An Analysis of the Voting," in David Butler and Dennis Kavanagh, *The British General Election of 1979* (London: Macmillan, 1980), pp. 408–409.

5. Angus Campbell and Warren E. Miller, "The Motivational Basis of Straight and Split Ticket Voting," *American Political Science Review* 51 (June 1957): 293–312; Donald E. Stokes and Warren E. Miller, "Party Government and the Saliency of Congress," *Public Opinion Quarterly* 26 (Winter 1962): 531–546; Warren Miller and Donald Stokes, "Constituency Influences in Congress," *American Political Science Review* 57 (March 1963): 45–56; Morris Fiorina, "Congressmen and Their Constituents: 1958 and 1978," in Dennis Hale, ed., *Proceedings of the Thomas P. O'Neill, Jr., Symposium on the U.S. Congress* (Boston: Pusey Press, 1982), pp. 33–64.

6. For U.S. figures, see Lyn Ragsdale, "Incumbent Popularity, Challenger Invisibility, and Congressional Voters," *Legislative Studies Quart-*

erly 6 (May 1981): 201–218. For British comparisons in an earlier era, see David Butler and Donald Stokes, *Political Change in Britain,* 2d. ed., (London: Macmillan, 1974), chapter 17.

7. To illustrate, consider a strong Democrat in an open seat. The modal Carter rating in this category is good. Thus, from Table 7.1 the predicted z-score for such an individual is $-.39 + .92 + .08 = .61$. This translates into a probability of voting for the Democratic congressional candidate of .73 (using the standard normal table). If the seat is held by a Republican incumbent, subtract .45 from .61, and if the seat is held by a Democratic incumbent, add .85 to .61. The corresponding probabilities are .56 and .93 respectively.

8. On congressional perquisites, see David Mayhew, *Congress: The Electoral Connection* (New Haven: Yale University Press, 1974); Cover, "One Good Term Deserves Another,"; Parker, "District Attentiveness"; Albert D. Cover and Bruce S. Brumberg, "Baby Books and Ballots: The Impact of Congressional Mail on Constituent Opinion," *American Political Science Review* 76 (June 1982): 347–359. On dollar values of congressional perks, see Austin Ranney, "The Working Conditions of Members of Parliament and Congress: Changing the Tools Changes the Job," in Norman J. Ornstein, ed., *The Role of the Legislature in Western Democracies* (Washington, D.C.: American Enterprise Institute for Public Policy Research, 1981). On British campaign finance, see Michael Pinto-Duschinsky, *British Political Finance, 1830–1980* (Washington, D.C.: American Enterprise Institute for Public Policy Research, 1981).

9. Thomas E. Mann, *Unsafe at Any Margin: Interpreting Congressional Elections* (Washington, D.C.: American Enterprise Institute for Public Policy Research, 1978); Barbara Hinckley, "The American Voter in Congressional Elections," *American Political Science Review* 74 (Sept. 1980): 423–439; Gary Jacobson and Samuel Kernell, *Strategy and Choice in Congressional Elections* (New Haven: Yale University Press, 1981). In the postwar period there has been a steady upward trend in the proportion of MPs whose records show prior electoral defeat before they ultimately attain office. Anthony King, "The Rise of the Career Politician and Its Consequences," *British Journal of Political Science* 11 (July 1981): 249–286.

10. Gary C. Jacobson, *The Politics of Congressional Elections* (Boston: Little, Brown, 1983), p. 111. On problems associated with model specification, see Fiorina, "Some Problems"; John C. McAdams and John R. Johannes, "Does Casework Matter? A Reply to Professor Fiorina," *American Journal of Political Science* 25 (Aug. 1981): 581–604.

11. Mayhew, *Congress,* pp. 49–77.

12. The American equations also were estimated using name recognition in place of name recall. Whereas the former usually has a somewhat larger and more highly significant effect, the overall fit of the equations is no better, and other effects are no more than .02 different. Thus, only the equations using name recall are reported in order to maximize cross-national comparability. Campaign spending is also included in the American equations, but it fails to have significant effects. Spending presumably purchases contacts and visibility, but direct, individual-level measures of visibility

already appear in the equations, thereby rendering indirect district-level expenditure reports superfluous.

13. Unfortunately, .evaluations of the member's voting record did not appear in the 1980 NES/CPS election survey. Fortunately, the 1978 estimates suggest that job ratings of congressmen incorporate the effects of attitudes toward the congressmen's voting record.

14. Incumbent contacts were not included as challenger contacts in the equations, since doing so increases collinearity to the point where the estimating routine will not converge.

15. Attempts to include both expectations of helpfulness and job ratings encountered the same problem—including both items in the equation increased collinearity to the point that the estimation procedure would not converge.

16. The category "Labour MP, Callahan rating poor," was suppressed. The coefficients of the other five interactions measure departures from this baseline.

17. Bruce E. Cain, John A. Ferejohn, and Morris P. Fiorina, "The Constituency Service Basis of the Personal Vote for U.S. Representatives and British Members of Parliament," *American Political Science Review* 78 (March 1984): 110–125.

18. Parker, "District Attentiveness," p. 455.

19. The equation is for the 1978 vote because the American interviews were conducted during the second half of 1978 and pertain to activities as of that time.

20. Butler provides the initial formulation of swing. David E. Butler, "The Relation of Seats to Votes," in R. B. McCallum and A. Readman, *The British General Election of 1945* (London: Oxford University Press, 1947), pp. 277–295. For the effects of multiparty elections on the concept, see Ian McAllister and Richard Rose, *The Nationwide Competition for Votes: The 1983 British Election* (London: Frances Pinter, 1984), ch. 11. For the 1979 results, see Curtice and Steed, "Appendix 2," p. 395. For the regional results, see Butler and Kavanagh, *The British General Election of 1979*, "Appendix I: Statistics"; *Times Guide to the 1979 Election* (London: Times Books Ltd., 1979).

21. For the rationale for including the demographic variables, see Ivor Crewe, "The Voting Surveyed," in *Times Guide to the House of Commons* (London: Times Books Ltd., 1979).

22. Williams did not have available a measure of constituency effort. Rather, he sought more generally to estimate the personal votes of "familiar" Labour versus "familiar" Conservative MPs. A familiar MP was defined as one with eight or more years of service. Williams, "Personal Vote," p. 25. Curtice and Steed estimate the actual personal vote in a sample of *marginals*, whereas these figures represent the potential electoral difference between a very low level of constituency effort and a very high level, averaged across both marginal and safe constituencies. Curtice and Steed, "Appendix 2," p. 409.

23. Ivor Crewe, "Do Butler and Stokes Really Explain Political Change in Britain?" *European Journal of Political Research* 2 (1974): 47–92; John

Curtice and Michael Steed, "Electoral Choice and the Production of Government: The Changing Operation of the Electoral System in the United Kingdom since 1955," *British Journal of Political Science* 12 (1982): 249–298; McAllister and Rose, *The Nationwide Competition*.

24. The 1958 SRC study had two open-ended questions: "Is he the right sort of person to be a congressman?" and "Is there anything else that might make you want to vote for him (against him)?" The 1978 NES/CPS study relied on the "anything you like about" and "anything you dislike about" questions. In Britain, the Butler-Stokes studies questioned the bases of incumbent job rating. The 1979 Gallup study used the American "anything you like (dislike)" format.

25. The fact that independent leaners are classified as partisans and pure independents turn out at lower rates than partisans accounts for the 90 percent figure.

8. Particular Interests and General Benefits

1. On constituency pressures and congressional voting, see Julius Turner, *Party and Constituency: Pressures on Congress* (Baltimore: Johns Hopkins University Press, 1951); Duncan Macrae, Jr., *Dimensions of Congressional Voting* (Berkeley: University of California Press, 1958); David Mayhew, *Party Loyalty among Congressmen* (Cambridge: Harvard University Press, 1966); W. Wayne Shannon, *Party, Constituency, and Congressional Voting* (Baton Rouge: Louisiana State University, 1968); David W. Brady, *Congressional Voting in a Partisan Era: A Study of the McKinley Houses* (Lawrence: University of Kansas Press, 1973); Morris Fiorina, *Representatives, Roll Calls, and Constituencies* (Lexington: Lexington Books, 1974). On presidential influence as a function of district voting outcomes, see George C. Edwards, III, *Implementing Public Policy* (Washington, D.C.: Congressional Quarterly Press, 1980), ch. 4. On congressmen and national responsibility, see Morris Fiorina, "The Decline of Collective Responsibility in American Politics," *Daedalus* 109 (Summer 1980): 25–45.

2. Richard F. Fenno, Jr., "If, As Ralph Nader Says, Congress Is 'the Broken Branch,' How Come We Love Our Congressmen So Much?" in Norman Ornstein, ed., *Congress in Change* (New York: Praeger, 1975), pp. 277–287, 280; Richard F. Fenno, Jr., *Home Style: House Members and Their Districts* (Boston: Little, Brown, 1978), ch. 5.

3. See "Outlook—Oklahoma," *Congressional Quarterly Weekly Report* 42 (Feb. 25, 1984): 408. For incumbents' efforts to stave off challenges in 1984, see the *Congressional Quarterly Almanac* 60 (1984), p. 14-B.

4. Randall L. Calvert and R. Mark Isaac, "The Inherent Disadvantage of the Presidential Party in Midterm Congressional Elections," *Public Choice* 36 (1981): 141–146.

5. John Schwarz, "Exploring a New Role in Policy Making: The British House of Commons in the 1970s," *American Political Science Review* 74 (March 1980): 23–37; Philip Norton, *Dissension in the House of Commons, 1974–1979* (New York: Oxford University Press, 1980); David Robertson, *A Theory of Party Competition* (London: John Wiley, 1976), ch. 5.

6. Glenn R. Parker and Roger Davidson, "Why Do Americans Love Their Congressman So Much More Than Their Congress?" *Legislative Studies Quarterly* 4 (1979): 53–62.

7. Geoffrey Smith, "Parliamentary Change in Britain," in Norman J. Ornstein, ed., *The Role of the Legislature in Western Democracies* (Washington, D.C.: American Enterprise Institute for Public Policy Research, 1981), p. 38.

8. Actually, the effects of inflation performance are significant, though smaller, even for Republicans. Americans may tar all congressmen with the same brush irrespective of party control of the presidency. Cf. John R. Hibbing and John R. Alford, "The Electoral Impact of Economic Conditions: Who Is Held Responsible?" *American Journal of Political Science* 25 (Aug. 1981): 423–439.

9. Granted that the executive may be the target of negative personal reactions as well, but not many people attain the highest office in their political system without having personal characteristics that are on balance more favorably than unfavorably regarded. Carter and Reagan are cases in point. They are more positively evaluated as people than for their competence or policies. On U.S. presidential ratings, see John E. Mueller, *War, Presidents, and Public Opinion* (New York: John Wiley, 1973); Fiorina, *Retrospective Voting*, ch. 6. For the British case, see David E. Butler and Donald Stokes, *Political Change in Britain* (London: Macmillan, 1969); James Alt, *The Politics of Economic Decline* (New York: Cambridge University Press, 1979).

10. Fenno, *Home Style*, p. 168; Morris Fiorina, "The Presidency and the Contemporary Political System," in Michael C. Nelson, ed., *The Presidency and the Political System* (Washington, D.C.: Congressional Quarterly, 1984), pp. 204–226.

11. This is not impossible to imagine, however, for the modern British party system is a product of the past century. Parliaments in the first half of the nineteenth century evidenced the kind of fragmentation and electoral disaggregation characteristic of the contemporary United States.

12. Turner, *Party and Constituency*; Macraw, *Dimensions*; Mayhew, *Party Loyalty*; Shannon, *Party*; Brady, *Congressional Voting*.

13. Legislative party membership is essentially defined by how a member of Congress votes on the organization of the chamber at the beginning of each Congress, although in 1965 two southern Democrats in the House were stripped of their committee assignments and ejected from the party after supporting Barry Goldwater for president. Congressmen who consistently desert their party on critical votes suffer disadvantages on matters like committee assignment requests. On emerging British patterns, see Mark N. Franklin and Michael Tappin, "Early Day Motions as Unobtrusive Measures of Backbench Opinion in Britain," *British Journal of Political Science* 7 (Jan. 1977): 49–69; Robertson, *Theory of Party Competition*, ch. 5; John R. Hibbing, "Parliament without Parties: Voting Patterns of British MPs on Free Votes," Paper prepared for delivery at Annual Meeting of American Political Science Association, New Orleans, Aug.–Sept. 1985; Smith, "Parliamentary Change."

260 / Notes to Pages 207–213

14. Norton, Schwartz, and Crowe all combine cross-voting with abstention. See Philip Norton, "The Changing Face of the British House of Commons in the 1970s," *Legislative Studies Quarterly* 5 (Aug. 1980): 333–358;
Schwarz, "Exploring a New Role"; Edward Crowe, "Cross-Voting in the
British House of Commons, 1945–1974," *Journal of Politics* 42 (May 1980):
487–510.

15. The results are not dependent on this particular index. They also
hold for the factor analytic index and for a number of the activities examined
separately.

16. The weaker relationships for abstention may reflect the lower frequency of the behavior. Particularly on the second and third measures of
abstention, the behavior is too rare to justify statistical analysis. On the
generally greater prominence of the constituency role in British conceptions
of represention, see Donald D. Searing, "The Role of the Good Constituency
Member and the Practice of Representation in Great Britain," *Journal of
Politics* 47 (May 1985): 348–381.

17. Robert Crandall, for example, estimates that protection in the steel
industry in the mid-1970s cost American consumers $1 billion in order to
save 12,000 jobs. Crandall, "Steel Imports—Dumping or Competition," *Regulation* 4 (July/Aug. 1980): 17–24.

18. See Bruce A. Ackerman and William T. Hassler, "Beyond the New
Deal: Coal and the Clean Air Act," *Yale Law Journal* 89 (July 1980): 1466–
1572; R. Shep Melnick, *Regulation and the Courts: The Case of the Clean
Air Act* (Washington, D.C.: Brookings, 1983). Although representatives who
adopt the role of trustee may choose to pursue the general interest, the
political reasons not to adopt such a role reduce the importance of this
possibility. The only dependable way to induce representatives to act as
trustees is to design institutions which make it in their interest.

19. See e.g. John R. Johannes, *To Serve the People* (Lincoln: University
of Nebraska Press, 1984); Arthur Maass, *Congress and the Common Good*
(New York: Basic Books, 1983).

20. Mancur Olson, *The Logic of Collective Action* (Cambridge: Harvard
University Press, 1965); Russell Hardin, *Collective Action* (Baltimore: Johns
Hopkins University Press, 1982).

21. Fenno, *Home Style*, ch. 6.

22. Joseph Cooper and William West, "Voluntary Retirement, Incumbency, and the Modern House," *Political Science Quarterly* 96 (Summer
1981): 279–300; John R. Hibbing, "Voluntary Retirement from the U.S.
House: The Costs of Congressional Service," *Legislative Studies Quarterly*
7 (Feb. 1982): 57–74; John R. Hibbing, "Voluntary Retirement from the U.S.
House of Representatives: Who Quits?" *American Journal of Political Science* 26 (Aug. 1982): 467–484.

9. Implications for Political Institutions

1. Bruce E. Cain, "Blessed Be the Tie That Unbinds: Constituency Work
and the Vote Swing in Great Britain," *Politcal Studies* 31 (March 1983):
103–111.

2. Burdett Loomis, "The Congressional Office as a Small (?) Business: New Members Set Up Shop," *Publius* 9 (Summer 1979): 35–55; Robert H. Salisbury and Kenneth A. Shepsle, "U.S. Congressman as Enterprise," *Legislative Studies Quarterly* 4 (Nov. 1981): 559–576.

3. David Mayhew, *Congress: The Electoral Connection* (New Haven: Yale University Press, 1974), pp. 81–82. Tom McNally, an MP and former special adviser to Prime Minister Callaghan, commented on the tensions in Britain: "'ministers are not much interested in having legislation scrutinized by the House of Commons. They want to get it through as quickly and as quietly as possible. Therefore, when discussing giving powers to select committees, it is important to realize that a large body of members of Parliament have no interest whatsoever in increasing the power of the backbenchers. When I told my erstwhile boss that I had signed that motion, he simply said, 'You will regret it one day.' " See Norman J. Ornstein, *The Role of the Legislature in Western Democracies* (Washington, D.C.: American Enterprise Institute for Public Policy Research, 1981), pp. 124–125.

4. Philip Norton, *Dissension in the House of Commons, 1974–1979* (New York: Oxford University Press, 1980); Leon D. Epstein, "What Happened to the British Party Model?" *American Political Science Review* 74 (March 1980): 9–22; John Schwarz, "Exploring a New Role in Policy Making: The British House of Commons in the 1970s," *American Political Science Review* 74 (March 1980): 23–37.

5. For a discussion of the change in congressional careers, see H. Douglas Price, "The Congressional Career—Then and Now," in Nelson W. Polsby, ed., *Congressional Behavior* (New York: Random House, 1971). On the evolution of the Appropriations process, see David Brady and Mark A. Morgan, "Reforming the Structure of the House Appropriations Process: The Effects of the 1885 and 1919–1920 Reforms on Money Decisions," Paper delivered at Annual Meeting of American Political Science Association, Chicago, Sept. 1983; Charles Stewart, III, "Structural Cycles: The Case of Budgetary Reform in the House, 1865–1921," mimeo, Stanford University, 1985; Nelson W. Polsby, Miriam Gallagher, and Barry Spencer Rundquist, "The Growth of the Seniority System in the U.S. House of Representatives," *American Political Science Review* 63 (Sept. 1969): 787–807; Lawrence C. Dodd and Richard L. Schott, *Congress and the Administrative State* (New York: John Wiley, 1979).

6. Maurice Duverger, *Political Parties: Their Organization and Activity in the Modern State*, trans. B. North and R. North (London: Methuen, 1954); William H. Riker, "The Two-Party System and Duverger's Law: An Essay on the History of Political Science," *American Political Science Review* 76 (Dec. 1982): 753–766.

7. Ivor Crewe, "Do Butler and Stoke Really Explain Political Change in Britain?" *European Journal of Political Research* 2 (March 1974): 47–92; James Alt, *The Politics of Economic Decline* (New York: Cambridge University Press, 1979).

8. On the rise of political parties, see Mosei Ostrogorski, *Democracy and the Organization of Political Parties*, vol. I, trans. Frederick Clarke (London: Macmillan, 1902). Cf. Hugh Berrington, "Partisanship and Dis-

262 / Notes to Pages 219–220

sidence in the Nineteenth Century House of Commons," *Parliamentary Affairs* 21 (1967–1968): 338–374. On the assumption of procedural control by the Cabinet, see Peter Fraser, "The Growth of Ministerial Control in the Nineteenth-Century House of Commons," *English Historical Review* 75 (1960): 444–463; Valerie Cromwell, "The Losing of the Initiative by the House of Commons, 1780–1914," *Transactions of the Royal Historical Society* 18 (5th series, London: 1968): 1–17; Gary W. Cox, *The Efficient Secret: The Cabinet and the Development of Political Parties in Victorian England* (Cambridge University Press, forthcoming).

9. A British academic remarked, "One of the papers that we are discussing today mentions the famous episode of Brian Walden and John Mackintosh, who defeated or emasculated the Callaghan government's dock labor bill. Both men were able to destroy that legislation on the floor of the House, not through a committee system, but because each had a very strong constituency base. They knew that the ties of party loyalty would not constrain them, that their constituents would not care if they defeated their own government on the floor of the House." Ornstein, *The Role of Western Legislatures,* p. 126.

More generally, Smith and Polsby anticipate the first link in our argument when discussing the more likely effects of adopting the direct primary in Britain: "An M.P. would know that he could afford to disregard the views of a few powerful figures in the local party, provided that he stood well in the eyes of the voters; and his public reputation could sometimes be enhanced by taking a bold and independent line in Parliament. Once this new electoral relationship was established between M.P.s and their constituents, members would be all the more eager to develop their own parliamentary institutions as a means of keeping an eye on, and even influencing the policies of, the government of the day." They are more cautious about asserting the further connections we assert in the text. Geoffrey Smith and Nelson Polsby, *British Government and Its Discontents* (New York: Basic Books, 1981), pp. 140–141.

10. J. Theodore Anagnoson, "Home Style in New Zealand," *Legislative Studies Quarterly* 8 (May 1983): 157–175; Allan Kornberg and William Mishler, *Influence in Parliament: Canada* (Durham: Duke Univeristy Press, 1976); S. R. Maheshwari, "Constituency Linkage of National Legislators in India," *Legislative Studies Quarterly* 1 (Aug. 1976): 1–12.

11. Given the well-known implications of collective action problems, one might expect to find little constituency service activity in proportional representation systems. In brief, because individual members of the group have little incentive to contribute to the collective good, the group enjoys less of the collective good or suffers more of the collective bad than the members would collectively prefer. Mancur Olson, *The Logic of Collective Action* (Cambridge: Harvard University Press, 1965); Russell Hardin, *Collective Action* (Baltimore: Johns Hopkins University Press, 1982).

12. The German elector has two votes, one to indicate a preference among the contending district candidates, another to indicate a preference among the party lists. The vote achieved by the list determines the proportion of Bundestag seats to which a party is entitled. If the party wins a greater

proportion of seats, a smaller proportion of its list candidates are elected, and vice versa. Gerhard Loewenberg, *Parliament in the German Political System* (Ithaca: Cornell University Press, 1967).

13. On the differences between MPs elected from districts and those elected from lists, see Jeff Fishel, "On the Transformation of Ideology in European Political Systems: Candidates for the West German Bundestag," *Comparative Political Studies* 4 (Jan. 1972): 406–437. Cf. Gerhard Loewenberg and Samuel Patterson, *Comparing Legislatures* (Boston: Little, Brown, 1979), p. 175; Loewenberg, *Parliament*, pp. 73, 77.

14. For a survey of constituency service around the world, which should be read especially by those who believe the essential stuff of politics is the clash of great ideologies, see Michael C. Mezey, *Comparative Legislatures* (Durham: Duke University Press, 1979), ch. 9.

15. Douglas W. Rae, *The Political Consequences of Electoral Laws*, rev. ed. (New Haven: Yale University Press, 1971); Enid Lakeman and James D. Lambert, *Voting in Democracies: A Study of Majority and Proportional Electoral Systems* (London: Faber and Faber, 1955).

16. "What the parties do to enhance the size of the local vote (and to mitigate competition within their own ranks) is to arrive at bargains settling the exact boundaries within which each candidate will canvass most heavily, and where the local party apparatus will urge its clientele to give a man first preference, i.e., a system of individual bailiwicks. Such bailiwicks function not only at election time, but in the interim between elections as well. Elected representatives thus have distinct areas which they service, the constituency being parceled up among members of the same party." Paul M. Sacks, "Bailiwicks, Locality, and Religion: Three Elements in an Irish Dail Constituency Election," *The Economic and Social Review* 1 (July 1970): 542. See also Basil Chubb, *The Government and Politics of Ireland* (Stanford: Stanford University Press, 1970).

17. Eric M. Uslaner, "Casework and Institutional Design: Redeeming Promises in the Promised Land," *Legislative Studies Quarterly* 10 (Feb. 1985): 35–52.

18. Philip Williams, *Crisis and Compromise: Politics in the Fourth Republic*, 3d ed. (Hamden, Conn.: Archon Books, 1964), pp. 341, 346.

19. P. A. Allum, *Italy—Republic without Government?* (New York: Norton, 1973); Sidney G. Tarrow, *Between Center and Periphery: Grassroots Politicians in Italy and France* (New Haven: Yale University Press, 1977), p. 124.

20. The Scandinavian systems are proportional representation systems with party list ballots and average district magnitudes of six or more. At least in Norway, "being elected to the Storting makes it more likely that one will give up office at the local level." From 1961 to 1977, just over 60 percent of those seeking re-election were returned to the Storting. Johan P. Olsen, *Organized Democracy: Political Institutions in a Welfare State: The Case of Norway* (Bergen; Oslo: Universitetsforlaget, 1983), p. 54. In Sweden, however, members of the Riksdag commonly retain membership in local assemblies. M. Donald Hancock, *Sweden* (Hinsdale, Ill.: Dryden Press, 1972), p. 95. In Sweden the re-election rate is somewhat higher, ranging between

75 and 80 percent. Nils Andren, *Modern Swedish Government* (Stockholm: Almquist & Wicksell, 1968), p. 70.

21. John Fitzmaurice, *Politics in Denmark* (London: Hurst, 1981), p. 53; Erik Damgaard, "The Function of Parliament in the Danish Political System: Results of Recent Research," *Legislative Studies Quarterly* 5 (Feb. 1980): 101–121.

22. Proposals to establish a national ombudsman periodically are introduced in Congress, but they do not receive serious consideration. John R. Johannes, *To Serve the People* (Lincoln: University of Nebraska Press, 1984), pp. 213–316. In Britain, a national ombudsman was established in 1967 after a period of considerable controversy and threatened backbench rebellion. As the price for passage, backbench MPs imposed the requirement that constituent requests and the ombudsman's responses both be communicated through the MP. The requirement concerning constituent requests has been relaxed. For useful discussions, see Roy Gregory and Alan Alexander, " 'Our Parliamentary Ombudsman,' Part I: Integration and Metamorphosis," *Public Administration* 50 (1972): 313–331; William B. Gwyn, "The British PCA: 'Ombudsman or Ombudsmouse?' " *Journal of Politics* 35 (Feb. 1973): 45–69.

23. Private member bills accounted for a third of the enactments in the 1956–1958 period, and they sometimes stimulated government legislation. Williams, *Crisis and Compromise*, p. 261, 275.

24. Between 1948 and 1958, "approximately three of every four bills approved in either house of the Italian Parliament were approved by committees *in sede delibarante* . . . it is argued that the procedure is used only for 'unimportant' legislation or for highly technical legislation . . . such technical matters often involve important economic interest, such as export and import regulations, the governance of state-owned industries, tariffs, and similar measures." Mezey, *Comparative Legislatures*, p. 73. See also Allum, *Italy*, p. 133.

25. Tarrow, *Between Center and Periphery*, p. 90. See also Robert Leonardi, Raffaella Nanetti, and Gianfranco Pasquino, "Institutionalization of Parliament and Parliamentarization of Parties in Italy," *Legislative Studies Quarterly* 3 (Feb. 1978): 161–179.

26. Interpellations are "the time-honored method of forcing debate on a matter of public urgency." They have survived in Scandinavian countries in part because interpellations do not lead to a vote of confidence; whereas ministers are not required to respond, they do so in virtually all cases. Mezey, *Comparative Legislatures*, pp. 109–110.

27. See Olsen, *Organized Democracy*.

28. Fitzmaurice, *Denmark*, p. 59; Damgaard, "The Functions of Parliament."

29. Hancock, *Sweden*, p. 174; Joel D. Aberbach, Robert D. Putnam, and Bert A. Rockman, *Bureaucrats and Politicians in Western Democracies* (Cambridge: Harvard University Press, 1982), ch. 7. For U.S. national policy making, see Randall B. Ripley and Grace A. Franklin, *Congress, the Bureaucracy, and Public Policy*, rev. ed. (Homewood, Ill.: Dorsey Press, 1980); Keith A. Hamm, "Patterns of Influence among Committees, Agencies, and Interest Groups," *Legislative Studies Quarterly* 8 (Aug. 1983): 379–426.

30. Heinz Eulau and Paul D. Karps, "The Puzzle of Representation: Specifying Components of Responsiveness," in Heinz Eulau et al., ed. *The Politics of Representation* (Beverly Hills: Sage, 1978), p. 63.

31. Theodore Lowi, *The End of Liberalism* (New York: W. W. Norton, 1969); Nathan C. Leites, *On the Game of Politics in France* (Stanford: Stanford University Press, 1959).

32. Johannes, *To Serve.*

INDEX

Barker, Anthony, 80, 111, 112
Bochel, John, 168
Burnham, Walter Dean, 6
Butler-Stokes study, 22, 113–115, 190

Callaghan, James, 155, 170, 171, 205
Calvert, Randall, 200
Carter, Jimmy, 205
Casework, 57–71; measures of, 94–96; citizen evaluation of, 102–104
Congressional careers, 7, 12–13
Congressional elections, 4–6; advantages of incumbency, 4, 10, 98–100, 169–174; swing ratio in, 4; influence of party identification, 9; economic conditions in, 10; presidential coattails, 16–17; midterm elections, 200
Congressional staff, 60–61, 74, 99
Constituency service, 3, 50–51; citizen evaluation of, 38–40, 41–42, 136–148; and seniority, 142–143; member reputation for, 148–153
Constituents: evaluation of members, 45–47; communication with members, 53–54; expectations of helpfulness, 54–57
Cook, Timothy, 121
Cox, Gary, 218
Curtice, John, 168, 188

Davidson, Roger, 203
Denver, David, 168

District offices, 60–61, 99
Dowse, R. E., 66, 80, 112
Drayson, G. Burnaby, 110

Erikson, Robert, 4
Eulau, Heinz, 50

Feldman, Paul, 122, 130
Fenno, Richard F., Jr., 36, 50, 51, 54, 80, 121, 123, 198, 200, 205
Fitzmaurice, John, 226

Gregory, Roy, 147

Hattersley, Roy, 81
Home style, 36, 43, 47, 80

Isaac, Mark, 200

Jacobson, Gary C., 29, 121, 123, 128, 174
Johannes, John R., 122, 123, 130
Jondrow, James, 122, 130
Jones, Jim, 198

Kavanagh, Dennis, 168
King, Anthony, 15, 80–81

Labour Party, 87, 168–169
Loewenberg, Gerhard, 220

Mayhew, David, 4, 175, 215
McAdams, John C., 122, 123, 130

O'Neill, Thomas P. (Tip), 198

Parker, Glenn R., 203
Parliamentary elections, 6–7;